About the Author

CHRISTOPHER KENNEDY LAWFORD is the author of the *New York Times* bestsellers *Symptoms of Withdrawal* and *Moments of Clarity*. He has worked extensively in Hollywood as an actor, lawyer, executive, and producer. He lives in Los Angeles, California.

Moments
of
Clarity

ALSO BY

CHRISTOPHER KENNEDY LAWFORD

Symptoms of Withdrawal

CHRISTOPHER KENNEDY
LAWFORD

MOMENTS
OF
CLARITY

Voices from the Front Lines of

Addiction and Recovery

HARPER

NEW YORK · LONDON · TORONTO · SYDNEY

HARPER

A hardcover edition of this book was published in 2009 by
William Morrow, an imprint of HarperCollins Publishers.

HarperCollins books may be purchased for educational, business, or
sales promotional use. For information please write: Special Markets
Department, HarperCollins Publishers, 10 East 53rd Street, New York,
NY 10022.

First Harper paperback published 2010.

Designed by Mia Risberg

The Library of Congress has catalogued the hardcover
edition as follows:

Lawford, Christopher Kennedy.
  Moments of clarity : voices from the front lines of addiction and
recovery / Christopher Kennedy Lawford.
      p.   cm.
  ISBN 978-0-06-145621-3
  1. Lawford, Christopher Kennedy, 1955–   2. Recovering addicts—
United States—Biography.   3. Actors—United States—Biography.
I. Title.
  HV5805.L3939   2009
  616.860092'273—dc22   2008035531

ISBN 978-0-06-145622-0 (pbk.)

10 11 12 13 14   ID/RRD   10 9 8 7 6 5 4 3 2 1

*For my father, for my cousin David, and for
all of those who die from this disease
so the rest of us can get sober*

His craving for alcohol was the equivalent on a low level of the spiritual thirst of our being for wholeness, the union with God.

The only right and legitimate way to such an experience is, that it happens to you in reality and it can only happen to you when you walk on a path, which leads you to higher understanding. You might be led to that goal by an act of grace or through a personal and honest contact with friends, or through a higher education of the mind beyond the confines of mere rationalism.

—From a letter from C. G. Jung to Bill Wilson,
cofounder of Alcoholics Anonymous

Contents

Foreword

by PATRICK KENNEDY

In his last book, *Symptoms of Withdrawal*, my cousin Chris Lawford shared his very personal tale: a tale of his struggle with his brutal addiction to alcohol and drugs. In publishing *Symptoms* Chris boldly brought to light what it is like to succumb to the disease of addiction, and also what it is like to recover.

When Chris described his concept for another book, I was impressed by the approach he proposed for his follow-up to *Symptoms*. He told me that as he had traveled promoting *Symptoms*, individuals had come up to him asking him about his moment of clarity. Many, he said, also shared their own experiences and their own personal moments of clarity.

Instead of writing a follow-up book focusing solely on his own story, Chris decided to compile a collection of stories, essays, and anecdotes accumulated over the course of the last several years. In doing so, Chris has removed the focus from himself and created a book that illuminates the lives of the hundreds and thousands of Americans who suffer from addiction, thus confronting this societal epidemic from a grassroots level.

The recoveries and renewed lives you'll read about in this book are only possible because each contributor had that moment of clarity, a moment in which they realized they suffered from a disease, a moment that would forever alter their lives, because—through treatment, friends, family, faith, and a never-ending commitment to being healthy—they would build the strength to confront the disease and live a sober life.

My moment of clarity was a little different. In fact, I've had more than one, and both were very different. The first moment was when I realized I had a problem I couldn't manage by myself and so I sought proper treatment.

But months later, I experienced a second moment of clarity, an epiphany if you will. By the very nature of my profession, by serving in public office and having a public life, my public admission that I was in trouble appeared on TV, the Internet, and in newspapers all around the world. I have never experienced anything more frightening than having to admit to myself, my family, and the world that I was struggling to stay healthy. Standing in front of those cameras and admitting my faults was one of the most difficult things I have ever had to do.

It was a moment of pure fear. But it also was a moment in which I realized that I didn't have to hide anymore, I didn't have to try and deny to myself or others that I was suffering from this disease. In front of all those cameras, I took a great step forward in my life, and I shed the burden I had carried for so many years.

My travails began when I was younger, and they had been chronicled in the media. Based on the pattern of my behavior, most people could have guessed where I was headed.

A few years ago, I realized I was having a problem again. I was able to hide the problem from my friends, family, and my constituents because I was still functioning at a high level, but at some point I realized I couldn't get better on my own. I was fortunate to have the resources for and access to treatment, but as I would learn a few months later, I was not fully free of the weight of the disease and the pressures it imposed on me. Not until that day before the cameras.

That day in front of the cameras had been building for a long time. And at that moment, with everyone watching, it all came to a head. Finally I was exposed; finally my problem was revealed; finally my weaknesses were laid bare. There was a sea of TV cameras and a huge cavalcade of press outside my office. My capacity for denial had been enormous, but there was no way I could keep up the denial after that. I sat in my office and watched news anchors from CNN and FOX-TV deliver the story and scour over my past and present. It was impossible for me to deny the pattern; it was all being documented to the world.

Soon after my three-minute statement in front of the world, I realized the burden had been lifted. I no longer had to deal with my disease in the shadows. I was able to live my life without the fear of stigma that I have fought so long to erase. Instead of living in a constant state of anxiety, I am now constantly reminded of those things in life that are worth staying sober for. I'm not proud about how this all happened. If I were writing the script I would write it differently. But I wouldn't change the ending.

There are millions of Americans with stories just like mine and just like Chris's. What Chris has done is to bring some of them together, and in doing that, in a sense, he's brought us all together. In sharing these moments of clarity, Chris is helping to expose the problems that persist in our society, and the good that can come from working together to achieve a larger national, cultural, and societal moment of clarity; a moment in which we can all admit to ourselves that this disease plagues our families, our friends, and our neighbors. This disease plagues our national soul and our national conscience.

Shortly after my own recovery began, my dear friend and Republican colleague Jim Ramstad and I launched a nationwide tour promoting our legislation and investigating the state of mental health in America.* Having met so many people during that process, many like those chronicled in this book, I am left bewildered about the inability in our culture to value people for who they are as human beings. That basic idea is both universal and necessary for the survival of our culture and our society. Every time I speak now on domestic or international issues, it all starts from the contentment I feel in being my own self in the world. The fact is that I can't be totally self-reliant, none of us can. We are dependent on others; we've got to be engaged with our neighbors, in our world; we can't

---

* In 2007 Kennedy and Ramstad held hearings around the country to support the Paul Wellstone Mental Health and Addiction Equity Act. The bill seeks to broaden health-care access by preventing insurance companies from setting discriminatory restrictions on treatment for psychological afflictions, including addiction. It would require insurers to offer ordinary Americans the same coverage available to all members of Congress. As this book went to press, the bill had passed the House and was awaiting a vote in the Senate.

be just out for ourselves. Think about what might happen if we took the values of humility and service and, as a country, applied them to our policy domestically and internationally.

For too long, stigma has kept those with this disease in the shadows of our society. I am living proof that—with the care of others—clarity, recovery, and a better, healthier life are possible. There is a tenet of the twelve-step program: in helping others who are afflicted with the same disease that we all suffer from, we help ourselves. I have dedicated myself to helping erase the stigma and remove the discrimination inherent in our health-care laws.

In the spirit of our family's tradition of public service, Chris has dedicated himself, through *Moments of Clarity,* to improving people's lives in a meaningful way. By publishing this book, he underscores that this is a problem that spares no family and no community in this country or in this world. Chris bravely shared his own story in his last book; he now humbly shares the stories of many others, all in an effort to change the way we think about this awful disease.

Chris has gathered the stories of everyday people from everyday walks of life. No matter who we are, how much money we make, or what neighborhood we grew up in, we and the people we love are susceptible to the disease of addiction. In compiling these profound stories, Chris is again adding to the dialogue and moving our nation forward; he is making it acceptable to confront these issues and care for one another.

I hope that in reading his book, you too are able to learn from and identify with the millions out there who have been struck with this affliction. And I hope you too can experience grace and find that inherent link we all share, and help us all work toward a brighter day in this world.

INTRODUCTION

Stand upright, speak thy thoughts, declare the truth thou hast,
that all may share; be bold, proclaim it everywhere.
They only love who dare.

—Voltaire

The biggest mistake, sometimes, is to play things very safe
in this life and end up being moral failures.

—Dorothy Day

After writing my memoir, *Symptoms of Withdrawal*, the last thing I wanted to do was write a book about recovery. I thought I'd covered that already. When I first contemplated writing *Symptoms* I was seventeen years sober, recently separated from my family, living in a teardown on the Westside of L.A. that my cousin owned and was letting me squat in until I put my life back together. My career was in flux and I had just begun therapy for hepatitis C, embarking on a course of treatment that would save my life but leave me feeling really angry and depressed for close to a year. My only friend seemed to be a mouse that lived in the decaying chimney of the practically empty house I was living in.

One morning I received a call from a writer who was doing another in a long line of books about my family and he wanted to talk about what it was like being a Kennedy male. I wasn't in the mood and told him to write me a letter explaining why the world needed another book about the Kennedys. He recalled what he thought was a heroic story involving one of my cousins. I didn't know the story, nor did I think it particularly heroic. I told him if he'd said he needed the money or was trying to impress a girl I would have talked to him, but the only reason that story needed to be told was if my cousin wanted to tell it. And then I had a flash—maybe I had a story to tell and maybe I should write it before the virus attacking my liver killed me. That was the moment I *had* to become public about my recovery because any story I told would in large part be about my recovery from addiction to drugs and alcohol. I also knew any publisher who might publish that story would insist I do my part to promote it—publicly.

Two months and fifty pages later I received another phone call. This time it was a treatment center in Indianapolis that wanted me to come speak at their annual fund-raiser. I had been asked many times to do this, the offers usually coming with large sums of cash attached. I had always said no, firmly believing that my recovery was private, anonymity a preference if not an obligation. I said yes to the good people in Indianapolis not because of a conversion in my thinking but out of necessity; I would have a book to promote in a year and the sooner I was comfortable speaking publicly about my recovery the better. At six o'clock the morning of my speech, I found myself in an Indianapolis television station being interviewed by a well-meaning young news reporter who wanted to know what it was like being a heroin addict.

"Oh my God," I thought. I didn't want to be on TV talking about *that*. What had I done? Why did I open my mouth? Maybe I shouldn't write a memoir after all. *How the hell am I going to get out of this?* These were the thoughts racing through my mind as I settled into the hot seat at my next interview in a radio station studio, facing the large picture window that looked like something on the *Today* show. The host of the radio program picked up where the TV reporter had left off: "Did you take LSD, Chris?" I'm sitting there thinking "Beam me up, Scotty!" when a homeless man walks up to the window holding a sign that reads, "Can you help me get sober?" His name was Lawrence, he was fifty years old, and he'd been living drunk in a Dumpster for five years. In an instant I knew why I was on the radio and television that morning. I was there to speak to Lawrence and others like him. I haven't shut up since. So, I told *my* story of recovery, and found, surprisingly, that that was the part of my life that fascinated people the most—the part that resonated more profoundly than any other. Everywhere I went on the *Symptoms* publicity tour, I was asked the same question: "What happened to you on the morning of February seventeenth in 1986?" I had written about that day as the moment I had the revelation that resulted in my continuing sobriety and people wanted to hear more. In fact, they asked me about that moment with a need to know bordering on desperation. It seemed like they were dying for me to share the secret that allowed me to change from hopeless addict to someone who had stayed sober for twenty years, lived a productive life, and written a book about it all. Everywhere I visited, I ran into folks thirsting for some reassurance that change might be possible. It was clear there was a powerful need for a message of hope and inspiration.

I had told *my* tale, but recovery is a bigger subject than just one person; there's a community of voices out there, and each voice has a different story. The message couldn't come only from me. I knew a lot of people who had put down the booze and chemicals—people who took their own path toward sobriety—and all these different experiences were important. I realized that a collection of these stories, in different voices, would be more meaningful and powerful than any single recollection could be. There were two things that united us all: one, we were all addicts, and two, as recovered addicts, we had all experienced some form of what I call the "moment of clarity." So I decided to interview those people I knew who had something to share and who were willing to open up their lives in order to serve as inspiration to others.

I sent out e-mails to four people I knew in recovery. The response surprised me, leaving me with a sinking feeling that getting people to share an intimate, profound moment that altered their life forever might not be as easy as I had imagined. The movie star I had known for years and who I was sure would say yes—said no! He didn't want to make pronouncements about recovery or pose as an expert. The other movie star, someone I barely knew at all, said yes without reservation. A man I'd known in recovery who had a story to tell wanted to keep it private. Then there were the journalist and the rock star, both of whom I never heard back from.

Clearly the road to getting people to open up about their "moment" was going to be bumpy and full of unexpected turns.

A good friend told me, "Don't worry, Chris. Whoever's meant to be in the book will just show up." And that's pretty much what happened. I kept asking people, looking for people, letting people show up.

An old friend I had no worries about pulled out at the eleventh hour, saying, "I just don't want to dredge all that up again. The last time I talked about my recovery the newspapers crucified me." Several others had second thoughts as well and pulled out of the project at the last minute. I began to understand why it is so difficult to change the way we view addiction in this country. If accomplished, talented, well-thought-of members of society are wary about the stigma of the disease of addiction, what about those with less power and standing?

I came to understand in doing this book just how difficult it is for addicts and alcoholics to stand up and talk about their disease, whether because of stigma, misunderstanding the tradition of anonymity in twelve-step programs, or the very real threat of losing one's livelihood or insurance coverage. Claiming one's recovery publicly is an act of moral courage often resulting in nasty consequences, occasionally coming from those in the recovery community itself. A friend sent me an e-mail where he went on a bit of a tirade about the "racket" of the new wave of "I'm in recovery," where addicts and alcoholics play fast and loose with programs founded on anonymity. I didn't write back to explain that the tradition of anonymity in twelve-step programs didn't mean one could not speak publicly about their recovery but that it simply governed their anonymity with regard to their membership in the particular twelve-step program. In fairness, though, there is a more fundamental aspect of anonymity than whether you tell your story or claim your recovery publicly. I interviewed someone who's very open about his recovery, and also a great storyteller. I sent back the edited interview and he said, "I can't do this. Reading the words on the page, I realized that my story is really just for the guys in my recovery group, not for anyone else."

Saying you're an alcoholic or a drug addict, claiming your disease in public, is one thing. Telling any part of your story *to* the public is another. There's something very powerful about the telling and sharing of stories from one addict to another. It's powerful enough to change lives. The guy who decided not to participate because he didn't want to dilute that power has a point, and I can't say he's wrong. The question of anonymity is important, not solely in the sense of whether one is publicly known as an addict or alcoholic but because sometimes it's difficult to reconcile the spiritual remedy to this illness with a public profile—difficult but not impossible, as those in the pages that follow have demonstrated.

Finally, I did what I've learned to do in my recovery: I turned the problem over to whatever higher power is out there. If the book was meant to happen, it would happen. And so it has, and for that I am very grateful.

I made the decision to be public about my recovery when I recounted my story and my moment of clarity as part of my memoir. My intention then was to begin a career as a writer, not to make a statement about recovery. The forty-three individuals in this book and the tens of thousands who stand up every day to claim their recovery publicly have no other motive than to share their experience, strength, and hope with others in the hope that it may be of some help. I am humbled by their willingness, awed by their courage, and grateful beyond measure for their participation.

It seemed as though whenever I doubted the wisdom of doing this book, a lightning bolt of inspiration would be delivered in the form of one of those I interviewed. I cried with Jamie Lee Curtis in gratitude and solidarity over our common path. My faith in my humanness was bolstered by the unwavering courage and integrity of Martin Sheen. I sat in wonder at the energy and unquenchable desire for betterment of Elaine Stritch. I was amazed and inspired by a Native American woman named Marie Morning-Glory, who endured unspeakable tragedy only to transcend it brilliantly in a life of love and service. And Jim Vance, who after reading the transcript of the interview we did together sent me an e-mail saying, "Damn, it is rough seeing that stuff in print, but it's true. I sure do hope the guy was right, whoever it was who said the truth will set you free."

The risk of doing this book was worth it because of those who are in it and because I've seen the desperation in people's eyes when they asked me, "What happened? How did you change?" I heard them tell me to write about recovery so that others might get the message and find what I have found.

There are an estimated 22.6 million people in this country (9.2 percent of the population age twelve and older) struggling with substance abuse, and many more family and friends who often are just as tormented by the addiction as the person who is afflicted. It became apparent to me that with so many suffering and fewer than 10 percent getting any treatment at all, a book like this might not only be useful to those touched by addiction but also be instrumental in the effort to change public health policy, and to address the bigger question of what we, as a nation, pay attention to.

I remember showing up on the Washington Mall in the shadow of the U.S. Capitol to interview my cousin Congressman Patrick Kennedy, who excitedly told me that in 1969 Bill Wilson (the cofounder of AA) had spoken in front of a subcommittee of the United States Senate where he said that in the future, "AAs" would be free to express opinions about alcoholism if they spoke not as members of the group, but as private citizens." That future is here.

The doing of this book was both a giant pain in the ass and a gift of indescribable proportions. Asking for and scheduling the interviews was just as bad as I'd thought it would be, but every single time I sat down with one of these brave human beings, all the frustration fell away and I got caught up in the great drama and beauty of their "moments." Each conversation, for me, was a spiritual experience, one that enriched my own journey.

Based on his treatment of alcoholics, the psychologist Carl Jung was convinced that recovery was impossible without "a transforming experience of the spirit,"* and that was my focus of inquiry with each of the interviewees. I asked them to describe their moment of clarity—when that transformation began—in as much detail as possible. Then we talked about the changes in their daily lives, and what they understood about

---

* In her biography of Bill Wilson, founder of Alcoholics Anonymous, Susan Cheever quotes from a letter Jung wrote to Wilson, discussing this idea of spiritual transformation. Jung comes up with a great summary: "Alcohol in Latin is 'spiritus' and you use the same word for the highest religious experience as well as for the most depraving poison. The helpful formula therefore is: *spiritus contra spiritum*"—spirit against spirits.

their transformation now that wasn't obvious to them then. Many of the people in this book felt it important to contextualize their experience of spirit and tell, to one degree or another, what it was like *before* their moment occurred. I left portions of these passages in, so far as they illuminated the experience.

These moments are as unique as the people who experienced them, and that's part of the magic. Some people embrace the notion of a Christian God, while others explicitly reject organized religion. Some are led to sobriety by dramatic, even near-death experiences, and others begin the journey with purely internal changes. But these moments share a deep, profound power, one that ignores class and celebrity, changing the lives of those in desperate need.

That change isn't—*can't* be—instantaneous. In that moment, we feel something powerful at work, and yet, being addicts and being human, we don't fully trust it. We fight it, we question it, we fear it's just one more dead end. Still, that moment is all we have to believe in. Over time, the real miracle happens, as the influence of that moment not only persists but lives and grows in us. It's only in retrospect that it becomes *the* moment, the beginning of a new life. In a way, it's like the first sight of someone you fall in love with, or your first glimpse of your child. Those moments are precious in and of themselves, but their deepest value and meaning comes from the journey that follows, the path they set us on. In this case, it's a journey away from isolation and addiction toward profound peace.

The stories in this book were told to me directly by the people who experienced them. I chose that approach because I wanted to get as close as possible to having readers *hear* the intensity in their voices as they talked about those first steps out of the darkness.

Then, as it often does, something unexpected happened. Over and over, people told me that talking about their experience one-on-one, answering questions about it, brought them fresh insights and enriched their own understanding of their journey. Jim Vance told me after our time together "that all of what we talked about was only a snapshot. There is so much more that, in fact, needs to be revisited. Recalling it helps me not to repeat it." I didn't want to miss out on that, so I decided to use the same method to tell my story. I sat down with my collaborator, Jan Werner, who asked me the same questions I'd been asking all these other people. It was a valuable experience for me, and I hope you gain something from it too. Here goes. . . .

By February of 1986, I'd been trying to get sober for nine years; for two of those years I'd even been going to mutual support groups. There was a program for recovery, which I was trying to do piecemeal, trying to do my way—again. I'd use Valium for a couple of days, then narcotics, and then I'd use booze for a couple of days, so I didn't get addicted to any one substance. That was my whole thing—I was always concerned about the physical aspect of addiction, not the mental or spiritual. I was desperately trying to control my usage so that I could function a little bit and not be completely physically dependent.

I was white-knuckling it and it was absolute misery—worse than being a stone-cold junkie, because at least the other way you can be out of it all the time. But I couldn't do that anymore, because the little recovery I had ruined my terminal uniqueness. See, I thought that I was the only one with these problems, that I had gotten myself into this mess and therefore only I could get myself out of it. As addicts, we really believe we are the centers of the universe. Nobody feels like we feel, nobody understands us, nobody can do it but us. All of that *me me me me* thing, which is the thing that kept me sick.

When I went to this group, I sat in a basement with a bunch of other people who were just like me and yet they'd found a way out, and it ruined my drinking and using. I could no longer just lie in the gutter with a needle in my arm. At the same time, I was *incapable* of understanding what I needed to do. Basically I had to accept that I had a spiritual malady as well as a physical malady. That meant surrendering, which I was unwilling to do.

I didn't want to be "addicted," but I couldn't give up, couldn't surrender my will. I just wanted to be out of myself, because all I'd ever wanted was to *not* be here. If that's how you feel, then being here without knowing *how* to be here, and trying to control your use of the only thing you've ever known that helps you cope—that's a recipe for putting a gun in your mouth, which is basically what I was left with.

I was thirty years old, and my whole life had been a series of "This isn't *so* bad." I graduated from law school. So I didn't learn anything, so what. So I was arrested for buying heroin in Roxbury. That's not so bad. At least it was in the *Boston Globe*, not in the *New York Times*. The morning of February 17, I woke up, as usual, with that weight in the pit of my stomach, knowing that all I had in front of me was another day of dancing with the 800-pound gorilla of addiction. I got out of bed and walked over to the windows that looked out onto Commonwealth Avenue—I was living in one of those beautiful old Boston brownstones, and it had giant picture windows, floor to ceiling. I just stood there and stared out at the city. Everything was gray, gray and bleak and freezing cold, and that matched what I was feeling inside.

I thought, "This is bad. This is as bad as it can get." What I felt was just a little bit darker than what I'd felt the day before, but that little bit was enough to finally put me over the edge. I knew I could not exist anymore in that state. I had to either die or change, and I didn't have a gun to put in my mouth, so I had to change, and the only way I could change was to surrender. So I did. I said, to whatever was out there, "You know what? I give up. I absolutely, unequivocally give up. I'm not talking about, 'I give up so I can fight another day.' Whatever you want me to do, I'll do it." And I realize now, that was it. That was the opening through which grace entered my life.

What grace looked like that morning was me walking across the room and picking up the phone. I called a cousin I admired, with whom I had competed my whole life and who was the last guy in the world I wanted to listen to. A couple of years before, my cousin David had died of an overdose. David and I had been best friends our whole lives, which of course involved drinking and drugs, but a few months before he died, I started pulling away from him . . . part of my plan to cut back on using, but I didn't tell him what I was doing. I thought, "It'll help him too. He'll figure it out for himself." Later, I realized David was becoming the version of me I didn't want to see. And my pulling away just made him more isolated, and I felt like it pushed him down into the abyss faster.

So after David died, this cousin I called said, "You know, we've gotta stay sober." He'd gotten sober a while before and was actually the only person who'd said something to me, tried to stop my downward spiral. He had made a quantum leap ahead of me, and on some level I probably knew that, but I wasn't willing to admit it. And so when he said that, I just said, "Fuck you. I'm not staying sober through this. My best friend just died. If you think for one minute I'm gonna lose my other best friend too, you're crazy."

But on the morning of February 17, I called him up and said, "Tell me what to do. Just tell me what to do. Whatever you say, I'll do." And he told me to go back to that group of people who were in recovery and to do what they told me to do. If I hadn't completely surrendered I would've said, "I've already done it, it didn't work." Instead I said, "Okay." And I did it.

There was an enormous relief in the surrender. I remember feeling that something changed, something shifted. I had tried many, many times to get sober, so I didn't completely trust this. But there *was* something deep down inside me, just a glimmer, where something shifted. I didn't understand it, I just had some awareness of it and how profound it was. God, or whatever you want to call it, had given me a glimmer of hope. So I knew intuitively there was something different going on, just a sliver of understanding, something so deep that it was undeniable, and it was totally different from anything that I'd ever experienced before. Just a glimmer. Just a taste.

And it grew exponentially every single day, because the surrender gave me the key of willingness to engage this new life. It's like a starving guy who gets to have a little piece of something, and that's when he realizes just how ravenous he is. That's what it was like, pulling my seat up to this new table and beginning to eat, and then just stuffing my face. Which proves I'm an addict. I'll stuff my face with anything.

The woman I was with was using at the same time, and she didn't stop right away. She tried to get me to use with her. She said, "Do you want to take this?"—a Quaalude or whatever. And I was like . . . "No." I had never said no in a context like that before, *ever*. When somebody handed me something, I put it in my mouth, always. But at that point I could say no.

Even so, the obsession was not lifted immediately. The thing that had driven me for seventeen years, ever since I was twelve years old and I took that first tab of acid—"Oh my God, I want to do this *again*," "*When* can I do it again?" "How can I get *more*?"—that *thing*, which is the obsession, which is the 800-pound gorilla, which I know is the weight that no human power could relieve (because I had tried everything), that thing didn't disappear right away. That thing was still there.

I remember coming to New York, which was always the place I'd go to get high, and I had a lot of prescriptions still. And there's this *thing*. I was enmeshed in recovery, talking to people, and this guy said to me, "You need to get on your knees." I went, "Wh-what?" And he said, "No, you need to get on your knees, and you have to ask to have that lifted. If you have to, throw your shoes under your bed as a way of getting you on your knees. Whatever you need to get down there. To humble yourself. To actually, physically humble yourself. It's all well and good to think about it, but unless you do it . . ."

I did it. I went to my mother's apartment and I was humiliated and I was terrified but I got down on my knees and I asked for this thing to be removed, and it was. Not immediately, but within the next couple of months, it was gone. That thing that I was absolutely powerless over, that had vanquished me for seventeen years, was lifted out of my life. And it hasn't come back since, in over twenty-two years.

The moment I realized it was gone, *that* was like a burning bush. That was nothing short of a miracle.

Bill Wilson, the guy who founded Alcoholics Anonymous, said, "You sober up a horse thief, and you've got a sober horse thief." And that was the case with me. I came to sobriety thinking I was a pretty good guy who hadn't done anybody any harm. I came in with that kind of self-delusion and also an enormous sense of entitlement, of self-centeredness. And I still have all that. I've chipped away a little bit at those faults, and I keep trying, but I'm the same flawed human being I was. The difference is, now that I'm sober, I'm closer to realizing all parts of who Chris is, the good and the bad. That's the great gift of recovery. To discover yourself and also where you come from—it really is a remarkable gift.

If the darkness is down there below and the light is up there above, I'm going from darkness to light. It's not a straight line and it's not a fast journey, but it's going up. I have a set of spiritual principles that I try to live by. Very imperfectly, but I try. Try to do no harm. Have a power greater than yourself to rely on. Serve other people—that's a big thing in terms of your contentment. And clean your house. Clean your own house, and don't worry about other people's houses.

What I realize now is, I could not navigate my life. I couldn't do it. I didn't understand how people *did* the world. I was a law school graduate, I had this résumé I'd managed to put together, but the basic mechanics of navigating the world—I had no idea. You schedule a business meeting and you show up. You get a part in a movie and you show up. Even if you're terrified, even if you're afraid you'll fail. Even if you *do* fail. You show up.

Right now, I'm a productive member of society. I'm involved in other people's lives, I have three great kids, I write books, I make movies, I speak all over the world. I get to do all this stuff because I'm in recovery and I've learned how to put one foot in front of the other. Normal people probably already know this on some level. Addicts and alcoholics, we've got to *learn* all that.

What I think happens for a lot of people, people who've had a road like mine, is that at the end you're hanging out with users and dealers only. At the end I just had drug dealer friends, so I stopped calling them. It wasn't like they were big losses when they were gone, although there was a part of me that thought, "What about that guy, that really nice pharmacist that I used to know?" Because you have to come to terms with the fact that your relationships aren't really friendships, they don't really mean that much, they're just accommodations to the 800-pound gorilla.

The other thing that's hard is the whole family thing. This is not an individual disease, it's a family disease. Even if there's just one alcoholic in the family, everybody's affected by it on some level. I had a difficult time with that. Even though people were very happy that I wasn't ending up in emergency rooms or on the front pages of newspapers anymore, they didn't like *how* I was different. My mom once said, "You can't make the daiquiris anymore?" She didn't get it. "That's great you're not going to shoot heroin anymore, but that doesn't mean you can't drink, right?"

Plus other people who may have problems have to look at their own stuff when you're around. You become like a giant mirror. People start projecting their worries and problems on you. The fact is, I'm too busy worrying about my own problems to pay attention to yours. But if *you* decide you want to get sober, I'm your guy, on whatever level, whatever I can do—because what I've learned is that in order to keep this thing, I've got to give it away.

Somehow I was picked to move from the darkness into the light. I don't know why. I didn't do anything for it, I didn't "earn" it or "deserve" it. At all. At *all*. I just stayed alive. I stayed alive and I stayed connected to some kind of treatment, or some motivation, some goal. I hung on to hope, and hope opens you up to change.

That's what this book and the stories in it are about, and that's what I want people who read it to take away from it—the hope that *this thing can change*. No matter how long it's gone on, no matter how bad it is. And also, these are interesting stories. Lives that are transformed inexplicably are interesting. They're interesting to read about, they're interesting to ponder, they're interesting to meditate on.

But more than anything else, they show us that what's right in front of us is not all there is. There's something else going on out there. I have evidence of it in my life, the people in this book have evidence of it, and it's reinforced for us over and over again, as long as we keep ourselves open to it. And that is grace.

Moments
of
Clarity

JIM VANCE

❧

Jim described himself this way: "I'm a cocaine addict, a father, a husband, a man trying to make a difference in the world." Jim also anchors the nightly news at WRC-TV in Washington, DC, where he's worked since 1969. He was one of the first people to break the color barrier on TV, and he's earned seventeen Emmys and a spot in the National Association of Black Journalists Hall of Fame. He's also one of the stalwarts of the DC recovery community. A couple of things stand out to me about his story: his humor in telling it, and the way he feels most ashamed when he's being recognized for his success. That sense of being a fraud is so common among addicts.

I haven't known hopelessness since 1987, but I remember very well what it felt like. I had a total, complete, full conviction that I was going to die. I did not believe that I had a chance at getting a decent life. I knew I was going to die, and not just die, but die a miserable death. I had decided that if I could get any "good" out of this misery, it would be that I died more miserable than my father. My father died in 1951. I was nine years old. He was thirty-eight. He died of cirrhosis and DTs. I don't know a worse way to die than DTs. Jesus, what agony. But my condition in April 1987 was that I'll find a way to die worse than he did.

I think that speaks to the hopeless state of mind that I was in. I didn't want to die, but if I was going to die, then let me die even worse off than my father was. What kind of insanity is that? That, my friend, pretty much defines hopelessness.

I'm a broadcast journalist and I had been the anchor at the NBC station in Washington, DC, since 1972. In 1987, in August, somehow or other I was still hanging on, but I had been missing in action for two days again. I was down in Southeast DC, where people were living hard lives, and still are. There was a public housing complex that had been abandoned or determined to be shut down—huge, as most of them were, from an urban renewal program in '62. In one of the buildings, there were two apartments that were still occupied. There were no utilities: no water, no electricity, no telephone, no anything. There were some mattresses on the floor. And for two days, I was in one of those apartments, desperately trying to get one more hit off the pipe. I'm in that apartment, I didn't have any clothes on, couldn't get an erection, and couldn't get high. I don't know how that is for most normal people, but for this colored boy, that was as low as he could get. You couldn't get your dick up and you couldn't get high. What is left?

I finally got out of there at some point. I didn't have a car because my car had been repossessed. I went back to where Kathy, who later became my wife, was living and I got cleaned up. She had nothing to say, because by that time, there was nothing else *to* say. There comes a point when silence becomes deafening and cruel. I mean, silence can cut like a knife.

I went to work and got through it, I don't know how. I have some pictures from back then, and I'm not sure why they allowed me to go on the air. Cheeks sunken in, eyes way back in the sockets, dark circles around the eyes because I hadn't slept in probably three days. My teeth were falling out. Literally falling out, because my gums were deteriorating and the bone under the gums was deteriorating. I had to talk in a certain kind of way just to keep my teeth in my head.

On a Thursday night, I did the six o'clock show and I left work at seven o'clock. Richard, who worked at the station, had loaned me his car. I was supposed to turn left to go home but I turned right. I drove around for a couple of hours, stopping every now and again at some phone booth, trying to get somebody to get me something. I finally got a guy in another part of Southeast Washington. I went to his place and got an eight ball* and fired it up. Didn't even pay him, just smoked it right there. When the ball was smoked up, at this point I was geeking. You got to get more. You

---

* An eighth of an ounce of cocaine or methamphetamine.

can't be still, you're bouncing around, kind of like when people want to speed. *Geeking* was the term at that time, and I was geeking.

I told the guy, and he said he had more but he wouldn't give me any more without seeing some cash. I said, "Let me go over to the money machine." I walked out of the apartment and I left the keys to Richard's car because I was just going to walk over to the bank right across the street. But I hailed a cab. As it pulled out from the curb, I saw the guy running out of the house. He had a pistol in his hand, and he ran this way and ran that way looking for me. I got down in the cab, and the guy was still running around when we turned the corner. Oh, he was pissed off.

I got home and got Kathy to pay the cab. She went to bed. I went downstairs, got the shotgun, took Kathy's car, and went to Great Falls Park. The Potomac River runs through it, and there's a serious drop that creates some big rapids. The Olympic kayaking team practices at Great Falls. I was upstream, where you don't have the roar of the river as it drops off the precipice. It's more brooklike, more tranquil, but on that night it was deafening where it should have been melodic and soothing. Deafening and discordant. Jagged and unnerving. It was a violent noise that didn't really exist. My, it was horrible!

I loaded the shotgun—it was a Remington 1100. I used to do bird hunting. Remington 1100 twelve-gauge number four shot. I loaded it, and I had the stock between my legs, against a rock, and I had my thumb on the trigger, and I was ready to go, man. I was ready to go because I just couldn't stand the pain anymore. I had heard tales of heroin addicts when they're trying to kick it, this agonizing phase that they go through when every cell in their body was on fire. Every cell in my body was not on fire, but it seemed like every cell in my body was in pain, just physical pain. I couldn't think of any other way to stop the pain except to just check out.

Why didn't I pull the trigger? I think probably there are two reasons. One is because of what I choose to call God. The other reason was, I had the thought of Kathy or one of my children being asked to come and identify the body. I knew what number four shot from a twelve-gauge shotgun would do. I knew what they would be forced to see, because somebody would have to identify this body. That seemed like such a punk-ass thing to do. I thought about how much I had already devastated them, hurt them, almost destroyed them, but that I could not abide. Even in my total insanity, I couldn't abide the thought of one of them seeing me with the back of my head blown out. And I relaxed my grip.

Oh man, did I cry then. I just lay down in a fetal position and I cried and cried. I don't know, truly, how long I lay there crying. I know it started raining and I was soaking wet and freezing cold. Finally I got up and I went back home. The next day I went down to this place called the Metropolis Club, a real old-school recovery support group, full of old-time drunks. When you go in the building it's just an old rickety door, and when you open the door, what you see are these crumbling old rank stairs. You go up those stairs for a long time. I remember standing there looking up those stairs, thinking, "These are drunks in here." You know what I mean? I'm standing there thinking, "I'm not going in with these fucking drunks."

For whatever reason—and I truly don't remember why—I did climb the stairs and I walked into the meeting room. It was almost full. I don't remember who was speaking at the time, but he looked over to me and there was this little grin on his face, and then he turned around and he continued. I just slunk down the wall to the back of the room, as far back as I could go. When I got back there—talk about things happening as they do—all eyes followed me back, they all knew who I was—and when I got to the back of the room, there was a small guy sitting there, and he said out loud so that everybody can hear, "We were wondering when you were going to get here." And he broke into this big grin and got up and came over. He grabbed me and hugged me, and I swear to God it was like being filthy and then being washed clean. It was energizing. It was fulfilling. It was comforting. It was every wonderful thing you can think of. He didn't let go. He didn't let go. He stood there and he held me, I don't know, a couple minutes. And nobody else said anything. They grinned and smiled all around the room, and I sat down. I don't know that I've ever been anywhere where I ever felt more loved.

That was my first support group meeting.

I got to tell you, it took a while to get comfortable in those groups. I was comfortable in the first moment because I was comforted in that moment. But it took me a while to get comfortable because every time I went in there for the next couple of months, I went in there as Jim Vance, the anchor guy. It was a little while before I went in there as Jim the Junkie. Jim Vance sitting in there, he never had a chance of getting clean. Never had a fucking chance. Jim Vance is convinced "I got this. I can handle this because I have been through as much fire as you and I've had many challenges as you. I have overcome all of them and I have prevailed. And I will prevail over this too, no matter what it is, because I got what it takes and I can beat this." That's Jim Vance. That's Jim Vance with his finger on the trigger. That's Jim Vance crying in a fetal position in the rain because he's desperate and out of answers and doesn't know what else to try except maybe death. Death might work because nothing else was working. That guy isn't going to get clean. That guy is going to die.

Jim the Junkie, he had a chance, because Jim gave the fuck up. I'd like to be more eloquent, but that's what it was. Jim gave the fuck up on everything. "Whatever you say, I will do. I'm done. I got no answers. I got no solutions. I got no hope. I got nothing." That's the guy that got clean. That's the guy that gave himself a chance to become clean, because Jim Vance was a dead man walking. Jim the Junkie just needed a way he could go on. Jim the Junkie needed to sit down, shut up, and listen. And that's what the Metropolis Club was all about. Some hard-core dudes in there, and to this day I bless them one and all. I will bless them until the day I die and then beyond that, because their full thing was "You've got nothing to say that we need, and we've got everything that you're needing. So shut up, sit down, and listen."

It could not have happened sooner. It happened when it happened because that's when it was supposed to happen. One thing I will never forget is something a guy named Reggie said to me. I was miserable, just geeking again one day, this time without dope. I called him, and I was telling him that I'm in a miserable state of being and I am not liking this shit, and I am not liking you either, Reggie. He chuckled and said, "You are exactly where you're supposed to be." I'm like, "What the fuck are you talking about?" He said to me, "Vance, everything that happens does so because it's supposed to. If it doesn't happen, it's because it isn't supposed to." I wanted to go all Descartes and Nietzsche on him, I wanted to pull out my philosophical library on this guy. Jim Vance was pissed, but Jim the Junkie, he didn't try to argue that. I accepted it. I really did, man, and I remember it was like a wave crossing over me. I accepted the fact that I'm supposed to feel like this today. But just because I feel like this now, that doesn't mean that at four o'clock I'm still going to feel like this. This is what it is *now*. I'll deal with this.

That's as close as I got to an epiphany, that willingness to accept whatever was happening at that given time. There was no bolt of lightning. There was no revelation of any kind. It was simply the fact that I had begun the process and embraced the process of surrender, which was foreign to me, by the way. Surrender, my ass.

My grandfather was a plumber. He had sixteen kids, nine sons including my father. I was an only child, but I had tons of uncles, aunts, and cousins. From the time I can remember walking until I left home, I remember one or another of my uncles chucking me under the chin and pushing my head back up. The point being, "Hold your head up. Never let me see you cry."

I remember tearing up my knee one time. I had a brace on it, and my Uncle Spunky went to the hospital with me to get the brace taken off, and he brought me back to the house. I was going up the stairs to my house, climbing the stairs with a stiff leg. And he's like, "Why are you walking like that?" I said, "I can't bend my knee." And he hit the back of my knee, to make it bend, and it hurt—not a little bit, it hurt like hell. I started to cry, and his words to me were "Do you think that hurt? I can do some hurt that'll make you really want to cry." I walked up the stairs like a man. Now that sounds cruel. That sounds abusive. It was not. Those people were loving me just as hard as they possibly could. They were black men in 1950-whatever who got shit on every which way they turned. All they were saying to me was "Little Jimmy, stand up. Man up. Never surrender." You see what I'm saying?

So when I get to this dope thing, and all of a sudden these guys are telling me "You have to surrender," I'm like "What the fuck are you talking about? There's no way. I got here by being a stand-up kind of guy." And their thing was "Yeah, you'll kick the rest of the way only if you surrender." It just didn't connect. It only connected at the point when Jim Vance went away and Jim the Junkie came in.

Jim Vance died in 1987. Jim the Junkie is the one that lived. Jim Vance is the one who killed himself then. And that's how that works.

I surrendered, but Jesus, I was scared. For days and days and days, I had to adjust as the embryo of the new Jim grew. As a colored man, it was the first time in my life that I didn't try to assert some control over my life, or at least make some effort to manage the forces coming at me, whatever they might have been. I had no strength, no power. I had no will. And that all put me in a state of terror. I remember being afraid like I have never been afraid before in my life.

And there was something else too—crying. God, I never cried so much in my life. I could be on the way to 7-Eleven and I'd sit in the parking lot and just break out in tears. Unreal, sobbing tears. And that would terrify me, because I wasn't even sure why I was crying. "What the fuck is happening to me?" I felt shifting and changing shapes and lines and colors and shadings. The word that comes into my head now is *rebirth.* That's a little melodramatic, I think, but it's not that far off what my feeling was. I really was being reshaped, reconfigured, remolded, maybe even reborn. But whatever it was, the change was scary.

That night in the park with the shotgun is still the most absolutely painful recollection that I have, and I don't revisit it often. When I do, it's not because I seek it and go there. I think it's because of the bounty of blessings that have come my way. The memory of that moment usually comes up when I'm about to be celebrated. I remember there was a celebration of my twenty-five years at the station. This was twelve years ago. It was at the Four Seasons. It was a big go-to-hell blowout thing, and people are making speeches and giving tributes and stuff. When it's finally my turn to take the mike, I swear to God I remember Great Falls. Whenever Jim Vance is about to come back in, that's when I remember.

The guy at the Metropolis who hugged me, I do remember him. I was not a hugger when I went in at the start, and I was a little bit uncomfortable with all these guys. For one thing, some of them didn't smell that good. And I was just uncomfortable with all the hugging, a lot of hugging. I got over it. I got over it and I began to appreciate the benefit of a good hug. They're not all as overwhelmingly meaningful as that first one, when I first walked into the Metropolis Club, but they all have something significant to them. I do recall the hug way more often than I recall that moment in Great Falls. And frankly, I'm grateful for that.

How do I deal with people in my life who need help? Carefully, quietly, respectfully, and deliberatively.

My experience teaches me that you can't gorilla—that's the word we use in the hood—you can't gorilla an addict into doing what you think the addict ought to do. Nobody could gorilla me into doing anything. That's the quietly and respectfully kind of thing that I'm talking about.

And the carefully. I will always be accessible to someone who needs what I have to give. But I was so full of shit when I was using that I think I have an antenna for those who are full of shit. I make no judgments, but I will not let someone bullshit me. My time is too valuable and there are too many people who do need some help. I won't be wasting it on some asshole.

And deliberatively. You can't rush that shit. I have taken guys to recovery meetings who got arrested two weeks, three weeks later. When the brother came out of jail, I not only took a call, I picked him up. "Are you ready now?" And it doesn't happen all that many times, but sometimes—yeah, he's ready now.

God, to me, looks like Amani. He looks like Dawn. He looks like Brendon. Those are my three kids. God, to me, looks like my wife, Kathy. We just celebrated our twentieth anniversary. God, to me, looks like Sumo. Sumo is my Akita, and I admire him because it occurs to me that that dog is telling me something every single day. Dogs don't think about yesterday. They don't think about tomorrow. Dogs live in the moment.

I look for God everywhere. I see God everywhere, and I'm grateful for the vision. I always believed in God, but I didn't have a clue what God is about. I thought God was in heaven, and that was one of my biggest mistakes. I lived for years with that mistake. God isn't in heaven. He's in my dog, among other things.

SUSAN CHEEVER

In the early nineties, friends started telling me stories about a brilliant, funny woman who was one of the most supportive, enthusiastic, and visible members of the New York City recovery community. She's probably best known for two memoirs: one, Note Found in a Bottle, *describes her battles with alcoholism and eating disorders, while the other,* Home Before Dark, *is a tender, honest recollection of her father, the writer John Cheever. But my favorite is her wonderful biography of the cofounder of Alcoholics Anonymous Bill Wilson, entitled* My Name Is Bill.

After more than a decade of hearing people sing her praises, I finally met Susan in 2005, when we were both onstage at the 92nd Street Y in Manhattan. I was on tour for my own memoir, Symptoms of Withdrawal, *and she was interviewing me in front of four hundred people who were there to hear tales about Camelot, the Rat Pack, and yes, that 800-pound gorilla she and I both wrestled with. Her questions were surprising, playful, and insightful—everything you hope for but usually don't get from an interviewer—and all of it was pure Susan.*

One thing that struck me about her story was its basic contradiction: despite her intelligence and perceptiveness, she was completely incapable of seeing, much less dealing with, the reality of her situation. It's such a familiar, human dilemma, and she recounts it with great humor and grace.

I really believe that there's a level of harmony in the universe, which I call God, and I do think that everything happens exactly the way it's meant to happen. Often not the way *I* want it to happen, often not the way I think it *should* happen, but there's a holiness to what actually exists, as opposed to what I think should exist and which is not holy.

. . .

For me, it wasn't just one moment of clarity, it was several of them, over several years, and they're all about other people because I don't like to think about myself, what might be wrong with me. Those moments are very vivid to me, and I think about them a lot. At the time, they were all about other people's addictions, not mine. It's embarrassing to me now. It was like, how many ways can my finger point before I finally get it, that it's me.

My first moment was about my daughter, who was about a year old. When I had my daughter my whole life changed. I mean I just had had no idea what life was, no idea, for all my yak, yak, yak about everything. And the moment I had that little girl, I knew what it was to care about someone else more than you care about yourself.

But then my father died—after seven years of sobriety—and I was having a difficult year, so difficult that when my dog died I didn't even notice. I was in some kind of numbness. I did quite a bit of locking myself in the bathroom or shutting myself in a room with absolutely no light. On the outside, life looked good. We had a nanny and a babysitter, and I was writing a book about my father. I would cross the park to my studio on the East Side and get a six-pack of Tab and a bottle of vodka. I would drink Tab and vodka and write all day, and then I would get home at about four o'clock in the afternoon and take care of my daughter. I was totally unaware that my drinking was anything other than completely normal. I just thought I was a thirty-nine-year-old with a young kid and a handsome husband, and my father had died, and I was having maybe a hard time with that. I knew I definitely was not an alcoholic. My father was an alcoholic. He was a bisexual seventy-year-old man, and I was this *very* heterosexual girl, so how could I possibly be what he was?

I would go to mutual recovery support groups with my father and I would say, "I'm sorry, I'm not an alcoholic, although I attend these meetings," and of course everybody was adorable. Everybody said, "You are in the right place. We are happy to have you. Come anytime." And the level of honesty in these groups was so electrifying, and the stories were just amazing. So I went to the meetings and I felt this intense connection with these people, but I'd listen to their stories and I always just thought, "This is not for me, because I'm not an alcoholic, because I don't do any of these things."

Anyway, that first moment. I was sitting in the kitchen with my daughter. She's in her high chair, and I'm watching her drink her milk out of a cup, and there's something *weird* about the way she's drinking her milk, I swear. There's just some extra hunger there in this little baby. And I think, "Oh my God, she's an addict. What am I going to do? Okay, I'll go to recovery meetings for her because she can't go."

So I started going to a support group for people with eating disorders, and I completely identified—I have an eating disorder. And I definitely got the message that I was *not* an alcoholic. One woman said, "When you're hungry, just have a drink." So I did, and it was great. I was able to control my eating disorder with my alcoholism, with my sex addiction, with my many disorders. I had so many disorders that I was able to hide each one behind all the others.

Then I started going back to the groups I'd gone to with my father, because there aren't as many of the eating disorder meetings. I'd go these meetings for people who drank too much and they would say, "How long have you been having problems with drinking?" I would say, "Oh, I'm not an alcoholic. I'm in another program, but I just come to these meetings because I like them."

One of the friends I made in these peer support groups suggested that I stop drinking. When I did, I suddenly felt that my life had come into focus. All of a sudden, like I'd stepped off a curb. I saw that my marriage was dead, for instance. All these big questions were suddenly answered, very clearly, but not in a spiritual way. I think clarity without spirituality is a very dangerous thing, and that's what I had.

I was sober for about three years, went to a lot of meetings, did everything they suggested—except I ran my own life. In those three years, I left my second husband and married my third husband, who was an alcoholic. I thought that was fine. That's how well I was running my life. I thought that his drinking wasn't my business, that I could be sober while he was an alcoholic.

The next big moment was when I was pregnant with my son. At home, my water broke and my contractions were ten minutes apart. My husband could see that I was in a lot of pain so he handed me a glass of champagne.

He said, "Here, this will help," so I drank it, and then I went happily through the bottle. My contractions completely stopped. The pain entirely went away and I went to sleep, and actually what woke me up was the doctor calling and saying, "Where are you?"

So that was a moment, when my husband handed me that glass. I thought, "Okay, I'll go back to meetings of those peer support groups. So I drink a bottle of champagne in childbirth. It won't be a big deal. I'll go back to meetings and it'll be gone." I had my son—thank God, he's healthy—and when he was about a week old, I started going back to meetings. But I did not get it back, that precious connection, that feeling I'd gotten in the meetings I'd gone to before. I couldn't get it. I would go, and I would feel like I didn't belong there, and who *were* these people? When I went with my father, I was feeling so good there, and then I had the same thing when I went back after I saw my daughter with the milk. But then I lost it, I could not get it back.

So then I drank for two and a half years, during which I gladly trashed a lot of important things. But I did have rules. I only drank wine. I never drank in the morning. I rarely drank alone. I didn't drink every day. I did all the things you have to do to prove you're not an alcoholic. At the end of two and a half years I was living in this nightmare house with two little kids and my husband, who was getting drunker and drunker and less and less reliable, and of course for kids you need reliability. I just wanted to die all the time.

One night I looked at my husband and thought, "He's an alcoholic." I felt like I had just met him. "He's ruining my life. *He's* why I'm having a hard time." So I decided to do an intervention. I went and talked to all the intervention people and eventually one of them said, "You know, why don't you get sober and it'll be good for the intervention."

On April 3, 1992, I went back to a meeting I had been to many times. A handsome guy walked me home and I said, "I'm not an alcoholic. It's just wine." And he said, "Of course you're not an alcoholic. Here's a meeting list. Here's my phone number. Call me tomorrow and we'll go to another meeting." I called him and we talked and I went to another meeting and I started going to a meeting every day. Within about a week this handsome man had a sober woman call me and take me to meetings. He got me there, and I started to get better. That connection was there, that feeling of being at home.

I was so scared. As I began to get better, in spite of myself—because I was only there to stop my husband from drinking, right?—I began to see that I had to leave that house. I couldn't live with a man who was drinking a bottle of liquor every day. I began to see all these things, and very slowly things began to happen. People came with me to look at apartments. People came with me to a divorce lawyer. I mean it was the most amazing time. People came and helped me. The intervention with my husband never happened. He's still drinking, whatever it is, sixteen, seventeen years later.

But I got through that time with God's help. Up to that point, I didn't really think there *was* a God. I mean I was Christian and I went to church, but I didn't think God was interested in *me*. Now I have what I consider scientific proof that God exists, because before, whenever there was a glass of red wine, I drank it. I always tried so hard *not* to have that glass of wine, and I always drank it. I knew that I couldn't stop on my own. So every night I *didn't* drink that glass of wine, I began to believe that there was another force.

And slowly, very slowly, I began to believe that I was an alcoholic. I began to believe that an alcoholic can be a person who only drinks wine. I began to believe that I didn't have to go to jail and have DTs, like my father did, to be an alcoholic.

I remember the first time I heard the Saint Francis Prayer, the one that begins, "Lord, make me an instrument of your peace." I was married and I was having an affair with a married guy, and the two of us were hanging out with another woman with whom he was also having an affair, who was also married. The other woman's uncle died, and we all went to the funeral. I was there with my husband, and this man with whom I was sleeping was there with his wife, and of course the woman who was also sleeping with him was there with her husband. It was her uncle's funeral. So ridiculous, I can't stop laughing about it now. She stands up and speaks for her uncle and she reads the Saint Francis Prayer. She gets to the part that says, "Lord, grant that I may seek to comfort rather than to be comforted; to understand, rather than to be understood; to love, rather than to be loved." I hear that and I think, "That is crazy. That is *craziness*. Who wouldn't rather be loved? Who wouldn't rather be comforted?" I thought it was a joke.

Now I love that prayer. It gets me through *everything*. I taught it to both of my children, and we've recited it before meals for years and years and years. That's how I live my life now.

Before, for all my moments of ecstasy, for how good I looked and how many fantastic clothes I had . . . I was very, very unhappy, because it was all about getting. And once you get, then you want more. My whole identity was a person who *got* stuff and *had* stuff. I wanted to be pretty. I wanted to be fancy. I wanted to be sexy. I wanted to be rich. I wanted to have whatever anybody else had. I thought all that would make my life good.

And it didn't, and the only way I was able to live like that was by using these addictions. I was afraid the whole thing would come down like a house of cards, which is exactly what it was, and then I wouldn't have anything. All the things that I thought made me happy would be gone. And to some extent, they are. That thing that I used to do with men before, I can't do that sober. A lot of what happened was over a lot of very good wine. There are moments when I miss that, being able to operate in that way. I think it's important to say that. I *did* lose a lot of what I was afraid of losing. But what I got in return is so precious that I really don't mind.

Here's the beauty of getting sober late. I slept with everyone. I traveled everywhere. I drank thirty-year-old scotch and I took heroin. I did all that stuff and you know what? It didn't make me happy. So in a way I'm a little grateful that I got sober late because I tried everything else and it added up to nothing. And now I know that.

Now I have peace. I feel like I'm at peace with the world most of the time—not always, but most of the time. I know how to behave most of the time—not always, but most of the time. And if I *don't* know, I can just remember that it's not about me, it's about you. Then I can just behave in the way that would be of more service to you, and that really works out well for both of us, right? I just know how to live now in a way that makes me extremely happy. I'm very content. I'm very grateful. I go to bed every night and I say to God, "Thank you."

CHRIS GEROLMO

Mississippi Burning *put Chris on the map as a screenwriter. Since then, he's written and directed the HBO movie* Citizen X, *about Russian serial killer Andrei Chikatilo, and he and Stephen Bochco cocreated the FX Network's series* Over There, *about the U.S. troops in Iraq. Chris is also a talented musician; he wrote the theme for* Over There, *and has an album out called* I'm Your Daddy. *Chris and I went to elementary school together in Manhattan but we didn't reconnect until we both became members of the L.A. recovery community. He's both smart and thoughtful, and I knew he'd have something interesting to say about recovery. I interviewed him in his office, and while we talked, he strummed his guitar. He wrote his own sound track to his story while he told it.*

I'm a dyed-in-the-wool atheist and have been since I was ten years old. In fact, I was an atheist altar boy. So I don't think of my recovery in spiritual terms, although I do believe there is a spiritual component to what has happened to me. William James, in *The Varieties of Religious Experience*, wrote that the basis for all the world's religions is that oceanic sense of connection to all living things. Sensing it gives you the same kind of awe and wonder and excitement and even terror you can get from looking out at the ocean.

I don't believe in any religion whatsoever, but I do acknowledge that oceanic sense of connection. I tend to think of it more in scientific terms, of course—that we are all made out of DNA—so it makes perfect sense to me to feel that connectedness to all living things. I feel it when I go to a meeting. I feel it when I share with other alcoholics, other human beings. An hour later, when somebody turns left from the right lane and cuts me off, I can temporarily lose my sense of connection to all living beings, but it never totally goes away, and I still acknowledge that it's a part of the change that's going on in me. It's not so much about myself and my own tiny, private, desperate corner of the world anymore. It's more about taking my place at the table with everybody else.

There wasn't really one moment when I realized I had to get sober. It took a long time, and I really was kicking and scratching and clawing, trying not to realize it. I can tell you about some of the moments that *didn't* do it for me, as remarkable as they were.

First, I never considered myself an alcoholic. I knew I had a cocaine problem, but alcohol was just something I drank to go to sleep at night. One morning I woke up in the most excruciating pain. It was like a 9 on a pain scale of 0 to 10. So I was really in excruciating pain, and I ended up at my doctor's office and then in the hospital, where I remember being really paranoid about falling asleep. I was on Demerol in the hospital, but normally if I didn't have my vodka, I had a lot of trouble sleeping. I remember demanding that they give me something to help me sleep.

I remember waking up that first night in the hospital, in the middle of the night. I was looking down what looked like a row of beds, although there was only one other bed in the room, and I decided that I was in a Vietcong hospital and I was a prisoner of war, chained to my bed. I got up and tore off all my chains, which meant pulling out the IVs and spraying blood all over the walls. Then I woke up out of this haze and, being a very neat drug addict, I cleaned up all the blood before I pressed the button for the nurse. I did quit drinking after that, but only because I'd had pancreatitis and they said I had to stop drinking to avoid a recurrence of the pain. I didn't stop taking cocaine.

What I needed then was something to replace the alcohol to go to sleep with, and I discovered the Pill Lady in the Valley. I was doing very well in Hollywood at that time, and I'd drive my custom-made Porsche convertible to the Pill Lady in the Valley and I'd ask her what she had. She'd say, "Well, I have two hundred of these and they are Mexican, two dollars each, and I have fifty of those, they're five dollars and they are really good, and I have seventeen of those and they are ten dollars each. I have some of this black tar heroin too. You can try that." And I'd just say, "I'll take it." I would clean her out of everything she had every time I visited. I always pitied the poor drug addict who showed up after me, because there was nothing left. I would be back four weeks, six weeks later and she'd say, "Jesus, you didn't do all that yourself, did you?" I'd say, "Oh no, I have a lot of parties." But basically, I was just using it to go to sleep. Anyway, *that* didn't make me quit either. That might have been a warning sign to somebody else, but not to me.

The moments of real despair came when I couldn't sleep. When I had taken too much cocaine, or run out of alcohol, or didn't have the right pills, or just couldn't get the combination right, I would end up awake in bed for hours, sometimes all night. I was desperately alone and miserable and occasionally suicidal at the end of a long night after not being able to go to sleep.

I decided I needed to have a pistol in the house, so I got a Glock 17 and kept it between the mattress and the box spring. My head was on the pillow, always twelve inches away from the Glock. I thought about that Glock often in those days, when I couldn't go to sleep. But that wasn't a wake-up call for me at all.

I used to take a lot of drugs on the road. I remember once coming out of that haze when I'd taken too much cocaine and had drunk everything in the house and I was dozing. I remember waking up with a start, every muscle clenched, sitting up halfway in bed, absolutely convinced that I was dwindling in stature, literally. I was sure that every time I breathed out, I was shrinking a little more. And that when I inhaled again, I wasn't reexpanding. I sat in this clenched position for like forty-five minutes in a total panic, a total drug-induced psychosis. I was sure that I was going to die by dawn. Then it went away. I was able to lie down, roll around, be miserable, go to sleep. *Still,* that was not a wake-up call.

I remember once waking up in a hotel in New York with slurred speech and it didn't go away all day. So the next morning I went to the hospital to talk to a doctor about it, and he said it was from taking a lot of drugs. The slurring persisted for a couple of days, and that was pretty scary. I thought I was going to be permanently debilitated, but then that went away, so that was not a wake-up call either.

Nor were the nosebleeds, which were regular toward the end, but eventually, somehow, I had this gradual, dawning realization that I have to do something about this. That the only responsible thing is to do something about this. I basically had alienated everybody in my life.

The whole time all this was going on, I had a therapist who knew I had a drug problem and was waiting me out. I sometimes lied to him, told him I had stopped for weeks at a time, blah, blah. He knew what I knew, that it was just a matter of time. We talked about it regularly, and I gradually realized that the only responsible thing to do was to go to rehab.

Finally there was one summer, the summer of 1998, when I acknowledged, okay, it's time to make a plan. I was going to go to rehab early in 1999. Marty, my therapist, was going, "What do you mean? Why are you going to wait till January?" I explained that I was so important in the movie business—by the way, I was the only person in the movie business who thought that—I was so important that I couldn't take a month off and just disappear. In the past few years I had been taking a month off in the winter to go skiing in Aspen, so I would take the same month off this year and go to rehab instead. I had this all worked out in my mind. Now if you say to people in the movie business in L.A., "I'm renting a house in Aspen for a month," they'll immediately ask you, "Well, when can I come for a weekend?" So I said I was going to Canada, because I knew they'd say, "Well, it's cold in Canada. Have a good time."

I finally had a date—February 7—and I let everybody know that I was going skiing. My parents decided they wanted to come and stay in my house while I was away, for a kind of winter vacation. Fine, fine—only they got these super-saver fares and they had to come out three days before I was leaving. Now that's a bad idea, because I had a lot of narcotics to take before I went to rehab, and if my parents were staying with me I couldn't stay up all night, get whacked out of my tree, and play the guitar. So that was my last three days, waiting for my parents to go to bed at nine thirty, waiting for my nose to stop bleeding so that I could snort more cocaine and play more guitar and get ready to go to rehab. The rehab wasn't very real in my mind. It was on the schedule, that's all.

Of course, the day arrives and I'm supposed to leave at seven thirty in the morning. I try to sleep for an hour at five thirty, then I get up at the last minute. Because I had this whole charade going about skiing, I had to pack all this shit, my skis and everything, and I am wearing an enormous parka, waving good-bye to my parents, who were in their own Norman Rockwell dream, and my friend David is there to pick me up, with my parka and my enormous bag of ski stuff, and of course I am going to rehab in goddamn Arizona.

I hated rehab. When I saw they had this higher-power thing going on there, I was really pissed off. My brother had been sober for many years, and at the time I didn't get along with him at all, and I assumed that everybody in the recovery program was just like him, so that was bad. It took a week or two before I really turned my head around and realized how great this experience was going to be for me.

I remember Marty—who I later found out was in recovery himself—telling me before I went that I should try to say yes as often as possible. I was like, "What do you mean? Why?" He said, "Because there are going to be people there who have seen a lot of people like you come through the process. They are going to try to help you, and the more you can say yes and just do what they suggest, the better off you will be. Just don't question everything, and don't start with no as the answer to everything."

That stood me in good stead there after my first week. I was basically detoxing and pretty hostile, and they keep you that first week in rooms right off the nurses' station so they can take care of you. I was not a very good patient. But then you move into the other buildings with roommates, and I started meeting people and listening a little more. At some point, I realized I was forty-five years old and I was done. It wasn't going that well for me, and I didn't want to be here in rehab five or seven times. I didn't want to start again, I didn't want to be lying there at four in the morning thinking about that Glock again. Gradually I realized those people were there to help me, that they had very specific knowledge of exactly what I was going through in that moment, and they knew how to help me get through that moment. And I really made some good friends there. By the time I left rehab, I really wanted to stay sober; I really wanted to. I was willing to do whatever it took.

Marty had said, "We have to have an aftercare facility," so I went to this outpatient rehab facility called Matrix two or three times a week. Most of the people there were just trying to get sober, but some people, like me, were using it as outpatient aftercare. I was there for a couple of months, and then, when I was six months sober, I asked if I could stay there and be a volunteer. In each group there are the therapist and the clients and then a coleader, which is this volunteer position. Marty had told me you have to do two things to stay sober: go to recovery meetings and help other alcoholics. So I did this volunteer thing, and I have been doing it for eight years now, and I go to meetings still.

At first I hated the meetings. I stood in the back, I wore my sunglasses, I folded my arms, and I kept my jacket zipped up so that nobody dared say hello or anything. But I just kept going. I did it. Marty had told me that I had to do this to stay sober and so I did it.

Why did it work? Well, as part of the program, we're often asked to tell our stories. You're trying to make sense of your life, so you tell the story of your life in such a way that *you* understand it. When I was in rehab, I remember very vividly feeling that I did not know how I'd gotten there. I just did not know how I'd started out as a promising young screenwriter and ended up in rehab at forty-five, an alcoholic and a drug addict. And I very vividly remember sitting in that circle of sixty people in rehab, recalling this thing that had happened to me years before in L.A. I had written *Mississippi Burning,* and I came to L.A. and I bought a little gray Porsche, and I was really cool in my own mind. I remember driving down Sunset in my little gray Porsche on a sunny day and I'm at a red light, and a bumblebee landed on my windshield wiper. I am looking at him, and the light changes, and I take off, and of course this bumblebee is trapped in this kind of little vortex of air behind the windshield wiper and it can't get out. It's getting bounced around like it's in a washing machine. I go for a mile till the next red light and then the bumblebee flies away, and I'm looking at it and going, "Now what does he think just happened to him? How can he find his way home? What was that all about for him?"

I remember that coming into my mind in rehab, and this sense of knowing that I am that bumblebee. "I am here now and I do not know how I got here." We tell the stories of how we got here to ourselves and to other people all the time, because what I believe recovery is, at its essence, is that I talk to you about what happened to me and you talk to me about what happened to you. I tell these stories, and I've told them all a hundred times. I tell them for therapeutic reasons, both for me and for the recently quit addicts that I talk to regularly, just so they hear what happened to somebody else. I think of what happened to me a lot, because it's so important to an alcoholic to remember where you were in order to stay here where you are now and not go back. If I started thinking that everything was cool, I'm fine now, I could get in trouble again.

Because that was the main lie of my life as a drug addict—I'm cool, it's cool, everything's cool. I dress like a bum now, but when I was a practicing drug addict I dressed very well by the standards of Hollywood at that time. I wore black Armani suits. I drove a convertible Ferrari. I dated the most spectacular-looking girls I could find. Illusion was everything that I had, the illusion that everything is cool. I'd end up at home with an eight ball and a bottle of vodka and two packs of Marlboro Lights, but that was my private problem. Now I don't want to go back to that sort of pretending. Now I'm just trying to be a good citizen, insofar as I can. I'm trying to do my job and be a good husband and be a good father. I'm just trying to take my place at the table.

AIMEE LIU

❦

Aimee Liu suffers from an eating disorder. Her first book, Solitaire, *described her experience with anorexia, at a time when eating disorders weren't on most people's radar. Since then she's become a successful novelist and teacher. In 2007, she returned to the issue she'd first explored nearly thirty years before in her book* Gaining: The Truth about Life After Eating Disorders. *It's estimated that 8 million Americans have an eating disorder—7 million women and 1 million men. And though eating disorders have the highest mortality rate of any mental illness, Aimee's story demonstrates that there is a way out.*

If I could talk to my previous self, I'd say, "Pay attention to what you love. Give yourself permission to focus on what you love and act as if the rest of the world doesn't exist. Just focus on what gives you delight, what gives you pleasure, what really makes you tick, and also, learn to understand yourself. Look deeper than the obvious." So much of who each of us is really comes down to our DNA. We are all born with very particular temperaments and tendencies, and some of that you can change and adjust, and some of it you can't.

There were three moments for me. The first one occurred when I was between my sophomore and junior year of college, when I really hit bottom with my eating disorder. There was another one that occurred when I was in my late forties, when I realized that I had been living in a kind of a half-life of eating disorder for over twenty years. And there was a third one, which was the turning point to real clarity.

The most obvious turning point was the first one, which propelled me out of the real depths. It was 1973, and very few people really knew anything much about eating disorders. I was in a period of profound, self-imposed isolation, living my life basically to satisfy the eating disorder. In order to protect my weight loss and to prevent the world from pushing any food in my path, I had elected to spend that summer in New Haven by myself. I was a painter, painting self-portraits all summer long, by myself. I was living on a single bag of oranges, which I stretched for as much of the summer as I possibly could. I was walking several miles a day, to and from where I was house-sitting to the gallery where I was painting. I didn't talk to anybody, I didn't call anyone. It was the summer of the Watergate hearings, but I didn't turn on the television or pick up the newspaper, I didn't listen to the radio. That was the world I created for myself that summer.

One afternoon, in August, walking back to the house, I was in the middle of Cross Campus, which is bordered on one side by Beinecke Library Commons and on the other side by Sterling Library—it's an enclosed quad—and it was very, very hot in that dirty, polluted, claustrophobic way that New Haven can get. The humidity was high and it was about 97 degrees. Everything felt very polluted and very still. Halfway across the quad I was just struck by the *silence*. It was a moment that stopped me in my tracks. It felt like the entire world had emptied out. There wasn't a sound. Not a bird, a whisper, a car, a truck. There was nothing. I don't know why, but I suddenly was completely shaken by the realization that I had pushed everybody that I cared for away from me. That there was all this life out there, all the people I knew from school were off living a life filled with things, with their summer. I felt like I was the last person in the world, and I didn't want to be the last person in the world.

At the same time there was a recognition that I had completely created this situation myself, I had basically isolated myself. I suddenly came up against the recognition that my life was totally empty, *I* was absolutely empty, all my senses and all my emotions just blunted. That was probably the most hopeless yet hopeful moment I can remember. It was a state of despair and—I don't want to say guilt—a recognition that I was responsible for what I had done to myself and to my life, that nobody else was responsible, and that the only way I was going to be able

to change it was by making and choosing a different path for myself going forward.

The first thing I did was call some friends. I tried to locate people and
tried to make plans to reconnect with people. I was specifically trying to
think of people who were healthy, people who were joyful, people who
ate, people who laughed, people who cared about themselves and about
what they were doing and about other people.

I had always denied that I had a problem, and I'd always defended my . . .
well, there was no name for it then. Nobody at that time called it *anorexia*.
It wasn't until years later that I heard that term for the first time. But I
defended my choice to maintain a minimal weight and to not eat and to
hide underneath that obsession. I had noticed that although there were a
number of other people on campus who were doing the same thing, and
there had been a number of other girls in high school also doing the same
thing, we were very much in the minority. The majority of people seemed to
be much better adjusted and more self-directed and more purposeful and
happier in their appearance. I had noticed that, but I didn't really pay attention.

That moment on that hot August day was really the first time that I'd
ever come face-to-face with the reality that something needed to change
dramatically. Instead of seeking out pathological, negative examples, I
started to look at life-affirming examples as role models. I suppose the
simplest way to say it is that instead of actively choosing to minimize everything about myself in my life, I started looking at the possibility of
maximizing my life.

I didn't know any treatment that one could get, and I hadn't come
from a family that had any use for psychology or psychotherapy, so unfortunately, when I had this turning point, my assumption was that I could
and should take care of business myself, and that I could do that simply
by choosing better role models and making different choices. Those are
both important, but in and of themselves they're not enough. What I realize now is that I sent myself into what I call the half-life of eating disorders. I didn't continue to obsess about food and weight as I had done

before, but I didn't acquire really good coping skills. I didn't fully come to terms with the wiring and temperamental aspects of my body and my mind, those things that were contributing to the eating disorder. I remained very compulsive, very obsessive; it just took other forms. Rather than obsessing about calories and losing weight, I became obsessive about performance, about other aspects of my life. For the next twenty years, I was in that half-life where I was still captive to the same kinds of thinking but with behaviors that didn't involve food.

I met my husband when I was twenty-five, and we've been together through most of the time since, but there were a lot of ramifications related to the eating disorder that affected our marriage and affected my other relationships. One of those ramifications is a real difficulty with intimacy and trust. Another big one is the inability to face conflict, the inability to stand up to another person and articulate my feelings, my emotions, needs, wants, fears—any of that stuff. I would run away from problems, I would hide, I would think that if I found another husband, then that would take care of the whole problem, rather than realizing that I was a big part of the problem. All of this went on for years.

Then in my late forties, my husband turned sixty, and he was under a tremendous amount of stress due to work. He basically said he wanted out. We got into counseling, and I kept telling myself that it was all going to be fine, and he kept saying, "No, I really need some time apart. I really need to be separated. I am not at all sure that I want to continue this marriage and I need to figure it out by myself." I thought that being in counseling would solve the problem, and I also thought that getting a new house would solve the problem. I mean, it's classic. It's the parallel of "Well, if I just lost five more pounds, that would take care of the problem," only I was thinking, "Well, if we just get a new house, that will take care of the problem." We did end up buying a new house, and I did keep thinking that as soon as the house was finished and we moved in, everything would be fine.

Well, my husband viewed the arrival of the new house as his opportunity to start the separation. I honestly didn't believe that he meant it until

I moved into the house alone. He refused to come. I went into total chaos then, and started exercising compulsively. I stopped eating. I went right back into the beginnings of a full-blown eating disorder.

The moment, the second moment—I remember standing in the new bedroom, in the middle of the room, in this house I was so sure would fix the problem, and it was quiet and calm but I was feeling as if I was internally spinning, and the lightbulb went on in my head. I realized, "Oh, my God! I am doing exactly the same thing." Only unlike the other time where I was just totally dead, this time I was completely agitated. There was a part of me that was able to split off and pull back and realize I was out of control. I was using the eating behavior to hide, to tell myself that "Well, I'm losing my husband, but at least I'm losing fifteen pounds, and that will make it all better." I realized that all these years, I had not been as really recovered as I told myself I was.

There's a phrase that I think is very useful: trying to live inside out instead of outside in. It's just a reminder to pay attention to your own standards, your own needs, not everyone else's. I was trying to live up to other people's definitions of who I was, trying to measure myself against standards that I was allowing other people to impose on me. I really didn't see that, as an individual, I had permission to live inside out, starting with who I was, starting with understanding what my various specific individual needs, abilities, desires, loves, passions were.

We also have to face the reality that there are some things that we can't change about ourselves. I have realized that I am fairly introverted and I am quite obsessive, I am quite compulsive. Part of that is in my makeup, and I can learn to manage it for better or for worse—that's my choice, and that's within my control. But I cannot turn myself into some sort of gregarious, outgoing personality; that's not who I am.

Perfectionism is a big part of most eating disorders, and that's something we're born with, to a large degree, and we can't change it. But we can choose to set our own definition of what is perfect rather than go constantly chasing after what somebody else says is perfect. If we create our own definition of perfection and keep it close and make it something that is truly gratifying so it gives us a sense of joy and accomplishment and purpose and meaning in life—then that's great. We can be as perfectionist as we need to be in that sense. But if instead we just blindly accept someone else's definition of perfection—for instance, as a thin model in a magazine—then that perfectionism will end up doing absolutely nothing for us, and it will make us sick.

The third moment . . . This was after I had been working with a therapist for a while, after the second turning point. Things didn't seem like they were going to work out in my marriage. I had been at an afternoon gathering with some friends, and I left early. I was driving through the Sepulveda Pass—not on the freeway, but down onto Sepulveda—and it was a spring afternoon and all the trees were just starting to turn green. I drove around this bend in the road, and I just looked at this wall of green foliage in front of me, and I felt one of those moments of absolute, intense pleasure. Just the beauty of the color and the quality of the light, and the way the leaves were moving. I couldn't tell you why, but that moment told me that whatever happened, ultimately my happiness didn't depend on my marriage, it didn't depend on my husband, it didn't depend on anything except this ability to feel this heightened sense of joy. In that moment I knew that I was going to be all right, and whatever happened, I was responsible for my own future. After that, everything really was different. That was the ultimate moment, and I haven't looked back.

I still have moments of depression and anxiety. I am probably never going to get rid of that, but I understand now that they are fleeting. I understand that the world isn't going to come crashing down. I have learned about mindful awareness and meditation, and I have this whole arsenal now of strategies I can use when I start to feel despair creeping up. And there are always moments when I notice the way the light falls, and the color of the leaves.

RON SMITH

❧

Ron is career military and one of the elder statesmen of the Washington, DC, recovery community. He's the former chairman of psychiatry at the National Naval Medical Center in Bethesda, Maryland, and both professionally and personally, he's an enormous inspiration to a lot of men and women in our armed forces who are struggling with addiction. He's also been extremely supportive to me as I've struggled with this book. He told me once, "As a therapist, I'm always waiting for these little windows, the moments when psychic change is possible. So I can point them out to whoever I'm working with and say, "Did you see that little window? What do you think might be possible in your life if you choose to look through that window?" These windows of change are not just the purview of addicts and alcoholics, but opportunities in the human experience. But addicts are lucky, in a way, that we have to pay attention to them because our lives depend on it."

I think I grew up buying into the American dream . . . what would make me happy was accumulating stuff, Mercedes-Benzes, race horses, women or Porsches or what have you. Then I got more stuff than I ever dreamed of, or needed, and I realized that another new car will not make me any happier. There's that hole in your soul, and then you'll hear a truth like that—that more stuff is just more stuff, that another drink won't fix it—that you just can't deny.

One of the earliest memories I have is when I was about four. I grew up away from my family of origin, essentially as the only child in this tribe of elders, a missionary community in Deer Lodge, Tennessee. I did have a lot of love and attention. There was nothing my grandfather couldn't do. I worked with him every day, and he really loved me and instilled a sense that I could do anything. He communicated a sense of competence and agency, autonomy and possibility. My grandmother was more candid about my powerlessness, my smallness and ignorance. So at one level I had a wonderful childhood, but also I felt somewhat isolated and alone. When you're very young and you're surrounded by adults, you can see where the real autonomy and agency in your life is. I didn't know how to live life, and I wanted to know.

One Friday afternoon, my grandmother and I went to the church to clean up a little. She went into the church, and I went into the library and looked around at the books. I remember an awareness came over me that there was wisdom or knowledge or a way to live out there, and I didn't know exactly what it was, but if I could look in these books I might find it there. I wouldn't have said *wisdom* or *knowledge* or any of those words. It's only looking back that I could fit it into words. But the feeling came over me of peace, and of excitement at the possibility of what was available in that room.

Thirty years later, I was attending a course on alcoholism for physicians at the Naval Regional Medical Center. I was a young intensivist, the first physician in the federal system trained in critical care medicine, and I was the director of the largest intensive care unit in the country. I had stopped drinking for about six months because it was that or end up in prison, but I wasn't in any kind of recovery. I remember the confusion and the loss, feeling adrift, and I was aware that I couldn't go on living the way I was living. I loved my work and I was very successful professionally, but my personal life was agony. My beautiful wife had left me, taking my two sons, and I was very lonely. I would come home at night to my suite in the Bachelor Officers Quarters, and not know where to go or what to do, and I was just lost. I'd thought that if I stopped drinking, things would get better in my head and they didn't. I remember riding up the elevator that day, feeling in despair, and then the elevator doors opened and I looked out into the room of the alcohol treatment program, into the joy of recovery.

My idea of alcoholism, unfortunately, had come from the movie *Days of Wine and Roses,* which is not a good picture of recovery. Alcoholics in that film were people down on their luck, people in desperate straits.

When those elevator doors opened at Long Beach, I saw real recovery for the first time. There were many sailors and marines, astronauts and people from Congress—people whose lives were working out. Everybody was talking honestly, talking about being vulnerable, about not having answers, about recovery and possibility and agency and autonomy and responsibility.

That moment, I felt a wave of belonging, of hope, of home. It was the same feeling I had when I was four and looked at the books in the library, and I recognized it again, the sense that there was a possibility, a hope, a journey to be taken. There were no voices, no euphoria. It was like coming out of a dark wood into the light.

I always wanted that "Paul on the road to Damascus" moment, the burning bush experience, where God or Yahweh would talk to me. I didn't get that, but what I got was a feeling of being on course in my life. I knew it was going to be fine.

That was thirty years ago, and I haven't had a drink since, and it hasn't been a struggle. It's been so much fun. Alcohol is no longer part of my life, any more than the baseball cards of my youth are. It's just not relevant to me anymore. I know I'm an alcoholic, and I know that I'm only one moment or one drink away from relapse, but I have not experienced the last thirty years as a struggle. It has been a search for joy. It has been ridiculously hard at times, and I have learned to love the suffering and the joy.

At both those moments, when I was four and when I was thirty-four, I was out of ideas. At four, you don't have any ideas yet, but I knew something was wrong in the universe and I was trying to figure it out, and when I came in that room, I knew, "Here's something that's right." And when I was thirty-four, coming off the elevator, I didn't have any ideas, I didn't have any solutions, I didn't have a new self-help book to read. If I'd known of another one to read, I would have. If I'd known of another philosophy, another church or synagogue, I'd have gone to it. I'd been looking, but I was out of ideas. I was emotionally dead, emotionally and spiritually bankrupt, and at that point I was receptive. Christ said, "Blessed are the poor in spirit," and I think that's what is wonderful about the receptivity to new ideas.

I don't think there's anything I could have done or said to get myself there any sooner. If I could, I'd probably be rich as an analyst, saying those words to others. It's like a rose blooming—you can't pull the petals apart to make it happen earlier, or faster. All of a sudden your brain cells are open and vulnerable and without knowledge, wanting knowledge, and then I think that's when the light gets turned on.

On that day at the Long Beach naval hospital, when I made the decision to turn my life and my will over to the care of whatever was in those rooms, two or three things happened. First, I was sure that whatever was there was better than where I had come from. Second, I knew it was going to be okay if I stayed in the room. And third, it was going to be a lot of work.

I think most alcoholism is a terrible form of breast-feeding into adult-hood. I was holding on to my bottle, almost like Linus holding on to his blanket in the Peanuts cartoons. It's your transitional object to soothe you, and I didn't know of anything else that would soothe me. I didn't believe and had no reason to believe what they said, that every feeling of comfort that you've tried to get through alcohol and drugs is available without that stuff. I'd never experienced that. At one level, you have to make a decision to stop using and drinking with no data, no personal experience. The only data I had was seeing those people when the elevator doors opened. I knew that alcoholism was fatal because I saw people dying of it every day, and then I saw ninety people who had that fatal illness who were alive. When I saw that, I decided I could let go of the bottle.

I'd say the capacity to recognize those moments, to be aware of them and then respond to them, to make the changes that are necessary, is of critical importance. I think that's the difference between people who live a good life, a successful life, and ones who end up badly, who are unhappy and miserable.

God looks like the awareness that gets handed to you when those doors open. I don't know if there's a visual component. It's almost like a medicine ball in the gut. I still have that Yahweh thing—I can't see him, I can't hear him, I just feel his presence. Early in recovery, I was agnostic and lost, and I'm still agnostic and lost. But as a result of doing the things they said, I get on my knees every day, and that's how I keep in touch with that feeling, the sense that things are going the way they're supposed to, that the universe is exactly the way it's supposed to be at that moment. That's what God is.

There are still moments when we come up against meaninglessness itself, when there is simply no way to construct a narrative that has meaning. How do you have faith then? And that's when you make a choice. Faith is a choice.

But it's also a journey, man, and it's terrific.

DAVID BLACK

David's a hell of a writer. As a journalist, he's covered Baby Doc Duvalier's secret police in Haiti and exposed a white slave operation in New York's East Village. His book The Plague Years, *about the AIDS epidemic, was nominated for a Pulitzer Prize in nonfiction, and his mystery novels have won numerous awards. He's written for* Hill Street Blues, Miami Vice, Law & Order, *and many more series, and wrote the screenplay for the feature* The Confession, *starring Alec Baldwin and Ben Kingsley.*

David's also one of my closest friends. He mentored me through the process of writing Symptoms, *and he's been tremendously helpful with this book too. David has an unusual, adversarial relationship with his recovery, and yet it works for him. I'm sure there are people out there who'll read it and think, "Yeah! That's me!"*

To this day, I'm not sure I'm recovered. I have to think of myself as a drug addict—a potentially *active* drug addict—every moment I'm alive, because the minute I think I'm recovered, I think, "Okay, I've taken the test and I've done well on the test and now the test is over."

Drug addiction and alcoholism for me were kind of a narcissism. Everything is about the self. Everything in the world relates to self. In recovery everything was related to the drama of trying to stop using, which is almost as good as the drama of using. So I had to realize that whether or not that drama existed, it was not the most important drama going on in the world. It was a sideshow. And I think you can only get that if you believe that there's a power greater than yourself and you're able to connect to that power . . . or at least see yourself in relation to that power and recognize yourself as just the sideshow, not the big top.

I grew up in a very left-wing family and always felt like a bit of an outsider. A Jew in a Yankee town in Massachusetts. A Trotskyist during the McCarthy era. A reader among people who didn't read. A bit of an oddball, which drove me to drink, not as compensation, but as kind of a badge of pride. I started trying to get sober twenty-five years ago. Took me about six years to finally do it. By then, I'd pretty much given up on myself.

I was a binge coke user mostly. I wouldn't use for two weeks, then I'd use for three days straight. Then I'd stop, but the pressure to use, to use, to use would start. I would go to mutual support groups, but they didn't help. The pressure would build up more and more and more, and finally I'd say, "Well, I'll just use once more. Just once more. Just once more." I really was pretty hopeless. I didn't even want to stop. I wanted to *want* to stop. And I just thought that that was it, I was going to commit myself to using, because whenever I had my first snort of coke or my first puff, I felt like "I'm home." To this day, being sober makes me feel I'm in exile. My home is that alternate state of consciousness, and I decided that was where I wanted to stay.

My father was a committed atheist, an old-fashioned leftie, so to even admit that I was interested in thinking about God might be the equivalent in someone else's household of ripping up a Bible. We were one of the last families I knew to get a television. TV became very, very important to me. I loved TV. Where we lived, we could only get one channel clearly, and there were only two other channels available anyway, but you had to turn your antenna in different directions to get the different channels. When I was nine or ten, there was a new gizmo on the market called the rotor. One component was a dial marked north, south, east, and west, which sat on top of the TV. You could turn the dial and turn the antenna up on the roof, so you could get all three channels. This was a big deal.

I started saving up. The rotor was thirty-nine dollars, I think. I saved up, literally, pennies here and a nickel there. I published a newspaper. I shoveled walks. I raked lawns. The whole time, I used to go visit the rotor at the television store in Springfield where I lived. Finally I had the thirty-nine dollars or whatever it was, but then there were taxes. So I had to go back and earn the taxes. I never forgave the government for that.

When I finally got enough money, including taxes, I called up the guy, and of course he knows I'm the kid coming in and worshipping at the altar of the rotor. I said, "I've got the money. Could you come over and install it?" He said, "Oh, it's Friday. I'm closing in an hour. It would take me too long to install it. I'll do it Monday."

For me—first of all, Monday was a lifetime away. Second, if I got it installed Friday, I'd have the whole weekend to play with it. Third, like every good alcoholic, I need immediate gratification. I wanted it *before* now. But he said he couldn't do it.

I decided, for whatever reason, I was going to pray. That's how extreme my feelings were. I went up into our bathroom. I remember the feel of the linoleum under my knees and the bright enamel and everything. It was like being in heaven, I guess. I think of heaven as being filled with bright enamel. And I start praying. I said, "If there is a God, this is a way you can prove it to me. If there is a God, have this guy come with the rotor today." I had no hope whatsoever that the guy was going to come. He had said no already, but I still prayed.

I was in the middle of the prayers when I heard my mother call and I jumped up, guilty. If she'd caught me jerking off, it would not have been more embarrassing. I think in our house, praying actually *was* more embarrassing than masturbating. I jumped up and I came running down to see what she was calling about. The guy was there, downstairs. He said he was on his way home, and he knew how much I wanted that rotor, so he figured he'd take a detour and just put it in.

At that moment, I decided there was a God. What my relationship to this God was, I didn't know. Whether or not this God cared about me or whether I had access to him, I didn't know. But I knew there was a God. He'd answered my prayers. I'd prayed and He'd answered the prayer, which was miraculous, because this rotor guy had said no.

Many, many years later, I was walking to my dealer's place, trying to convince myself I wasn't going to go and use. It was a beautiful day, one of those crisp New York days, sunny, not too cold. I was wearing my bomber jacket and jeans. I was aware that it was a beautiful day, but I was not able to appreciate it. I felt like I was in a fugue state, a kind of dream state where I would just keep walking. I mean, it was a *beautiful* day, and part of me thought, "God, if I weren't going to do drugs, this would be a great day to just feel alive." But I knew once I started doing the drugs, I'd be at a sleazy hotel with the shades pulled down and wouldn't see daylight for three days, beautiful or not.

Anyway, I got closer and closer to this guy's apartment, and I was still playing the game: "Well, I'm not really going over there. I'm just going to walk down the block. I'm really not going to his building. And when I get to his building, I'm just ringing his buzzer, I'm really not going up. And when I go up, I'm just going up to visit him, not to buy drugs. And when I buy the drugs, I'm really not going to use them. And when I use them, I'm only going to snort one and throw the rest away."

Just before I turn the corner, I remembered the moment when I was a kid when I prayed. I decided, "Well, I prayed once and it worked. The people I know in recovery tell me to pray," and I started to pray. I said, "I don't want to put you on the spot, God. But if I shouldn't be doing this, You better do something, because if it's up to me, I'm going to use. I'm turning it over to You." I really, really did not want to use, and when I said, "Okay, it's up to you," I really meant it. I couldn't have been more serious. This was a real challenge to God. Like "Okay, big shot, you're supposed to be the higher power, I'm supposed to turn it over, and that's supposed to help. Fine, I'm turning it over."

The minute I finished that prayer, it was like a switch went off. Suddenly I experienced the brightness of the day and everything. I mean, it was delicious, the feeling of being in the day and not trying to keep reality at bay. The awful burden of consciousness, which is how I used to think of it—the awful burden of consciousness no longer seemed a burden. It seemed a glory. And the need to use was gone. Miraculously. I mean it wasn't a struggle. It was just suddenly lifted. It was gone.

I turned around and I got giddy. I couldn't believe it. It's like God tapped me on the shoulder and said, "Back at you, big shot. Now you have to do a little bit of work too. I've shown my cards and I'm calling you. What are your cards?"

That was the turnaround moment. Suddenly it's like the lights went on, and the most sensory thing was really the feeling I had and still have every day, that the day is a gift and I don't have to hide from it. I really feel this, every day. A lot of my use was an attempt to turn down the volume, turn down the lights, get everything a little bit less intense—turn down the consciousness. I don't feel that need anymore.

So that was my moment of clarity. An absolute stillness and silence. And then into that stillness and silence is the stilling and silencing of all the static in my head. And then after a moment of stillness and silence, just the world, the wonderful sounds of the world . . . it's like a Cinema-Scope sound track suddenly turning on. I heard birds. I heard horns. I heard kids laughing. I heard muggers. But it was the sound of reality.

It's not like my life became that moment of clarity. A day doesn't go by when I don't seriously think about using. For me, coke and sex were associated, and when I quit, I felt like my libido was turned down low. Part of me says, "What if I just have a snort or two?" But I don't have the obsession. I don't get locked into that zombie state where I *have* to use. And just as every day there are moments when I want to use, every day there are moments of clarity comparable to that first one where I simply say, "Oh my God." I take a minute and I suddenly notice the day.

That used to happen a lot before I got drug-addicted. My drug addiction was meant to turn down that kind of intensity, whether it's intense joy or intense involvement in working. I don't regret the time I spent using, because I learned a lot, but I figure I've lost five books that I will never recover. Part of it was the intensity, which sometimes is the intolerable burden of consciousness—it's too much. But it's also where I live when I'm writing, when I'm consciously existing and feeling best about the world.

So every day I do have the desire to use, and every day I do have moments when I suddenly am grateful that I'm living in whatever passes for reality, but most of the time it's just the normal muddle out of which those two intense feelings pop. I think the big change after that moment of clarity was not that I then *lived* in a moment of clarity all the time, but that at least I had hope. I didn't have to give up on myself. I knew that there would be times when I really wanted to use, but I could decide not to. I wasn't quite sure if I could always get there in the same way, and I didn't want to. I have this image of God being very busy, and I didn't want to call on Him all the time. But it's like, He answered me once, and now it's up to me.

I would say I think about that actual moment when I felt God's presence maybe once every few weeks, but I'm aware of the experience of suddenly having a silence when the reality floods in every day. It gave me a model for experiencing the world in a way that the intensity, instead of being threatening, becomes joy-producing, physiologically. Joy and anxiety and excitement and fear—physiologically, the same neurology is going on. It's just our interpretation that differs. We describe it to ourselves as one thing or another, and so I'm learning more and more how to describe that feeling not as anxiety or fear but as joy. You can feel it as joy most when you're moving in the same direction that God is moving in the world. You're not in opposition to God's motion. When you're in opposition, it feels like fear and anxiety. When you're moving in the right direction, it feels like joy and bliss.

In a way, I don't believe in time. I think everything exists at once, and we experience that existing sequentially as time. Our moments of free will exist, but they exist in a pattern. Instead of being the people walking along the path, which is how we experience it, God looks down, sees the path and us and every moment on the path at once. Did I have to go through all that stuff to get where I was going? I guess I had to, since I did. It's part of the dance. It's part of the pattern of my life. That's how I got sober.

ALEC BALDWIN

According to Alec, he's "a middle-aged TV actor." I'd say he's a guy who might win an Academy Award, become governor of New York, or both. He's got that much energy and that much talent. I've known Alec since he was on Knots Landing, *when he'd show up at the Robert F. Kennedy Tennis Tournament at Forest Hills and drive all my sisters and female cousins crazy. For all these years, he's been a friend, a mentor, and an inspiration. I've watched with admiration as he cut his own path in his career and his life, regardless of the consequences, staying true to the principles that guide him. He was the first person I wrote asking to participate in this book. He turned me down initially because he didn't want to make any pronouncements on recovery, but when I told him how badly I needed him, he said yes. I'll be forever grateful to him for that and for his wonderful metaphor of the movie business as a crack pipe.*

There were times I did what I did because I was looking for God. There were times I did what I did because I was looking for a wife and a companion. And—this is the most dominant—there were the times I did what I did because I was looking for a family. I do believe in my heart that everything I did was to replace the family I lost when I grew up and left my house. I like being in a room full of funny, animated, un-self-conscious people. That was my family.

In the early eighties, in New York, there was a basic rule that you weren't even conscious of—you were just dysfunctional. Everyone was partying hard, or so it seemed. You were just living, and you weren't really examining it too much. Also, in New York, someone else is always doing the driving, so you could drink until you fell down, you could drink until you passed out. I didn't do that too often. I wasn't a crazy drinker.

Then in 1983, I was in Los Angeles. I'm driving on the Santa Monica Freeway at four o'clock in the afternoon with a plastic quart container that you get take-out Chinese soup in, filled with ice and half a bottle of Chardonnay poured over the top. And I'm driving down the road, I'm having a drink. It's four o'clock; I'm supposed to have a drink. But one day I went, "I don't see anybody else in their car with a plastic take-out container filled with ice and wine." They're drinking coffee, they're drinking Diet Coke, they're not drinking wine. So I think, "Maybe I should stop drinking while I'm driving."

So I switched from drinking to other things. What other things? Assume that I did everything. Make a list of every drug, and I'll say to you, I took that drug. I don't care, whatever you want to think. I did it all, all right? And that was when everything changed. I got into this white-hot period for two years from the spring of 1983 until the spring of 1985, and I had friends—you know, that's a big part of it. The influences. Always has been, no matter how much you think you outgrow that. They were guys who I would meet and we just wanted to have a good time. It was never anything sloppy or graceless. We're there and we're talking and we're laughing, and everything just suddenly appears, and the next thing you know the other people have gone home and gone to bed. It's two thirty in the morning and you're still going strong.

I'd find myself in a room with people, in a house with people, at events with people . . . and if you took away whatever it was we were having communion over—sex, drugs, booze—if you took that away, what was there? I didn't know them. I had so little in common with them. The room was full of people getting high and drinking and talking about all this bullshit. All those 3 A.M. conversations where everybody's talking, urgently talking about something that doesn't really matter. "Yeah, but the Warren Commission, man! You don't understand." Arguing about Dallas, Texas, all these years later, all jacked up on drugs and alcohol. I'd look around and I'd think, "Where do I belong? Where's the room full of people that I have some connection with, that I have something in common with, that I could have a healthy exchange with about something that means something to me and be myself and have a good time that doesn't involve this?"

I've had pretty bad insomnia my whole life, and around this time it was full-blown. I couldn't sleep regardless of what I did or didn't do, so I used to go to a video game parlor on Westwood Boulevard, this gigantic building, the old-style video game parlor back in the eighties, before everybody had Wii and Xbox and everything. It was a big warehouse, and there'd be this guy who just loaded a change machine, and some soft drink machines, and there'd be 150 video games stacked all around you. I'd be waiting at the door for them to open. I am not kidding you. This was the only way I could go "beta" and go into that state I needed to be, where I could calm down and take my mind off of everything. I didn't want to see anybody, talk to anybody, deal with anybody. I needed to get my soul in shape and I didn't know how, and so I'd go to the video game parlor. I would play video games from like 9 A.M. to 11 A.M., and I would wind down. Then I'd go home and go to bed.

My moments of clarity came when I'd be "acting out," shall we say, and then suddenly I'd see myself reflected in an unlikely mirror. That happened at the video game parlor. The guy that ran the place was a fifty-year-old Spanish guy named Julian. He didn't own the place; he was a guy who had a set of keys and a job, to come down and open up in the morning. I was doing a TV show then, making tens of thousands of dollars a week, which was part of the problem. That's part of the reason I was at the parlor at nine in the morning. It connects. Julian would put the key in the lock and open the door, and he would just kind of look at me, like "Wow, I'm glad I'm not you," and I'm going, "You got no idea, Julian. Julian, I need you. I need you to get that key and open that fucking door and let me in. I got to go play Galaga."

I met an actress then, and it was like the way Lenny Bruce describes Honey Bruce—I took one look at her and I said, "I have to have that, that must be mine!" All ego. She was the most gorgeous girl I'd ever seen in my life. We lived together for a while, and like a sweet young girl from Texas, she said, "Well, I don't think we should live together unless we're engaged." I think I ran all the way down to Westwood and bought an engagement ring that day—I flashed the ring and said, "You mean like this?"

She's a lovely woman and a fabulous person, and I remember she was doing a show in Denver, Colorado, with this young heartthrob—we'll change his name, we'll call him Tommy. I had moved there to be with her, and she comes home one day from work and says, "You're not going to believe what happened! These men came, the producers and some of their lawyers and other people, and they got Tommy in his dressing room. And Tommy doesn't really know the words to the songs, he hasn't really learned the dance numbers, because he's up all night partying and he's pretty screwed up. So they told Tommy they're going to break every bone in his body if he doesn't learn the songs."

And one of the first things I thought to myself was "Tommy's been getting high in Denver? Obviously I've been hanging out with the wrong person in the cast here."

So her driver is this big Hawaiian guy and you could tell—you get a kind of radar for people in that underworld.

"Hey, Big Kenny. I feel really bad about Tommy having all these problems."

"Yeah, it's real bad. They told Tommy they're going to fuck him up if he doesn't straighten out."

"Denver's such a nice town. They got a drug problem here?"

"Oh, man, a lot of drugs . . . bad, real bad."

I said, "Really? So if, for example, somebody wanted drugs, they can just pick up a phone and make a call?"

He's looking at me in the rearview mirror.

"Yes, that wouldn't be hard to do, Mr. Baldwin."

The next thing you know, I'm having brunch with my girlfriend and her grandparents, and these two are right out of Norman Rockwell. I get up and go to the bathroom like six or seven times during the brunch, and her grandfather is watching me, he's looking at me with that unmistakable look, like "There's just something not right with you." Sweat running down me like I had just gone through a triathlon, even though it's like 70 degrees and beautiful. I'm just looking at him like "What? What? What's up?"

❋

One of the first mutual support groups I went to, a guy spoke up and he said, "I told my wife I was sorry and I would never do it again, and the problem was that at the moment I said it I meant it, but I was not able to sustain it." That's what it was for me. I was incapable of being a man of my word, incapable of being who I knew I was. Whatever problems I've dealt with in terms of addiction, that all ended in February of 1985, when I was six weeks from my twenty-seventh birthday.

When I first went to the meeting, I had not read the book, but one guy referred to the "incomprehensible demoralization," and that was so apt for me. I was incomprehensibly demoralized. I was sick and tired of seeing myself, the person I had become, reflected in the eyes of other people, because I knew that's not who I was.

And then a guy in the meeting said, "You never have to feel this way again if you don't want to." That just landed on me like a bird landing on my shoulder.

I believe that there are people who come to this really tragic understanding of their lives . . . that's who they are. They are clinically depressed, they're deeply despairing and hopeless people. I remember saying to myself, "That's not me. I am not that."

I went to those mutual support group meetings, and I just remember I was there with people who were talking honestly and lovingly, and they were the family that I had been seeking. They spoke with humor and they spoke with humility. I remember thinking, "This is who I am. *This* is who I am." I'm someone who wants to be honest, I'm someone who wants to be connected, I'm someone who wants to live, I'm someone who wants to participate. I don't want to isolate. I'm someone that wants to communicate.

There's a list I saw early in my first year, a list of opposites: We drank to do *this,* and yet we were *that*. We drank to be social, yet we were isolated. We drank to be the life of the party, yet we were dull. I can't remember the whole list now, but I remember reading it and going, "Yeah, this problem, this pursuit, made me into someone that I'm not. That's not the real me."

God got me sober. That day, God was a black, sixty-five-year-old retired postal worker named Lenny. If you told me that Lenny was going to deliver the message for me, I would have said, "I don't think so." Lenny . . . well, he had that kind of preacher vibe to him, and I wasn't into listening to preachers. All those Lenny-isms . . . "Yesterday is history; tomorrow is a mystery!" But when Lenny said, "You never have to feel this way again if you don't want to," I remember sitting there thinking, "This guy really cares about me." And God to me is anyone who cares, who really cares.

You go into a recovery meeting and you realize people really want you to do better. That's what they're passing on, among other things—traditions and literature and so forth—but they want you to know they really do care and they really want you to get it.

They were my family. In that room I had many fathers and mothers; I had many brothers and sisters.

Sobriety ruined my career, and sobriety saved my life. The attitude that developed as a result of sobriety, the clarity that developed as a result of sobriety, ruined my career. One of the things that happened to me when I got sober was that I became almost unable—this is a pretty sad thing to say—I became almost unable to exercise the kind of selfishness and careerism that is demanded of you in order to make it in this business.

I'd been sober four years or so when I realized I hadn't done some of the things I might have done for my career. I'd lost the kind of vanity necessary to better my career, because I didn't *want* it enough. There was nothing I wanted more than the serenity and the comfort of sobriety. After I did *Hunt for Red October* I was in a phase where people were saying to me, "You're going to do this, and this, and this, and this, and it's going to be great." It was like they wanted me to get high again. It didn't feel like sobriety to me. This business has always been a tremendous challenge for me, something that I wasn't sure of. . . . Sobriety, I was sure of.

Another thing in this business is, you start doubting your instincts. Someone calls you up and says, "The following writer has written this material, the following director will direct this material, and the following actor is going to be your costar. It's the trifecta, it's all great, it's all good. This is the next thing you should be doing."

And I'd read the thing and I'd go, "This is a piece of shit." I had to live in my reality, that's what I'd learned. So I'd say, "I can't buy into what you think. I don't want to do that. I'd like to go do *A Streetcar Named Desire* on Broadway."

And they go, "You're not going to do the movie?" and I was, "Nah." I mean, this is an easy one. *Streetcar Named Desire* on Broadway with Jessica Lange, or a really mediocre movie script with a really mediocre director . . . And I said to myself, "It doesn't seem sober to me."

Stardom and fame and high-end entertainment careers come with little spiritual satisfaction. This is why it's usually a young person's game. Younger people seem to function fairly well without a reliable spiritual program. As you get older, you can't survive without that. I remember saying to myself, "These guys are all torching up the pipe and getting high on the movie business." And I'm going, "I'm not one of those people anymore. I don't give a shit about that." If you're in recovery, you know people who would get high with you and drink with you and then when you got sober, they didn't want to be around you. That's very common, and the same was true with my career. I don't want to do drugs and I don't want to drink alcohol. I want to live in the realm of the spiritual, of God. I transpose that into my work, which means I don't want to live in the world of the commercial, where I know that there's nothing nutritive for me, there's nothing satisfying. I want the world of art and the world of the spiritual, and the two became linked and have been inextricably linked for the last twenty years.

Now when I get offered a job, there are times I say to myself, "You want to give me a lot of money for one week's work to come and do this really shitty comedy?" and then I'll think, "I'm free that week. I'll take the money. You seem like a nice guy. We'll go have some fun." The movie is a steaming piece of shit, but every couple of years I'm going to step up to the griddle, I'm going to flip a shit patty this year.

And that will be fine. The money liberates me to do other things. I mean now I'm more comfortable with what I'm doing. Now I make a conscious choice. No one's manipulating me. Now I'm doing this TV show and these people say to me, "How do you feel? In your career, you did movies blah, blah, blah . . . and now you're doing this sitcom?" I say to them, "This is great." And it is. I'm almost fifty years old, and these people are paying me to go tell jokes in Queens for a couple of days a week. I said, "Where's the bad?" I am truly grateful for this opportunity.

When I went through the Sixth Sense phase,* I was miserable. And there was a constant stream of people who literally, in so many ways, would say to me, "I'm sorry . . . you must really feel like shit. Do you feel like shit? Because you really *ought* to feel like shit." I just kept telling myself, "That's their thing and that's not my thing." Now I don't even think about it. I never worry about what might have been. Never.

A friend told me once, he said the worst thing in the world for an alcoholic is to be misunderstood, which I think is true. And part of that also would be being falsely accused. And here in this debacle with my ex-wife, with this tape of me that got out—what really hurt me was this representation that I'm a bad father. Everybody who knows me knows I was a very good father, and I know very few men who put out what I put out. I'm always there, I set my ego aside, I showed up, I worked hard to be there.

It's been tough. It *is* tough. The business? That's not tough. This custody thing with my daughter . . . that's been tough. That has brought me to my knees. If it weren't for a spiritual program, I would have killed myself back in 2003. God kept me alive. For some reason.

---

* When you're dead but you don't know it.

JUDY COLLINS

❧

Judy's famous for that crystal-clear voice, captured in over thirty albums and compilations, including In My Life, Hard Times for Lovers, *and* Shameless. *She's also a tireless advocate, working on behalf of UNICEF, organizations to ban land mines, and family mental health. In 1987 she wrote her first memoir,* Trust Your Heart, *and later, in* Sanity and Grace, *she wrote about the struggle to heal after her son's suicide.*

Judy is legendary not just in music circles but in recovery communities too. I first heard her speak at a dinner in New York early in my own recovery, and I was touched by her story and profoundly affected by her ability to be so public about it. The fact that she's stayed sober through the most devastating blow a parent can receive says a lot about her strength, and the strength of her support network.

In the winter of 1977, my career was at the top in terms of what you could see from the outside. My records were on the charts, and when I did concerts, I was used to singing to huge crowds all over the world. The movie I had produced and codirected with Jill Godmillow, *Antonia: A Portrait of the Woman,* had been nominated for an Academy Award. On the outside, things looked wonderful. On the inside, I was in terrible trouble, and partly because of alcohol, I was beginning to have difficulty with my voice. During the previous year, friends began to call my mother, sobbing, saying, "She's lost it. It's gone." My instrument—the voice that had brought me success and saved my sanity—was coming apart. Drinking will do that, tear your life apart. Alcohol was bringing me to my knees.

My career was carrying on in spite of me, in spite of everything. I was working on the energy from my childhood—from the discipline and training I had been given, the studying I had done, as well as a strong sense of self-preservation. But I'd been drinking around the clock for about four years, and I was at the point where my blackouts were severe. I would pass out, come to, get myself together, and try to get ready to go out and do whatever I was doing, but I was really unable to work very much. I would go on tour and do a show, and the next day I would be too hoarse and too wrecked to go on, vocally. My band and I—musicians, road managers, drivers, perhaps my agent—would arrive at a hotel with a swimming pool, and I would swim and drink and go to a doctor for the voice problems I was having. I would be prescribed prednisone, which is a steroid, for a week or two weeks to bring down the inflammation, and it would help me through another round of concerts.

I had what the doctors called a hemangioma on the surface of my right vocal cord, and my doctor told me that I might not sing again. He said if there was any hope, it would be to have a new, unproven surgery on my vocal cords. And so, in October of 1977, I had surgery. I was very fortunate, as the laser in the hands of my wonderful doctor, Don Weissman, made a clean, perfect scar, and the problem—at least the physical problem—was gone.

But I was still drinking. In March of '78 I went to a fasting farm, where I took drugs to sleep, and although I did go ten days without drinking, as soon as I was home, I worked to get the alcohol level in my body back up. I could not stop drinking.

I remember my son, Clark, saw me one morning—it was early, eight o'clock in the morning—and he looked at my coffee cup, which he knew was filled with vodka, and he said to me, "Do you know what time it is?" That was all he said. It's funny how little things get you.

By then, I'd tried to get help in every single way possible. I'd been to a tremendous number of therapists for a number of years, and I was always looking for some way to get help, but I didn't know what to do.

Then, one day in April, I was reminded of a man I didn't know well at all personally, but I knew that he was a serious drinker, and when he was on a bender, he'd sometimes get into fights and wind up in the pages of the *New York Post* and the *Daily News*. His name was Patrick. I knew his wife a little bit because I was in a dance class with her. I was constantly exercising—dancing, running, swimming—just to keep a little ahead of the curve of the disease. I could usually show up and look okay, and my therapist of the moment would say, "You can't possibly be an alcoholic." They didn't know—they didn't understand the disease.

So I called Patrick's wife because I realized that I hadn't seen him in the papers for a long time. We exchanged a few social words, and then I said, "Patrick hasn't been arrested lately, has he?" She said, "No, he doesn't drink anymore." And before I asked, she said, "He'd be happy to talk to you about it."

She gave me his number in California and I called him up. He talked to me for about forty-five minutes. By then I knew I had to write everything down, write it down and date it, because otherwise I would forget it all. Patrick said, "You have to go and see this doctor, his name is Stanley Gitlow, and he will help you because he understands." So the next day I called Dr. Gitlow and made an appointment.

I felt completely out of control by this point. It was hard to look myself in the eyes, I couldn't fit into my clothes, I couldn't hold a conversation with anybody without having a few drinks. Up until then, I'd had a tremendous amount of deniability because I worked, I showed up, I was professional, I was always there on time. But that preceding year, with the surgery and the voice coming apart . . . everything had fallen away. I felt as though I was at the bottom of a well.

I had an appointment with Dr. Gitlow, but the day came and of course I was drunk, and I didn't show up. I called his office back to reschedule, and his nurse, Liz, said, "We don't do that. If you miss the first appointment, he won't see you." I was desperate enough that I begged. I begged and pleaded because something told me if Patrick wasn't drinking after seeing this man, then there was something about Gitlow that I must find out about. Liz finally agreed to rebook my appointment.

At that time I was wearing head scarves so you couldn't really see my face, and I remember having a pink scarf on. I was bloated, puffy, and felt maudlin as well as depressed—I felt melodramatic, but the truth was that many problems in my life seemed to have no solutions.

I walked into Gitlow's office, and there was this good-looking, trim fellow in a white suit. After a few moments of my telling him what I thought was wrong in my life, he said, "You're an alcoholic, and there's a way to help you."

Stanley Gitlow was not a man to mince words—ever! He had not even really said hello to me before he told me what was wrong with me. The next hour we spent talking about what I would do. He said, "You could check into a mental institution, that would be one choice. You could go on drinking and you'll soon be dead. Your liver is shot. The third choice is you can go into treatment."

I said, "Treatment?" Who ever heard of treatment? It was 1978, nobody was talking about treatment. But by the end of the session I had picked up the phone and called Chit Chat. (Chit Chat is a rehabilitation center in the farmland of Pennsylvania that, since my time there, has evolved into a center for the treatment of the family disease—the "ism" of alcoholism—but people still go there to get sober. It's also changed its name to Caron Treatment Centers, but I always think of it as Chit Chat.) The receptionist at the farm said, "Fine, we have a bed. You'll have to stay sober for seventy-two hours before you get here." I said, "I don't think you understand. That's not possible for me. I cannot stay sober for the next hour." She said, "I'm so sorry, we can't help you."

I hung up and looked at Gitlow, who shook his head. Perhaps I thought I was not going to have to get sober, but his face said otherwise. The phone rang again, and it was the woman at Chit Chat calling back to say, "It turns out we *do* have a vacancy in our detox unit." I told her it would take me a few days to get ready and said I could be there in a week.

The only people that were still talking to me were my assistant and my accountant, and God bless them, a week later they got up at I don't know what time in the morning and we took a 5 A.M. flight down to Wernersville, Pennsylvania. I was already drunk when I got on the plane. I had a suitcase full of books, and I had my typewriter and another suitcase full of clothes and vitamins and things, including a jelly jar full of vodka, and I got off the plane and drank the vodka in the bathroom of the Wernersville airport. I stepped into the stall and poured it down my throat.

April nineteenth is the anniversary of my last drink, there in the bathroom in the airport in Wernersville.

At Chit Chat they put me on Valium to keep me from going through the roof, and I was just coming off of my euphoric drunk, so happy to be in the country! Then the staff took my vitamins and my books and my typewriter away from me. I was in a complete fog, sitting around a table with a bunch of other people in soft slippers, and I remember being upset that they'd taken all my vitamins. All my books! A nurse came in and sat down and smiled and said, "Why don't you let us drive?"

I must have known I was in the right place. I heard what she was saying and I thought, "Oh my God, it's going to be all right." The next day is my sobriety date, the twentieth of April, the first day I did not have to drink.

Spring was just digging its way out of the mud in Wernersville and there were flowers everywhere on the farm, blooming, blossoming, practically shrieking with color. There were tulips and daffodils and forsythia and all these yellow and purple blooms. They told me there was a meditation meeting at 6 A.M. the next day—six o'clock in the morning! Who has ever heard of getting up to do something at six o'clock in the morning? Not in my lifetime. But I started getting up at five thirty and having my decaf coffee (they took us off caffeine, as well as all vitamins and all mood-altering chemicals) and I started going to this recovery meeting, and I'd look out the window at all the flowers while we read inspirational books and meditated on the words of the Saint Francis Prayer.

Everyone has a job at Chit Chat, and the woman who ran the job assignments, Carmela, said, "We're not putting you out in front of everybody waiting tables, believe me. We're going to put you someplace where people are not going to gawk at you. You are nothing special here, my dear, you are just someone who is trying to get sober, and the attention you might get in the dining room will not help you." She assigned me a job driving the garbage truck with Fred, another patient, who hauled the cans in and out of the back end of the truck. In between stops, we told each other our stories. I had a great time driving the garbage truck up and down the roads throughout Chit Chat, watching the flowers bloom, listening to Fred. Carmella might have thought twice about this job if she had known that I loved it, adored it. I even had my assistant send me my old leather driving gloves. It was fantastic to me, perfect.

The day I was going to graduate from detox and go into regular treatment and start doing all the things that one does there—going to the groups and getting a counselor and doing an intake—I remember taking a shower, getting out, drying my hair and looking in the mirror, and realizing that I hadn't been able to look myself in the eyes for years. I was suddenly dazzled . . . surprised to be alive but also so absolutely astonished at the world.

But it was up and down, in and out of anger and denial for a while. About a week and a half into treatment I got into a terrific fight with one of the counselors because I was making phone calls from the phone in the detox, where I had to sleep, since there was not yet a bed in the dorm. Dottie, who worked on the ward, gave me a hard time, and I said, "I'm leaving! This is the worst place I've ever seen!" For a day or so I was determined to leave, and I circled on my calendar when I was going to get out so I would know when I could drink again.

Then a couple of days later a man came to talk to us in our evening meeting. He was an African American from Alabama, he'd been on a chain gang, and he had a terrible story. He told us that at the end of his drinking he was in the kitchen on the second floor of the house where he was living, and he was cooking huge amounts of food for all these people who were coming to visit him. He happened to look out the window and he saw that they were all on stilts. He was having a major hallucination, and he realized he'd been having this hallucination for years.

There was another man, a man my father's age, who talked to me about my life as a drinking person and told me his story, and it was so horrible that I thought, "If he can get sober, certainly I can." He had a story like my father's, really. I felt so bad for my father and I still do. I always think of him battling against this disease with no tools, no tools at all, nobody to say, "You don't have to live like this."

When I got out of detox and was moved into the wing where the regular program took place, I had a roommate who prayed every night on her knees. I was embarrassed, and a little horrified. I was not in the habit of revealing my resistance or my surrender to another person. The inner life was not something I was comfortable with, and I certainly did not want someone to see me on my knees. I brought it up to my counselor, who told me that prayer on my knees might help me with the treatment aspects of not drinking. I didn't know how that could be, but they told me to do it and for a time, I did. They said it didn't have to signify anything. It was not about being Christian, it was not about being Jewish, it was not about being anything. It was about surrendering to something that was bigger than you were, bigger than your little problems with alcohol and love affairs and so on.

That was a big step for me. So I learned to pray. And the whole time I was at Chit Chat, I played an album of Joni Mitchell's called *Don Juan's Reckless Daughter*. I think it helped me get sober, and still find it's one of the most powerful influences on my life.

At the end of the twenty-eight-day program in those hills of Pennsylvania, I felt a stirring in my heart and my brain that had been dormant for many years. I will call it an experience of God. My brother, Denver, came to pick me up when I was ready to leave. He drove me to New York and he brought me to my apartment and he said, "I'm going to take out all the booze, every last bottle," and he did. I kept cases of booze, not just bottles. My brother carried it all out, and he told me later he dumped it all, poured it down the sink. He said he felt very superstitious about drinking any of it. I am so grateful he was there to help me with my reentry.

I was at Chit Chat for thirty days in all. Home again, I stayed close to Stanley Gitlow. He had a therapy group, and I started to get to know those people. I started to call people and make contact and stay connected with people who didn't drink—and that was really the network that began to feed my life. As soon as I could, of course, I made a new record, and throughout that and everything else, I stayed on the phone all the time. If I wasn't singing in the studio or on the road or on the plane, I was on the phone. This band I had—oh my God, half of them were drunks, half of them were addicted, and they used to laugh and say, "What do you do when you get off the plane? What are you doing on the phone all the time?" They teased me about talking to my bookie, when what I was doing was talking to other drunks who were not drinking, and that's how I did it. Many of those wonderful people got sober in the years to come and spent lots of time on the phone themselves. That kind of contact, of keeping in touch, continues to be an important part of the fabric of my life.

Because of my work, I have to be in places where there's alcohol. That's life, and I try not to tempt fate. For a few years I kept wine in the house for parties and special occasions, but after my son's suicide I had to get rid of it. I realize that this new life has been a gift, and if you get this experience of grace, you've got to keep your priorities straight, because you never know. The illness does not respond to rational thinking. I tried reason, and the intellect, and for me, they never worked. And who knew, if sometime in the middle of the night . . . anyway, it wasn't anything I wanted to take a chance on.

Spirituality was really the place where both my drinking and my musical life started. I always went to church, I always believed in another realm of existence. As an artist, I always believed in things you can't see that have tremendous power over your life and influence you—music, art, literature, and God. I believed in God. I sang in church choirs and school choirs. I believed in grace, in ideas of another dimension, and in the power of positive thinking. I had more than one healing experience, and I always found that the practice of yoga was powerful and would calm my racing anxiety attacks. But these were intermittent experiences that helped but never really sustained my feeling of serenity or peace. My deep fear, my anxiety, always returned, until at Chit Chat I glimpsed another way, and felt the peace come over me. Finally I was pushed over into the light in a surrender that I try to keep fresh every day.

Many of the philosophers I read speak of the need in our lives for solitude, for contemplation, for quiet. I was always looking for silence, for peace, but I never found the solitude that gave me solace without being alone, without feeling isolated and abandoned. I had been looking for it every day of my life. I think that for an alcoholic like I am, what alcohol does is to separate us from the forces that can really help us. I think removing that distance between myself and whatever it is that runs things—that was what treatment was all about. I believe in treatment, and I believe it does give people the opportunity for reflection and for support too, so that they're not off in a black hole, a black void. I could feel there was something new coming into my life, something shedding light, when I didn't have any way of moving in that direction on my own.

So I got that, and I got something else. I got joy. I was not a joyful person before. When I was drinking, I stood behind the microphone, played the guitar, and kept my eyes shut. Louis, my husband, has spent years helping me learn how to use the stage, how to move around, how to do things, how to talk. He literally has been a godsend. He's just amazing. I have more fun doing my work today. This could be illegal, having this much fun and enjoying your life this much.

One of the greatest gifts of sobriety is that I sleep now. When I go to sleep, I very often think about the first few days when I was detoxing, with this howling maniac in my head. I was hallucinating and frightened, and I think about that transition a lot, and how within the first few days a peacefulness descended on me. I am grateful that the serenity has never completely left me.

The tragedy that happened to me in sobriety came at a time when I was thirteen years sober and my beautiful son, Clark, took his life. I was devastated and not sure I could live through it, but I listened to people who had gone through terrible things and survived them and had not found it necessary to drink. I listened to what they said, did what they did.

I look back at that spring before I went to treatment. I was in misery, and I'd done almost nothing creative in terms of writing in nearly four years. I wrote two songs under huge duress, as well as the liner notes to a collection of my recordings called *So Early in the Spring: The First Fifteen Years.* I sweated over those pages. There were wineglass stains on those pages, and vodka stains, like tears. There probably *were* tears, as well. I had gone over and over and over those pages; it took me months. I told myself I was having a creative block. I was not having a creative block at all. I just couldn't stop drinking. I don't know how I got through those three or four years, because everything was so heavy and so dark.

Thank God my life isn't that dark anymore, but full of light and full of faith.

MIKE BINDER

⤬

Mike's an actor, director, and screenwriter. His first screenplay was 1990's Coupe de Ville, *and his directorial debut came two years later, with* Crossing the Bridge. *Since then, he's made several movies, including* The Upside of Anger *and* Reign Over Me, *and he also created and starred in the HBO series* The Mind of the Married Man. *Mike's a good friend and was one of my chief employers in my early acting days. We made three movies together:* The Sex Monster, Londinium *(also known as* Fourplay), *and* Blankman. *I've always appreciated his commitment to recovery, and his preoccupation with making movies that have something to do with sex.*

One of the questions I asked people was "Is there something you were afraid of that kept you from sobriety? If so, did that fear come to pass?" For Mike, it did—but it turned out not to be such a big deal after all.

My worst fear was realized, and it was the best thing that ever happened to me. I think that's one of the things that having a God-centered philosophy of life gives you. You get a sense of being in touch with the universe, getting the right signals, being in tune with a power greater than yourself. When I got centered, got conscious—I mean I still don't know what's the best thing for me, I just know that I'm going to do what my senses tell me to do today, and I'll take the ride where it goes.

I left Detroit and I came out here to be a comedian, and within weeks I got a job as a doorman at the Comedy Store. At the time, it was the center of the universe to me, a place that I'd read about and came out here to be close to. So now I had a job there, but I was miserable. I can remember leaving work, going home, and lying in bed and thinking, "I'm going to kill myself. I hate this life." I was broke all the time, and every time I got a chance to audition for something, I would blow it because I was high. I would reason to myself, I had these long talks with myself, every morning, every day—"I'm not going to do it. I'm not going to get high." And within an hour of getting up, I was high again and back on the treadmill of the things I needed to shove into my body to make myself keep going.

By the time I was twenty-four or twenty-five, I couldn't make a living. I had started with a lot of promise and I was on a lot of shows and I made a lot of money, but it was all gone. I was so hopeless. Day after day, after day, after day, after day—I was really at a low bottom in terms of pain.

My thing was marijuana and cocaine, together—I just needed them, and I would do anything to get them. I couldn't go half a day, let alone a whole day, without getting completely obliterated. It was really hard on me. I would ask myself, "Why am I so weak? What am I doing?" I saw all these other guys doing things, coming up with new routines and writing screenplays and getting acting jobs—I was just a slug. I remember thinking that, "I'm just a slug." I was overweight. I smoked two and a half, three packs of cigarettes a day.

I had an enormous desire to change, but it'd last about an hour and a half. And not only that—as soon as I would slip back into getting high, it wasn't "Okay, now I'm happy." I would just spend the next twenty-three hours miserable because I'm still doing what I don't want to be doing. This went on for years. That was helplessness to me; months and years of this saying, "Okay, I'm going to do it" and failing every day. I never had a day without the monkey on my back.

I knew a young guy, another young comedian, named Jesse. I'd smoked pot with him a lot of times and done a lot of drugs with him and I'd shared my shit, so I saw him one day and I said, "I need some payback. I've got nothing." He said, "I'm clean. I don't do it anymore."

It blew my mind, because I knew him so well and I knew *myself* so well and I didn't know anybody who would clean themselves up. This was probably '81 or '82, somewhere in there, and people didn't go to rehab. So this guy said to me, "I'm clean," and it just blew my mind. I remember walking away and coming back and saying, "What does that mean, you're clean?" I mean, that's how remote the whole thing was.

He said, "I've been going to these mutual support groups," and he started talking about it and I thought, "Oh, okay, that's obviously some Christian thing and I'm Jewish. It's not for me." That's the first thing I said to him. He was like, "No, no, it isn't organized religion at all. You got to come." In my mind I was thinking, "Well, probably they'll go into Bible readings or something. It's probably the hokiest thing I can think of." But I was in so much pain, I called him about a week later and I said, "What's that thing you were talking about, how you got off drugs?"

Jesse told me about a meeting in Beverly Hills and I met him at the place. I just thought it was worth trying. I was in so much pain, and I wasn't talking to anyone about it. I think the whole notion of getting help was so foreign to me that I thought, "Fine, I might as well try this."

I went to this thing and it was huge. I remember the guy was off to the left of the stage, and right away he started talking about God, and I thought, "I knew it. This is not for me." So I left.

Two guys from the support group followed me outside, and I remember thinking, "Here it comes, here comes the hard sell, these are Moonies." I started talking to them, and there were just these two guys. Their names were Mike and Nicky. They said, "Look, come on back into the meeting and just listen." So I went back in with them. Then after the meeting, they went with me up to do a set. It was the first time I had ever been straight to perform. I hadn't gotten high all day, and I really wanted to shake these guys so I could go and have a few drinks, snort something, and get ready to go onstage. They said, "Look, we're going to go with you. We're going to walk you through your first day."

So I went onstage, and sure enough, I just wasn't funny. I couldn't concentrate, I was sweating, and I came offstage and I was mad at them. They said, "Let's go get a cup of coffee and let's talk about it." They seemed really interested in the fact that I was in so much pain and there was no one in my life who really gave a shit about whatever was going on in my head, what I was thinking or feeling. I sat with them until like eleven or twelve that night and then they said, "Okay, let's go home and go to bed. Just do the rest of this day, this one day." They wrote down their phone numbers and they said, "Call us, wake us up if you have to, but just get through one day, and then tomorrow we will reconvene on the whole thing."

That was really my first day. It was just so rare at that time that anyone had any interest in me. I didn't have a girlfriend, my good friends were either completely in the same rut as I was or older and completely straight and didn't understand the problem, so I wouldn't talk to them about it. They would just tell me, "Drugs are bad, so don't do them. Your friends are losers and you're acting like a loser, but you are better than that," and that's the end of the conversation. No one ever said to me, "I know exactly what you are going through, I've gone through it. It's not easy, but it is what your life is now. You just need to make some changes, and here is what I did"—no one ever said that, until that day.

The guy I got closest with was Mike, who was a poet. I liked his writing. He was honest and he was a real artist, so I gravitated toward him, but there was still that God thing. I remember one time he said to me, "Well, have you gotten on your knees and prayed?" and I said, "No, never." That wasn't how I was raised. He said, "Even when you're in trouble or when you've been afraid, you've never said, 'God, please help me'?" And I said just, "No." God wasn't in my lexicon. That wasn't in my sense of the world, to get on my knees or just talk to God. I didn't want that aspect of recovery, and I told him that. I said, "I'm not the kind of person who thinks the God stuff is going to work for me. It turns me off."

Then I went back to Detroit to do a little movie there, *The Detroit Comedy Jam*. Mike kept sending me this literature, very God-oriented literature. God-says-to-me-to-do-this stuff, on some day-by-day-God's-plan thing—and this God, God, God really was very creepy to me. The whole time I was there, I stayed clean, getting ready for the show, and then the night after this show, I got drunk and everything started up again.

At the same time, there's all this stuff going on with my brother Jack. He's about five years younger than me and he was always a wild kid—wilder than I was. He was the brother that I was the closest to. He went to school at Michigan State, and he was kind of a lost kid. He got hooked up with these Jesus freaks at school. I never knew the full story, but they really got him to the point where he was a full-on Jesus freak for about three months. He was going to go to Mexico with them, just wander with the group.

My parents were really worried about him because he had quit school and he had given everything away and he was wandering the streets of Lansing, Michigan, trying to proselytize to bums and stuff. My dad called and said, "You need to talk to him. Take him out partying, get him high. Get the old Jack there." They were really worried.

My mother set it up so that Jack and I came to her house at the same time. He said to me, "Mike, have you ever asked God into your life, ever?" He was just so blazing with spiritual love that I was embarrassed by him. He was going to leave the next day for Mexico. I said to him, "I want you to do me a favor, and just agree that you are not going to go to Mexico for another month or so." He said, "Tell you what I'll do. If you get on your knees right now with me and you pray for God to help you, I'll postpone my trip to Mexico." And I said okay. I was willing to do anything just to get this guy to calm down a little bit.

So the two of us, in my mother's little house in Michigan, we got on our knees, and we prayed. I felt stupid. I was really glad that it was just the two of us. If there had been a third person in the room, I would have been making jokes about it. I felt like I was saving him. I was making a deal with him—"Okay, yeah, I'll do the praying thing and then you will get some help."

And you know, I was so relaxed that whole day. The next morning I woke up and I got right on my knees again. I rolled out of bed, got on my knees, and asked God to come into my life and help me with the pain I was in. I had another sober day, went back to Los Angeles, and started going to mutual support group meetings. Going on twenty-four years, I haven't had a drop of alcohol or any drugs. Every morning of my life I have been on my knees, asking God for some kind of guidance.

So that's really the story of how life went on through me. I was doing my brother a favor, and my father a favor, and my mother a favor. I really didn't even believe it. I was just saying, "Yeah, whatever it takes to get this loony nut to not go to Mexico." Which he didn't do, by the way. He dropped out of that group pretty soon.

But truly, the only thing I knew about praying was in the movies, like when you'd see frontier families praying before they were slaughtered by the Indians. But there was a psychic shift in my life from that day on. It hasn't been perfect, but from that day on, I've had absolute God awareness in my life. I absolutely know that there is a power that I need communion with, there is a force that I need to answer to, and there is a sense of something that I am connected to in the universe, into the past and present. I don't really see God as someone who is running the thing as much as the energy that's there to tap into, that will tell us, one man at a time, one woman at a time, one day at a time, what the next right move is. God is just a source, that's all. It's not a person and it's not a being, it's just a source.

I never had access to that source until that day, and I haven't lost it since. From then on, I really did feel like a different person. I have had a lot of rough times since then, times of anguish, times of doubt, but nowhere near what I had before that day. In the old days, I would have twenty-nine horrible days to one good day, and then it just slowly shifted to twenty-seven horrible days to three good days, and now basically, I have twenty-nine great days and one bad day.

What I wanted was to be funny and talented. I was funny for a few years because I had this wild drug-fueled energy, but I was so afraid I'd lose it. Everyone that I thought was good—Lenny Bruce, Robin Williams—they were all fueled by this wild energy. I thought sober people, people who didn't get high, were boring. Sure enough, the act that I put together after I got sober was very disciplined, and I worked on it, but it was boring. There was no spontaneity anymore, and I wasn't funny for a long time. I had enough tricks to make an audience laugh, but there was no greatness in it. There's wasn't anything close to greatness. So I let it go . . . gave it up, and I never did it again.

So my worst fear was realized, but it took me to the whole world of writing screenplays and making films. Once I got sober, and once I let go of the idea of being a great comedian, or even a good comedian, I really was able to put a lot of energy toward learning how to make films, how to write films and to study films. It's put me on the path that I'm on today. I still have not made a great comedy, but it's an absolute goal for me to one day write and direct a great comedy. It might be an elusive goal, but it's not one based on fear. There's no fear of not attaining the goal—it's just a challenge, a challenge to spend my life learning the craft and keep trying again and again and again to get a little bit closer to that spot on the horizon.

DALLAS TAYLOR

❧

Dallas was best known as the drummer on Crosby, Stills and Nash's debut album, Crosby, Stills & Nash, *(1969), and their follow-up with Neil Young,* Déjà Vu *(1970). Since overcoming his own addictions, Dallas now works as a substance abuse interventionist with recovering drug addicts and families. He specializes in helping musicians and entertainers with drug and alcohol dependencies.*

I totally believe that everything in my life has happened for a reason. There's absolutely a thread throughout the whole experience, from the loss of my parents, loss of my family, to the brief height of success, to the depth of depravity, to where I am today. I think it took all of that to humble me enough to be able to be a half-decent human being, which is really all we can be. All of that, it was God doing for me what I wouldn't do for myself, what I refused to do. That's how I see everything that's ever happened to me. It's always been the hand of God taking a shiny sharp object away from me and saying, "No, no, Dallas."

When I experience a loss or I don't get something that I think I really need or I really want, it sucks. And then looking back I see, "Oh, that's why. Because I was supposed to be over here." There has to be some kind of order to the universe is what I'm saying. There has to be some kind of power that we don't understand and shouldn't even pretend to. All the things I've done and gone through to come to this place, to be the guy people trust and invite into their home and share their deepest and darkest secrets with—that's a miracle. Human beings trusting and bringing out that intimacy in another human being, that's the hand of God. That's got to be the hand of God because it isn't me. Me, I'm a weasel dope fiend.

I accidentally discovered heroin while I was on the road with Stephen Stills and Manassas. I was sitting there and complaining, "Man, I can't sleep. I can't sleep." I'm sitting there doing coke, one line after another. I don't know why I can't sleep. A guy said, "Here, try this." I thought, "Just some more cocaine. What the hell," and I did it. It was China white, and it just put me where I wanted to be.

It's funny, because after I got sober, I remembered an incident with my mother. I was kind of a sickly kid. I had stomach problems, some real, some fake when it came to school—"I've got a stomachache. I don't want to go to school." I hated school from the first day. I hated myself and I hated my life, for as far back as I can remember. So my mother brought this stuff home called paregoric for stomach pain. I think you could get it over the counter then, even though it has morphine. She literally had to chase me around the house because it smelled so awful. She got me cornered, and I kind of gagged it down—and I swear to God, twenty minutes later, I went back to her and I said, "Mom, can I have some more of that?" I felt normal for the first time. I didn't equate it with being high. I equated it with finding that missing piece. The space that always seemed to be empty was filled. That's what it felt like when I did that first line of heroin on the road. "Oh yeah, this is what's missing. *This* is what's missing." It was a pain reliever when I was in a great deal of pain.

My career was going down the tubes. I got fired from Crosby, Stills and Nash and Young for a bullshit reason, a power play. Nobody stuck up for me, and that gave me a perfect excuse to lock myself up in my big house up on the hill and commit suicide by cocaine and heroin. I went through a million bucks pretty quick, and before I knew it I was out of dough, and I signed away all my rights to all those gold and platinum records on the wall in there. Then I was homeless, with my gold and platinum records, basically living off women I'd meet.

And I just couldn't stop. I couldn't stop. I just wanted to die, because my dream, the thing that I'd counted on to make me happy, didn't make me happy. Success didn't make me happy. Being rich and famous didn't make me happy. And when it hit me that none of it was going to work—that's when I really hit the bottom in depression. I proceeded to commit covert suicide by using just as much as I could. I remember coming to, with paramedics standing over me, and getting up, walking out, and doing some more. My friends were dying, but I couldn't kill myself. Keith Moon told me, "Dallas, man, you're just fucking crazy. I can't be around you. You got to leave." And so I ended up in the streets of London. He died right around the time I went into rehab. All my peers died, and for some reason I'm still here. I just couldn't die. I tried.

Around Thanksgiving in 1984, I had a moment of clarity. I was smoking freebase with this homeless guy in this garage. Me and my wife at the time, we lived in this little one-room shack. There's my gold and platinum records on the wall, in the scummiest fucking neighborhood that you can possibly get to. I had two kids that I wasn't allowed to see, and frankly, I didn't care. I loved them, but nothing mattered but getting high. Nothing. I had been on methadone for ten years, and now I was freebasing with a homeless guy. I decided to get some booze, and I went to this liquor store my wife's uncle owned. When I walked in, they were playing one of my songs over the PA. I said, "Do you hear that? That's Crosby, Stills and Nash. That's me. Somebody give me twenty dollars. Give me twenty dollars because I played on that fucking record." Everybody looked at me like I was crazy. My wife's uncle said, "Dallas, you got to leave, man. You got to go. You got to get out of here."

That was when I had this out-of-body experience and saw how far down I had really gone and that there was no further I could go. I had hit bedrock. It's not that I wouldn't have kept digging if I could have, but I'd run out of everything. I ran out of money. I ran out of willingness. I ran out of hustle. It was over. There was no way out except for death.

I made a conscious decision to go back to that little shack, and I grabbed the butcher knife and I stabbed myself in the stomach with it. My wife came in—I woke her up. I remember I said something like, "I'll show you." You know, that that's our addict's battle cry: "I'll show you. Fuck you." She came in, and I had stabbed myself right where they used to commit hara-kiri, and I remember saying, "If I'm still alive in the morning, take me to the hospital."

I came to the next morning. It was hot, flies everywhere. I was just absolutely horrified that I couldn't even succeed at killing myself. I was a failure at everything. I was a complete failure.

My wife got me to the emergency room, and of course the police showed up. I was smart enough to know that you don't tell the police that you just tried to commit suicide, so I said, "Oh, I was trying to open a tool kit with my knife and it slipped." So they went away. The doctor said it looked like a surgeon had operated on me. I missed the main aorta by one centimeter and took a little nick out of my liver. One more time, I couldn't die.

I'm in this hospital and it's Thanksgiving, and there was absolutely nothing to be thankful about. And this little guy kept coming into my room and just sitting there. I knew who he was. He was one of those recovery people. There was a treatment center just down the street and he worked there. He would show up every day and just sit and read the newspaper. One day I finally said, "What the fuck do you want?" He says, "Well, man, I'm here to try to convince you to go to treatment." I said, "I knew it. You're going to try to indoctrinate me into that cult."

So even at that point, even after all the shit I had experienced, I wasn't ready to surrender. They were giving me my methadone and Demerol and all my favorite drugs, so why the hell did I want to leave that hospital bed? It was like heaven.

I was in there a couple of weeks before they felt that the knife wound had healed enough that I could be discharged. They tried to do a little intervention on me with my wife, and for some reason I said, "Okay, I'll go." Just to get them off my back, I agreed to go. I was so fucked up I couldn't walk, so I arrived in rehab in an ambulance. I barely remember it. Later on, I worked for a little while with the nurse who did my intake. She said, "Boy, Dallas, you were . . . we didn't think you were going to make it."

Those first few days, I was like an animal. I hunkered down in a corner and nobody could come near me. I wasn't going to any fucking groups. I wouldn't do any of that crap. Don't you know who I am? Where's my private room? You know, all that ego stuff, that entitlement stuff that I developed through my little stint with success.

And I was up at the nurses' station every ten minutes: "I've got a headache. I'm sick. I need medicine." Well, no. I'm a dope fiend. I am a hope-to-die, to-the-curb dope fiend. I cannot be trusted with medication. I had a rough go of it through detox, and then that day came, the most frightening day of my life, when they said, "We're going to take you off your detox meds." But at some point I had come to my senses and realized, "Okay, if I can't die, then I have no choice but to try to live." I got a sense of hope from somewhere. I started thinking, "Maybe I can do this. I might as well take this train to the end of the line."

I think it was the experience of being confined with people you wouldn't normally hang out with, and then discovering that we have this incredible bond, and it's us against the world. And I remember they took us to a mutual support group and the people in there were laughing. They were alive and happy, and I thought, "Wow! This is pretty cool. These guys are okay." I noticed there was a couple of rock and rollers in there and I thought, "This might not be too bad."

So it wasn't the thunderbolt for me. It was these little things that started to build up and give me this sense of hope. Plus there was the absolute terror of going back to that night with the knife, because I never want to feel like that again. That night was the magic night. After that I was so terrified that I was in three meetings a day, morning, noon, and night. Sometimes four. Sometimes midnight meetings. I jumped into this with both feet because I didn't know what else to do. I didn't have anything else to do.

I had a friend in recovery, an old jazz musician named Buddy. I was trying to get back into the music business and it just wasn't happening. They weren't having me back. I remember calling my sponsor one night and saying, "Buddy, I don't know what to do." He said, "Man, you got to get a job." I said, "What do you mean, get a job? I've never had a job in my life. I wouldn't know what to do in a job." He said, "I'll give you two choices. I can get you a job at Pizza Hut or I can get you a job as a tech on the adolescent unit at this treatment center." I had no idea what a tech was, let alone an adolescent unit, but I knew I wasn't going to work at a Pizza Hut. Sure enough, somebody would come in and say, "Hey! You're that guy. Crosby, Stills and Nash. It's a long way down, isn't it?" So I picked the adolescent treatment center, and thus was born my middle life of being of service and helping other alcoholics, addicts, and families.

But I don't walk in thinking I'm going to do anything. I just walk in and try to be a channel. Either the universe is going help this person, or this person isn't going to take the offer. It's out of my hands. I can't take credit, nor can I take it personally if it doesn't work.

That might seem like a cold way to handle it, but it's the only way that I know how to do it. You can come aboard the lifeboat, but I'm not jumping in after you, because there are sharks out there.

ED BEGLEY JR.

❧

When I interviewed him in spring 2008, Ed's play about César Chávez, César and Ruben, *was getting great reviews in L.A. He's been in countless TV series, including* Mary Hartman, Mary Hartman; Arrested Development; Six Feet Under; *and* The West Wing. *He's had starring roles in* St. Elsewhere *and* Battlestar Galactica, *and the series* Living with Ed *chronicles his deep commitment to living green. My cousin Bobby Kennedy introduced us; they know each other through their environmental work. Ed's father was a Hollywood actor too, so we have that in common, as well as being on this recovery journey together.*

What impresses me most about Ed is his ability to let the slings and arrows of life bounce off him, to let the everyday hassles roll off his back and just be grateful. Those are the small, almost invisible changes in our nature that bring real recovery and the joy of living.

I had a very dark time through most of the seventies. Most of it was self-inflicted, but there were a lot of things that happened that were beyond my control. I found a body cut up in my trash, a human torso. When you come upon something like that, it's not like a movie—"Oh my God, it's a body!" You don't even process. You go, "Wow! What's this? Somebody must've hit a dog and put it in the trash can." And then you realize it's a person. That was the worst thing, but there were lots of other terrible things, and the common thread, the thing that put me in a lot of those situations and also made those situations worse, was my abuse—my addictions and abuse. That was the overriding influence in the seventies. I kept trying to get well and I couldn't. I had a very bad experience in 1976 where I had the DTs and I was very, very sick. I sought help, I got my twenty-one days sober, and then went out again. I got sick, I sought help again, I got forty-five days sober, and I started thinking, "That's enough for now," and I went out again.

That's what hopelessness was for me. I could not get well, and I was in a very dark period through much of that decade.

On September 30, 1978, I woke up with my wife slapping me. Ingrid was slapping me, saying, "Wake up, wake up. Your color is really bad. Your breathing is bad." They got me to the hospital and they put an IV in my arm and gave me some ipecac. I'd taken some pills to try to make the pain of the hangover and the DTs go away. "Oh, it was a suicide attempt," they said. I said, "If it was a suicide attempt, I wouldn't have taken them one at a time in the course of two hours. There wouldn't be any left. I was just trying to get some relief, so I took like eight Thorazine, along with all the liquor and everything else I've taken."

I passed out, and then I went to that place where you almost die. You send enough chemical signals to your brain to shut down, and things will shut down. Fortunately, my wife was present and she got me to Cedars-Sinai and I made it. The next day, Ingrid brought in our daughter, who was about to turn a year old. She and I had a great bond, a great affection, which we still enjoy. It was like day two of my recovery, and she had been away from me now for forty-eight hours straight because I was in the hospital.

I remember the beeping of a monitor, and I have an IV drip going into my arm, a nasal cannula, and the pulse thing on your finger to monitor that and the blood pressure cuff. There's lots of stuff on me. Ingrid was holding our daughter, and as soon as she saw me, she reached out to Daddy because she loved her daddy and I loved her. She reached out to me, she wanted to hold me, and I wanted to hold her, and she couldn't— I couldn't—because of all the tubes and everything. And I heard the nurse say, "You know what, this is not going to work." The nurse just kept saying that, and I never wanted to hear that again. I never wanted to go through that pain again, the pain of not being able to hold my daughter.

I'd hit that point where you're not really drunk but you're certainly not sober. You're in that netherworld where there's no relief at all from the pain. There's just this hell, where there's no drink, no pill that's going to make it better. And there's a bill that's past due. You just keep paying the interest, telling yourself, "I'll pay that next week. Let me get back to you," because you want to keep drinking some more and taking drugs some more. Suddenly you can't roll over the interest on that loan anymore. You got to pay the principal. That's the day you have the DTs. That's the day you wind up at Cedars.

That was as low as I ever went, but still I didn't fully dive into recovery. It was a year and a month later, and I tried it again. I drank half a bottle of wine. Half a bottle, and I'm sick as a dog. I went, "What happened?" My wife said, "You don't get it, do you? Your thermostat is broken and you'll never get back to room temperature. You've abused the privilege. You're never, ever going to be able to do this in a normal way, the way that you think other people can and some do." I realized she was right. Even supposedly normal amounts were a no-go for me.

That was the next epiphany in a series. I went, "This is over. This is over for me." The concept "Maybe I'll have some wine with dinner"—that option was gone, because I had so altered my metabolism. Was it my kidneys, my liver? I don't know. Maybe it was psychological. But I know there was a certain amount of grace involved in me surrendering for that year and a month, and then there was grace and understanding involved in me understanding that I had to make a change.

I think something physical happened with me long before that September thirtieth. I was kind of limping along with a broken thermostat and trying to make it work, and I think I broke it for good when I almost died. I only realized it when I opened that door again, and I just had to open that door because I realized I could no longer be funny. I couldn't be creative because really creative people, they got drunk. Richard Burton and those people, they were drunks and they were brilliant because they'd get in touch with the spirit. No coincidence, the use of the word *spirit*. Through drinking, you got that relaxation and you got in touch with authenticity. All the wonderful, talented painters and actors and writers, they drank. I wanted to be like them, and I couldn't possibly do it without drinking.

So then it was like some sort of biblical sacrifice. Abraham was asked to sacrifice Isaac, and he went for the whole thing before God said, "No, I'm sorry. I was just kidding. You don't have to kill him." I was willing to sacrifice my creativity, and I did. I just went, "Well, I have carpentry skills, I'll do that. And maybe, even though I'm no longer talented, maybe I'll get a job anyway." I did get a job. I got a job in the show *Battlestar Galactica*, the original one, playing Ensign Greenbean. That led to the next big epiphany, the biggest positive epiphany of everything I've mentioned so far.

I'm there on the set of the show, and I remember vividly other actors that I've been interacting with, working with and talking to, socializing with a bit since the first day. This is maybe the sixth episode, and I noticed we're all sitting in a semicircle, with our folding chairs. And then I noticed something. They were laughing really loud. They were laughing at something near me and I didn't know what it was and I looked around, and there was nothing that was particularly amusing. I realized they were laughing at me. I was being funny again. That gift was being returned. I was willing to give it up, and it was gone for a while, six months or something, and then suddenly I was funny again.

I went, "Wow! That is pretty good. Is this just for today?" It turned out it wasn't. I was in touch with an even greater depth, without the destruction or the haze of alcohol and drugs. It wasn't just the same, it was better, and that was that big gift. That was the biggest epiphany of all, that moment with those chairs in a semicircle, and those people laughing really loud. At who? At me. At me being funny.

I don't know why I got that moment, those moments, and why other people don't. I think it's part luck. Part of it might be my constitution, just being a big old 195-pound Irishman, to take that kind of punishment for that long, long enough to get to the moments. That was my blessing, but it was also my curse, because two days later, three days later, after the worst DTs, I start thinking, "I'm feeling pretty good. Did I have a problem?" Still, I stayed sober for that year and a month, until I saw that yeah, I did have a problem. Had one and still had it, always will have it.

I used to have this theory about the amount of pain that you're expected to endure in life. It wasn't just about the drinking, it was about all the other emotional pain that's a part of life. I was like, "Wow! Okay, life is this. Life is a ratio, it was 60 percent pain and 40 percent pleasure. Maybe worse, maybe 70/30. You got to put up with the 70 percent pain to get the 30 percent pleasure." Since 1979, when I finally started to really get well, that ratio has changed. It was more like 80/20 for years because I held on to other addictions, even though I'd given up drugs and alcohol. I held on to philandering as an addiction. I held on to gambling as an addiction. I held on to those, and that caused me that extra percentage of pain for a while. When I finally gave those up, the ratio went to 90/10, even 97/3, pleasure to pain. Bad things still happen to me, and I'm not suggesting otherwise, but I just don't go to that dark place anymore. When I think I'm supposed to paddle, I paddle, but the river takes me, and it turns out that is the way I'm supposed to go.

Alan Watts wrote an essay called "This Is It," all about how it's not going to be better later, this is it. This is as good as it gets right now. This is not some dress rehearsal for when you get that movie or when you get that Oscar. None of that really changes anything. So for me to sit in a 1,700-square-foot house in Studio City and have any complaints—I don't. I haven't had any in years. All my problems are quality problems, every one of them.

In 1998 I had my most challenging year in a long time. I got fired from the show. I'd never been fired from anything before. They picked up the options of all the other actors but not mine, and there was no reason given. They hadn't come up to me on the set and said, "You're doing this wrong." It was nothing but fruit baskets and love letters and everybody loved me until they didn't want me, and it was horrible.

Then the IRS lost the paperwork associated with my tax return and I had to pay them a lot of money. Then, through a clerical error, some neighbor owned my house through a quitclaim deed, so I couldn't borrow money on my house. Then my mother died. It was just a horrible year, but in the middle of all of it, I just kept saying, "This isn't so bad. Each problem I have is a quality problem. I have a house that'll one day be mine again when they figure out this paperwork. At some point the IRS will get their act together. Did I eat today? Yes. Did I sleep in a

Kelvinator box last night? No." Period. End of sentence. I have no real problems.

Having said that, talk to my wife; she may have a different perspective on how I handle it. And I do have my moments where I get into a bit of stress, but I will tell you they are quite rare, especially compared to the way it used to be. I mostly do not stress out.

KELLY McGILLIS

Like many men in America, I fell in love with Kelly McGillis after seeing her in Top Gun *and* Witness. *Kelly left Hollywood in the early nineties, and I figured she'd decided she'd rather raise some kids, or do any of the ten million things less maddening than making a living as an actor. She did have two lovely little girls, but unfortunately, most of Kelly's energy went into wrestling that 800-pound gorilla. Our paths crossed on a hot summer day in 2006, at the Caron Treatment Centers in Pennsylvania, where both of us were sharing our experience, strength, and hope with those still in treatment. That's when I learned about her journey.*

The story she shared with me that day, the story she agreed to share here, shows us a couple of things. First, beauty, talent, strength, and success do not immunize you from addiction. And second, you can recover from terrible trauma and addiction—and not just survive, but thrive.

In recovery, I've realized that life is about fun. It didn't used to be about fun, and it really should be, because I've only got this one chance. Work used to be my whole life, and I sacrificed everything for that. I wasn't ever present for my kids. I wasn't ever around. I was working or partying, and today I'm a full-time mom, and it has changed my relationship with my kids, and my life. We can actually talk, we can actually decorate the Christmas tree together and not have a major drama. Being able to laugh together. Those kinds of moments are things I've never had in my life. It's a tremendous gift to just be a parent and be here with them.

That's another thing I've learned how to do—to just *be* here, not always thinking and worrying and wondering. And those are the moments when I don't see God, the spiritual—I experience it. I experience it with you.

I experience it with my neighbor. I experience it sitting here being by myself. I experience it when I go hiking in the hills. I experience it when I hear a fabulous piece of music or see a beautiful painting. And I really was cut off from it before.

It took me twelve years to get sober. There were many things keeping me from recovery. One was the fact that I thought I could do it—I thought I could do everything—by myself. When I finally realized that I had a problem, still I thought, "I should be able to handle this. I've handled all these tragic events in my life and I can handle this one too."

I realized just how much I cannot handle and how thinking that I can handle things all by myself just isolates and alienates me from myself and God. And it's been freeing to know that I *can't* handle everything by myself. I don't know *how* to handle things by myself. I don't *want* to handle everything by myself. And that has enabled me to live with a sense of community, and I mean real community, not just a neighborhood. I think self-sufficiency was this huge problem for me, a kind of false, arrogant self-sufficiency.

When it was gone, it opened a place in my soul for who I really am to start emerging. That little door in my soul will shut down sometimes because I'm scared, because I don't understand—for whatever reason. It wasn't like the good fairy flew over my head and whacked me with her wand and all of a sudden I was a completely different person. It didn't happen that way. It's an ongoing process, and you can't just call up those spiritually connected moments when you need them.

Sometimes, when I've really been struggling, I tell myself to trust that if I keep on going forward, if I just purge myself of whatever it is I need to get rid of, there will be a huge gift on the other side. I don't need to know why, I just have to trust. I've had that miracle before. I've had lots of miracles in my life, but it took getting sober to be able to see them.

Those last few years, I knew I had a problem but I had all kinds of things that kept my denial intact. I had a lot of homes and I had a lot of handbags and I had a lot of friends. But even so, the last ten years or so, especially the last five, I was really trying to stop. I was going to mutual support groups, but I had this idea that if I just showed up at a meeting, I'd be struck by the sober fairy and that would be it. I never did anything that people suggested to me. Oftentimes, especially when I was on the road, I would just walk out of a meeting and go back to my hotel room and start drinking.

And then the drinking just got worse and worse and it started taking over. My kids would go on vacation with their dad and I'd think, "Woo-hoo, I can get drunk now because I don't have any responsibilities."

Finally, I lost everything. My marriage was over, my kids had been taken away from me, I had to sell my house because I hadn't worked in a long time, and so I decided it'd be a really good idea to kill myself. I was living in Florida by then, and locked myself in this little apartment with a bottle of booze and some sleeping pills. I don't know how many days I spent there—I guess maybe three or so—but every time I woke up I would just take more pills and drink more vodka.

I remember waking up at one point and I just heard this little voice speaking to me. The voice wasn't outside myself, but inside my being, inside my soul, saying, "Not yet." That was it, just this voice. I wasn't hearing it, because hearing is something to do with outside; I was *experiencing* this voice. Whenever I talk about it, I put my hand on my stomach, where my diaphragm is, because that's where I *felt* it, right at the center. I was feeling a lot of angst, a lot of despair, a lot of anger, a lot of fear, but after experiencing that voice, I felt a sense of peace. It was something I had never felt before, and I don't know if I will ever feel it again—an absolute peace and stillness internally. I just stopped fighting and I asked for help. Then the next time I woke up, a gardener had broken in the door, and I looked up at him and I said, "I have to go now. I need help."

This is what the disease of alcoholism is like. I'd just had this incredible spiritual experience, I'd asked for help, admitted that I needed help, and yet I spent five and a half hours in the car on the way to treatment trying to get out. My dearest friend had agreed to drive me to this place, and I made that whole trip hell because I was not ready to finally just *give up*. I kicked, I fought, I screamed, I cajoled, I begged, I pleaded, I did everything I could to get out of the car. I fought it, and I fought it, and I fought it, and then by the time I got there, I was just utterly defeated and I said, "I can't do it anymore." In that moment, I lost my desire. From that moment on, I have not had the real desire to drink or drug.

Which doesn't mean I haven't thought about it. That's part of recovery, learning new ways to deal with things. That was so foreign to me. When I had a fight with somebody for the first time sober, of course my thinking was "I gotta go get drunk now." You know how they say cows travel the same path until they wear it into the ground? Well, that's the path I was headed for, because after thirty years of thinking that way, it takes a little while to stop. But even though I thought about heading down my little cow path, I didn't do it. The compulsion, the absolute desire to do it, was gone. And having that taken away, that was a total spiritual experience.

Prior to that, recovery was an external experience, me trying to do it. After that moment, it was about *being* it and allowing things to happen. It doesn't mean that I didn't do things—I asked for help, I asked for a sponsor—but I wasn't dragging it behind me like it had a weight to it, the way it had always felt before. It was . . . not easy, not effortless, but *light*.

The people who saw me at the treatment center, my ex-husband, my girlfriend, the people who came to visit me, they all said, "There is something amazingly different about you." And I *was* different. I'd had a spiritual moment that I didn't ask for. I just gave up and made room for God. Plain and simple, that was the end for me. I had no will left, none. I had no more will to live, I had no more will to fight, I had no more will to *think*. I've always been a big thinker. I always knew what I needed. "I drink too much because I'm in New York and I need to move to L.A." Or "I drink too much because I've been working too much," then "I drink too much because I'm unemployed"—I mean, I was a *good* thinker. So at that point when I could no longer think, I just didn't know or care. I had no more will.

Now, whenever I'm around people I care about who are struggling, I don't push. I just try to stand by my integrity and sobriety, try to be of service and be helpful to people. Maybe it's because of my experience, where I felt that people shoved it down my throat, which just made me say, "Screw you." So I just practice being in recovery. I listen to what they share with me about how they feel, and it's really, really great to be able to say, "Yes, I used to feel that way too, and I'm really grateful that I don't today."

GERRY COONEY

❧

As a professional heavyweight boxer, Gerry compiled an impressive record of twenty-eight wins and three losses, with twenty-four knockouts. I've been a boxing fan since I was a kid, and I still remember his 1982 fight against Larry Holmes. Gerry slugged it out for twelve rounds, even after getting knocked down. He showed a tremendous amount of heart. The Spinks fight five years later, which he talks about here, was his last major fight in the ring—but he's continued to fight for sobriety, his own and others'. His organization, FIST (Fighters' Initiative for Support and Training), helps other retired boxers make the transition to the post-ring life, which often involves helping them with substance abuse problems similar to his own. He points out a basic truth about the journey: you have to face the darkness before the real healing can begin.

Where I ended up had a lot to do with where I came from and my upbringing. In my household I learned five things. You are no good. You are a failure. You are not going to amount to anything. Do not trust anybody. Do not tell anybody your business. That is what my father's father gave him, and what my father gave to me. Thank God, I did not give that to my children. I was given the cards I was given and I have to play them. I really wanted to give my children different cards.

At the same time, I grew up going straight from first base to home plate without going to second and third. I always found the shortcut. I was getting over and getting around, and that was my life. I did not hold fast to anything because none of it was real to me. I was just playing a game. In recovery, I found out that in real life, you got to go to first base, then second base, then third base before you come home.

It took two and a half years for the fight with Michael Spinks to happen. The fight was on, the fight was off, the fight was on, the fight was off. I didn't believe the fight was ever going to take place and I started drinking every day. When the night of the fight came, I still didn't believe it was going to take place and I was in no shape and in no condition. I got stopped in five rounds. With all that fear, anxiety, loss, I said to myself, "I will take a break for six months." I had a nice place out in the Hamptons and I'd hang out there every day with this old guy who'd go and drink with you anytime. I remember one day I'm driving home, and I figure that the transmission was going or there was ice on the road because I was sliding all over, but it was me, driving drunk. I remember going on dates, and I wouldn't be thinking about the girl, I'd be planning my drinking. Four o'clock or four thirty, "Where am I going? What am I going to have?"

I was a good drinker and I could handle my stuff pretty well, but I reached the point in life that I knew that I wanted to deal with this. I woke up one day, all alone in this beautiful beach house, and I said to myself, "I am scared. What is going on here? Who is in charge? What has happened?" I said, "I quit," and so I quit. Then the next day I woke at the same time, at eleven o'clock in the morning, the same way. I was on my bed, awake and hungover. What happened? I really got scared, and I realized that this is an illness that I have. That's the moment I cried out loud to God. I said, "God, please help me now. You got to help me out of this one."

I turned on the television, and there was a commercial for a center out in the Hamptons. I called them up because I thought I might have a problem. Three months into sobriety, this girl told me, "You better be careful because when you get five or six months sober, you're going to think you're better." I thought, "You got to be crazy." And after five months, I met this French girl, she was saying, "*Oui, oui,* let's go," and I got complacent and I fell down again, drinking.

Two months later, I'm driving down the road with my buddy and I say, "Let's stop for breakfast." I pull into the restaurant, and there was a guy in there I used to party with. He bet people that he could put a ciga-rette out on his hand—and he would. And now he was three years sober. Here I am, after a night of drinking, and he said to me, "Jerry, you know you never have to drink again." Now I'd heard that a thousand times al-ready, but I really heard it that day from him. I stopped drinking right there, and I still stay in touch with that guy. I mean I was twenty-nine years old. I'm thinking, "Hey man, time is running out on me here. I re-ally got to take hold, you know that?"

That was the best thing that could have happened to me. I thought I was the boss, and I found out in those two months, I am not the boss. The booze wasn't working anymore. It was no more fun. But I couldn't stop. I had such a fear that I'd have to go through everything sober. I used alco-hol for everything. No matter where I went or what I did, alcohol was my friend.

I had to look into myself and see that I made some mistakes. I never wanted to look at my mistakes, but you really have to look inside yourself and get down to the real source of the trouble in your life. When I was done fooling around, I was talking to this therapist and he asked me, "When you close your eyes, what do you see?" I said, "I see a dark hole." He said, "We got to go in the hole. You got to go in there. You got to feel around to see what is going on." I did not want to go there but I had no other place to go. I felt very uncomfortable, frightened, angry, but I did it, and then it gave me a little more courage to reach out some more, and then some more.

That's what you've got to do, and I know some great athletes who cannot do it. They cannot go into the hole and they cannot reach out. I give them information, I tell them my own experience, and I tell them I love them. That it's a great life that we have in sobriety and we're lucky to get it. There are those guys that you try and try and try and try, and after a while you got to say, "Well, listen, you got to find somebody else. You're not finished with your story yet, but I don't think I can help you more." Hopefully, some later day, if I can serve them, I am ready.

You can row the boat, but God's got to steer. When I first got sober I would figure, "Oh, I'll be done when I have three years. I won't have to work at it. Okay, I've got three years and I'm not done. I'll be done when I have five years." Well, I've got over twenty years now and there are areas in my life where I still have fear and I still have trust issues. But in recovery, I've had these amazing awakenings that gave me the courage to move. When I've got such pain that I feel like I can't keep going, there's always someone in the room to tell me how to get out of it. You work your program and you keep working it until you're done with that part of it. It's like a toothache. You go to a dentist and he takes out 98 percent of the cavity and fills it up again. Well, that cavity is coming back, just from that 2 percent that's left. It's the same with the program. You got to get 100 percent. So I keep working on my recovery. I want to work it. I do not want to go back to where I was.

My recovery is a fight, a great fight. I take my shots, but I get my shots in, and I know I will go all fifteen rounds. That's what life is about, being in the fight. When I was drinking, I was going around the circle. I wasn't in the fight.

STEVE EARLE

❧

Steve's one of these guys who always knew what he wanted to do with his life. He dropped out of school in eighth grade so he could move to Houston and get started in the music business. In 1975 he moved to Nashville and got his start writing songs and singing backup. He worked steadily and released his first album in 1986, but by 1993, addiction had caught up with him. In recovery, he's become enormously productive: setting up his own record label, producing about an album a year, touring constantly, writing a collection of short stories and a play. He is also very active in the anti–death penalty movement and does a lot of work with prisoners.

I met Steve not long after I came back from Cuba, when I was trying to get a movie made down there and he was involved in a musician's cultural exchange. I was impressed with his commitment to human rights; digging into his music was just icing on the cake. When we talked about recovery, he had a lot to say and was incredibly passionate about the idea of the human soul becoming unshackled.

The very first song that I wrote sober was "Goodbye," and it's still one of my most durable songs. People keep recording it. I wrote it while I was in treatment. There was a guitar there that everybody else was allowed to play, but I had to get permission, and I was not allowed to play more than a couple of hours a day. It was my own counselor who made that damn rule for me. That's how I wrote "Goodbye," and that song is the very first thing I created after being so spiritually bankrupt for so long. For four and a half years, I had not written a single solitary word or note.

I never believed that I was more creative when I was high. I tried to avoid performing when I was high and writing when I was high, but toward the end I didn't have a choice because I had to use all the time. I don't think I was afraid that I wouldn't be able to create if I stopped using. I believed I had a right to take drugs because it allowed me to stare into the darkness without blinking. When I look back at what I created then and what I create now, it's not that what I created before wasn't good. A lot of it was really good. But the way I wrote it, that's such an addict's attitude. The idea that numbing yourself out and preventing yourself from feeling what you should feel and then thinking that you're going to translate that into a piece of art that's worth anything—that is so flawed. It's cheating. You're writing *about* feelings and not really feeling them.

I grew up with the Serenity Prayer on the wall, literally. My step-grandfather, my mother's stepfather, was from northeast Texas. He went into the army and mustered out at the end of World War II and ended up in New York City. He was a tennis bum, basically, a ne'er-do-well tennis pro on Long Island. He was teaching tennis at different country clubs, and he would change jobs three or four times every couple of years, so you know what was going on there. He was a playboy, and he was really digging being a bachelor in New York City after World War II, but eventually he started to figure out that he was drinking differently than some of the other people that he knew.

Keep in mind, this is 1946 in New York City. Alcoholics Anonymous is eleven years old. My granddad was a real live old-timer who knew Bill W. and Dr. Bob. When he had about two years sober his father died, and as the only son, he goes back to Jacksonville, Texas, to run the family's hardware store. He went back kicking and screaming, and once there, he started most of the meetings in northeast Texas. He met my mother's mother in a meeting. She was an alcoholic who could not stay sober except in this program, and by the end of her life, she was running three halfway houses for women. After they got married, my uncle was born. The weird thing, for me, was that my uncle was only five years older than me. He gave me my first guitar and my first joint. I worshipped my uncle. He had this disease and it wrecked his life.

It took me a long time to really be successful. I was thirty-one when *Guitar Town,* my first release on a major record label, came out. But as soon as

I had money and was traveling where there was decent heroin, I had a problem. I stayed reasonably sober while I was actually performing. Most of the time. I'd have one really big drink of whiskey before I walked on-stage every night, but after the show was over I didn't give a fuck about alcohol anymore. It's an inefficient drug and I just didn't bother with it. Opiates were the deal. That being said, at the end, I smoked a ton of co-caine because I couldn't get high on heroin anymore. I had to resort to a methadone pill just to keep from being sick, and I spent hundreds of thou-sands of dollars and all day chasing after a drug that I don't even like.

Basically, the slow burn started when I got pulled over by the cops in a borrowed car with a tenth of a gram of really bad heroin wrapped up in piece of tinfoil hidden in the ashtray. After a whole bunch of bullshit, it ended with me going to jail, one year and eleven months hanging over my head. That was the twelfth of September, 1994. My bottom was probably sitting in front of a television camera that I allowed to come in because I thought I could make a public plea to get the judge to let me go back on a methadone program, because I thought methadone was treatment. I em-barrassed the fuck out of myself. By that time, I got no front teeth. I'm overweight even though I smoke crack every day because methadone does that. My diet was Dr Pepper and Cherry Garcia floats and those burritos they have in 7-Eleven. Those fuckers are good. Junkie food, no doubt about it.

This kid that worked in my lawyer's office finally said, "I can probably get you into treatment if you'll go." I said sure. I thought, "Once I get to feeling better, then I can walk out." This guy came to get me, and I still talk to him. His name is Chuck and he's a stalwart in recovery in middle Tennessee. His job then was to drive from Buffalo Valley treatment center, which is in western Tennessee, to jails all over the state to pick guys up and bring them in.

So I went to Buffalo Valley for no other reason except to get out of an orange suit. But something happened, and I have a hard time explaining it. I don't think I would have seen a flash of light even if there had been one, because I was really sick by that time. It began more subtly because that's what it needed to be for me.

First thing that happened was I started thinking, "Well, I don't think I can stay clean, but maybe I can stay here and get healthy. Then when I get out I'll do it better and I'll use it more successfully." Then I started seeing guys that I looked up to. They had twenty-six, twenty-seven days clean at the most, but they looked like they knew something, and at some point I started listening to them. Then two things happened right in a row.

At Buffallo Valley they showed movies in the common room, and the option was you could sit and read your fucking recovery book or you could watch the movie. So we were a bunch of inmates, we're watching the movie *My Name Is Bill W.* James Garner was in it and I knew who he was. In the movie he was Dr. Bob and James Woods was Bill W.

What happened was one of those feelings that you can only have when you're detoxing. Everything is so out of control. Most people when they get clean, they probably haven't cried in months, and then suddenly everything makes you cry. You cry at commercials. Great big hairy guys turn into little girls when they are watching movies in treatment. I cried several times during the movie, but it was weird—I would disconnect from the plot of the movie and go directly to my grandfather. Suddenly it dawned on me who those guys were that were sleeping on my grandfather's couch when I was a kid. That was old school back then, 1957 to 1961. There was no place to take anybody except for the state hospital, and my grandfather always had at least one of these guys staying with him, trying to get sober.

When I was a child I admired my grandfather, and I grew up with evidence in my life that recovery can happen, and I avoided it like the plague. But watching that movie, some gear shifted. I needed to figure out my connection to that history and where recovery comes from and how recovery works. In other words, how do you devise a spiritual system for both the spiritually bankrupt and people that are just too smart for their own good? It literally is a spiritual program of recovery for agnostics, a way to connect yourself spiritually to something.

Then the next day, I connected my grandfather to Chuck, this older gentleman that had picked me up in jail. Chuck comes in with some raggedy-looking motherfucker and I realized that that's what I looked like two weeks ago when I came in. Chuck goes, "How do you do, Steve?" and I said, "Well, I'm not in jail," which is my standard answer—"I'm too cool to be here, but this is better than being in jail." And Chuck said, "Yes. And you know what? You don't ever have to be in either place." It was like my grandfather talking to me, because Chuck was the age I remember my grandfather being.

And suddenly I filled in all the blanks. I never knew my grandfather to drink. I knew recovery was a big part of his life. He talked about going to meetings all the time. I've still got his Serenity Prayer, in a frame that he got on his tenth anniversary of being sober. My grandmother had given me a bunch of his stuff when he died, but it wasn't until that moment that I really felt it. It was like he was there, and he was the person that I needed to connect all of this history to me, personally.

I remember when I realized that I had turned some sort of corner. I did not want to say—hell, I was afraid to say—"Okay, I'm not going to use." For me, it was more like "I will not use today." But I also had to have some sort of admission that my ass was kicked. I had to admit that here's something I knew about all of my life and now I need it. I had to admit, "Okay. I'm the same thing that my grandfather was, and I'm the same thing that my uncle was."

The concept of anonymity isn't just about the neighbors not knowing that we're addicts and alcoholics. It's also about us being able to downplay our own self-importance long enough to hear God, to pay attention to what is going on around us. You think I ever went to the Anne Frank House before I got sober? They don't have any dope there, so no, I did not go. Amsterdam is a beautiful city, and I had no idea. I went to Australia and never even saw a fucking kangaroo. They've got the strongest heroin in the world, and I almost died there. That's all I knew about Australia.

This is why some people have to reach an absolute bottom and lose fucking everything. I think that the people that have the hardest time getting sobriety are the people that are the most individualistic, the people whose own identity is most important to them. And making art, you've got to literally not pay any attention to what other people tell you, to what other people do. That is a positive thing, it is a force of nature, but it has a pitfall. After a while you start believing that these special abilities that you have make you exempt from stuff that happens to everybody.

There were eighty-six or eighty-seven people in Buffalo Valley when I was there, and I am the only that has stayed sober continuously for thirteen years. Why me? Maybe it's as simple as this: For once in my life, I listened to those people. And maybe for once in my life, I do it exactly the way somebody else tells me how to do it. And you know what? I almost never fuck it up, because I am working with this huge body of experience.

Early on, the woman I lived with was using right in the house, and I had my head so far down in my recovery that I did not see it. She had a methadone habit going that I had no idea about until it went to code red. When I had less than six months of sobriety, I found a bottle of methadone under the front seat of my car, and that's how I found out about it. She went to treatment, and as soon as she got out, she started using again. At that point I had to go. I was not going to survive in that environment. Since then I've watched other people go through it, people that I really love a lot.

If you become aware of someone else's problem, then you've got to do something. You at least have to make yourself available. I just try to suit up and show up. Normally, if people aren't at least thinking about getting help and they know you're in recovery, they'll avoid you. You will never even see them. But if they start coming into your orbit repeatedly, if they're not avoiding you, then they're asking for something. At some point I will say something, and I have to say it for me, not for them. The two guys who started Alcoholics Anonymous literally started out by going to a fucking sanitarium and going up to some poor guy sitting there detoxing, and they'd sit down and say, "Hey! How are you? We don't drink anymore." That was really it. That was the whole spiel.

Do I believe in a God that plays dice with the universe? No, but what I believe doesn't matter. There either is a God or there is not. It has nothing to do with my faith, which is that there is a God and God really does love everybody, including people that don't believe that there is a God. I've seen a lot of damage done in the name of God in this world, so I understand why people are sensitive about it. I have seen the Catholic Church do horrible fucking things, I have read about them, but I lived in Mexico in the late seventies and I saw women go to church every Sunday, and I am absolutely positive that they were getting their God by doing that. Whatever gets you there.

Unfortunately, there are always going to be political entities. My friend in recovery said, "The best concept, which becomes a necessity in recovery, is the difference between spirituality and religion, because a lot of people are becoming traumatized by religions." You know—"Oooh, she said, 'God.' That's religion! I don't want to hear it." You have to try to convince people this is not religion, this is spirituality, it's something different. Eventually they're going to say, "What's the difference between religion and spirituality?" The difference is that religion is a group of people's agreement about what God is or, worst case scenario, what God is not. But it's an agreement, therefore it's political. That's the essence of what politics is, isn't it?

Spirituality is one person's individual, one-on-one relationship with God. It doesn't have anything to do with anyone else. People can get spiritual in a group, but really it's just like dying. You can have your family all around, all your friends, but when you go, you're going by yourself. Nobody is fucking going with you.

I am much more forgiving now, because I frequently have to forgive myself as I just stumble through the wreckage and try to recover. I have to be mindful of the fact that I'm forgiving other people because I have to forgive myself and vice versa. You can't do one without the other.

The biggest difference now is that I have to feel stuff and be there for it, and if I hurt somebody's feelings I have to deal with the consequences. Before, if I hurt somebody's feelings—and I'm sure I hurt lots of people's feelings—I was capable of living with it because I was high all the time. That's why people think we're assholes, because we are. We aren't out there operating with all of our senses, and we aren't operating with our hearts. We're operating with our brains and our "want to" and that's it. Recovery doesn't promise that you won't be an asshole, but most of the people that practice spiritual principles of recovery in all their affairs, they do get to be better people than they were when they came in. I may still be, relatively speaking, an asshole, but I know I'm better than I was, and that's because I have to be. It's absolutely necessary to my survival, and I don't do it for everybody else, I do it for me.

I hear people come into recovery meetings and share how they wish everybody had a program because this world would be a lot better place. I believe that, but I don't think it makes that much difference to my life. It's not about anybody else's program, it's about mine. It's the only thing that I can do. Is the world a better place if I don't succumb to this disease? Yeah, if for nothing else because I won't be driving cars upside down the wrong way along the interstate. All I can do is what I need to do to keep from ending up back where I started. The main thing about being sober is suiting up and showing up. Just the stuff that I have seen, the normal everyday stuff that I missed before, that's miraculous enough. Then you add to it capital-M Miracles—and those happen too. I have seen them.

STEPHEN BERGMAN
and JANET SURREY

❧

Both Stephen and Janet are clinical therapists at Harvard Medical School and at the Stone Center at Wellesley College. Together, they've written the book We Have to Talk: Healing Dialogues between Men and Women *(with Samuel Shem), as well as the play* Bill W. and Dr. Bob, *about the founders of Alcoholics Anonymous. My cousin Patrick suggested that I go see the play while I was visiting New York, and I was blown away. Janet and Stephen are the only married couple I interviewed for the book, and it was interesting to see how their stories connected and separated and reconnected again. There's another whole book there about recovery in relationships.*

JANET: There are four moments that really stand out in my mind. The first one got me to go to a mutual support recovery group, just open the door. It was an experience I had of letting go, just of tears.

It was a very nice summer day and it was hot, and I was in the house. I was eating chocolate cupcakes with white frosting and drinking Scotch. I was inside, it was a beautiful day, and there was just a real sense of being cut off from life, in isolation, and not wanting to be there. I just . . . for some reason, I let myself cry. I didn't do anything about it. I didn't go out, I didn't pick up the phone, I didn't do anything but stay with my experience. Just stay with what I was feeling for a really, really long time. It was the only time in my life I went to the end of my tears. And at the end of the tears, I felt this enormous peace.

I went outside and I had a sense of the skies opening up and the light pouring down. It felt like something really opened up for me, and I just surrendered to the depth of that feeling. I wasn't trying to make it better or tell myself anything about it. For once in my life, I let myself just feel what I felt. And it led me to the sense of peace, of *sumati*.

That was a Sunday afternoon, and I finally went back in the house and made a phone call to find out where there was a recovery meeting, and there was one a half hour later close to where I was. I had that miraculous feeling when things click.

I really believe that the universe rewards surrender—but you can't surrender *because* of that, because then it's not surrender. This idea of diving into the pain instead of running away—it's a surrender to the truths, the things you've been running from your whole life.

So that was the first moment. It allowed me to listen, and it made everyone at that meeting look like they were angels to me that night. That was twenty-eight years ago, and I still vividly, vividly remember what was said and what the speaker was wearing and what the light looked like. I could see the light in her. I could feel it in her story. I listened in a way that felt like "I'm home." I had this sense that I needed to really listen in a way I had never listened to anything else before. You know, like it says in one of the books we use in recovery, "As willing to listen as only the dying can be."

I did get a mentor in recovery, but I was doing that on the energy of that first moment, and just being a good girl. I remember hearing, "There will come a time when no power on Earth will stop you." I didn't know what that meant until later, when I was having cravings. I got on my knees because I was told to do that, and I asked for help and the craving was lifted. That was like an opening to a new reality, that I did not have to be controlled by the craving. To get through that craving moment, ask for help and feel something answer—it was just awesome to me. That was my second moment.

The third moment that really stands out to me was in another recovery meeting. Sunday morning, full of smoke, VFW hall. I was looking at the banners, you know, the slogans they used to have up in the rooms. One of them said You Are Not Alone, and I'd looked at it a million times, but suddenly I overwhelmingly *felt* for the first time that I wasn't alone. I had never known that I was living in aloneness, and suddenly I knew that the thing I wanted most in my whole life was to feel connected, and that was possible by being at this meeting.

That's not to say I always feel connected, because I don't. I struggle with that all the time. But I feel like something crossed over, something happened that made me understand both the possibility of connection and also the pain I'd been living in. Those moments of connection, they're bridges to something else. You won't be there forever, but once you've been there, you're never the same again.

One night I was at my house in Gloucester, overlooking the water. There was an incredible lightning storm, and this tremendous flash lit up the whole ocean and the whole bay. For a moment, you could see everything, and then it would get dark again. But once you've seen that flash, you never go back to total darkness. The light goes away, and yes, you're in the dark, but you have to cultivate the gratitude that you have seen the light and you might see it again. You can't have it all the time, because we're human and we don't live in those moments. But the moments open something for you, something in you. You get insight or expansion or illumination, or you see and feel what's real at a deeper level.

STEPHEN: I think that my struggle was different. It was really around—I mean there were two struggles I didn't know I was in. The longest one was alcohol. Jews aren't alcoholics; you know that, right? Only in looking back do I realize how many times I should have been dead, through various accidents or whatever. I didn't realize that I was living such a risky life. I just thought it was kind of normal, you know, after I started drinking.

And then the second struggle, which I only realized later was the spiritual struggle with self-centeredness, with ego. I was this society's definition of high achievement. I did Harvard College and I was a Rhodes Scholar at Oxford and then Harvard Medical School. It was really a pretty self-centered quest, and I didn't question it. I thought that was what you did. Then it caught up with me. I hit the wall after turning forty, and I realized all of these things had gotten so much more important than whatever one could call a soul or compassion.

I got depressed. Writing was the thing I wanted to do, but I was too depressed to write. I spent a year lying in a bathtub, you know, not knowing what I should do, because writing had gotten too important to me and I couldn't write.

Earlier, Janet had gone to a seminar by an Indian woman, a very wonderful teacher. I had met her here in the United States and I didn't think there was much in what she was talking about, but Janet was going to go off to a weeklong seminar with her in Holland. Janet and I were not getting along very well, but something made me say, "Well, I'm going with you." Janet was shocked, because we hadn't really been participating very much in each other's lives by then. She was living on the top floor and I was living in the carriage house, and we were not doing too well. Somehow I sensed that if she went to this thing alone, it might all be over, and I didn't want that. It just came out of me: "Well, I'm going with you." There was no calculation involved. I surprised myself by saying that.

So I went, and at first I still didn't get anything out of what this woman was talking about. We'd sit in meditation, and then she'd give a lecture. Then she gave a lecture on psychological suffering. I had majored in psychology at Harvard, I was a psychiatrist, I'm supposed to know about this. But she just put a whole different slant on the causes of psychological suffering and the ways to work through it.

I remember sitting there, with my knees aching and my back hurting. But I was, all of a sudden I was really *there*. I wasn't taking notes; I was just *listening* with this sustained attention. I had an hour's worth of sustained attention.

And it wasn't a lecture. It was really saying, "This is who you are. You don't know it, but I'm sharing with you because I know it." Janet said afterward—she was sitting in back of me—she said my ears actually got big.

So that was really the first moment. It didn't have anything to do with alcohol. It had to do with understanding and listening. She was saying that self-centeredness was the basis of psychological suffering—"Oh, of course. That's it. It's not your mother and father, it's not your toilet training." I had never understood that before. That started me on this Buddhist-practice path, and it's a remarkable journey.

Then one of my students was given the job of starting an addictions center and I became their doctor. I didn't know anything about recovery. It was never mentioned in medical school or anywhere else. So here I am, treating alcoholics, and I would tell them, "Oh, you've gotta go to this mutual support group." Then I thought, "Well, if I'm sending them to this recovery group that I've never gone to, maybe I ought to figure out what it is. Otherwise I'm bullshitting them."

I started going to meetings so I could see what they were about. Then I started to understand it, and then I could talk to people about it. I wouldn't take anybody in therapy unless they had "a meaningful connection" to the group. Then we would talk about what that means.

And I had very good luck with people, really. These people I worked with would do fine, which flew in the face of what I'd been taught as a psychiatrist. I'd been taught you work on their depression, and they'll stop drinking. Which of course is totally backwards.

So I'm going to meetings and holding these therapy sessions, many times a week, and doing this intense Buddhist exploration. Then I started to work with Janet on the *Bill W. and Dr. Bob* play, which involved me in learning and research into alcoholism and recovery in a really big way. But even through all that, I never put it together that I was an alcoholic.

One summer we were up in Gloucester, which has always been kind of a spiritual house for us, and we had not been getting along again. I started to see that there was a pattern in this—from my side, not from her side. Every day, late in the afternoon, I'd have a gin and tonic or two gin and tonics, and then we would have dinner, and I'd have wine with dinner. And every night, we'd have a fight after dinner. I'd get more and more irritable, we'd have a fight, and I'd conk out. Just fight and go to bed.

Finally all these different pieces came together. Not in a flash of lightning. In the play, there's this scene where Bob and Bill are really at each other's throats, and Bob says, "Maybe this thing can't rely on blinding flashes of light. It's like the body, human nature, like the rest of medicine. Step by step, you put the pieces of the puzzle together until finally the picture is clear before your eyes." And that's what happened to me.

That moment I said, "I'm not going to drink tomorrow." The next day I didn't drink, and I didn't have a real bad fight with Janet, and I didn't go to bed early. The next day the same thing happened, and I said, "Wait a second. There's really something going on here about alcohol." And then I looked back on my life, getting drunk, riding a BMW motorcycle without a helmet or a shirt or shoes to see if I could hit 100 miles an hour. There were lots of not only dangerous but totally humiliating episodes. Suddenly I went, "Jesus, that's been my problem here."

JANET: We should talk about the moment we had together.

STEPHEN: Go ahead. That's a good one.

JANET: It was really clear. We were standing out in front of the house, on a freezing night, and it was a terrible moment.

STEPHEN: Really freezing.

JANET: It was one of those moments where you knew if you walked away, you might walk away forever.

STEPHEN: Yeah, that's right.

JANET: I don't even remember the words, just the experience of having a shared moment of opening and surrendering. . . .

STEPHEN: Yeah. That's what it was, surrender.

JANET: It was the only time I have ever felt I wasn't alone. That shared moment, it had that sense of changing direction. It had a sense of "I have been here so many times. What just happened? What happened? I have been in that place how many times, but something just happened. What is that?"

STEPHEN: We really were on the edge of something, there was no question. I mean we were standing in the freezing cold, and we were about to move apart, but something else happened. That is the only way I have to explain it is something else happened that we both felt very strongly—

JANET: We both moved toward the relationship, moved out of self. And I felt you were in it with me.

STEPHEN: And I felt you, too. One of those clicks, and you are out of yourself. It's like a moment of awe. That's what it was, a moment of awe. You're not thinking in a moment of awe. You're not thinking of yourself.

You are in awe, and that's a state of love, real love. That was a remarkable thing.

JANET: Who knows why those moments come when they do? Or why they come at all? It's a mystery. I remember seeing this with an anorexic I was treating. She'd looked in the mirror a billion times and saw herself as fat, and suddenly she looked in the mirror and saw she was thin, and everything changed. I'll never forget that. I saw before me the mystery of that moment when something important gets reorganized, and it's not under our control. It's just a complete mystery, and it's transformative. And it's also truth.

That's the gift of desperation. Where you are is so bad, you have nothing left to lose, so why not try recovery? People tell that it will be hard, but you can get through it. People try by their human example to show you that you can lose and you gain things beyond your wildest dreams.

STEPHEN: Right, right. But that's the other side of it too, I think. I have found, in my experience anyway, that the things that I thought I needed to hold on to were actually the things I needed to let go of, and the things that I was terrified to let happen were necessary.

JANET: When someone needs help, I tell them my story. I try to get them to talk with someone. If not me, then someone else. And I try to carry the message in a quiet way. It doesn't always work, so I have to be very humble and not push. I have to find the right way to share and try to be sensitive, but not to expect much. Just trust you don't know where the seeds are going.

And if it helps, I tell people not to worry about "God." I mean I have so much trouble with the word *God*. So I think of it as G.O.D., the gift of desperation, because desperation brings us to the point where we can relate to the universe in a different way. It pushes us out of ourselves, makes us ask for help in a really fundamental way. Ask for help, and have something answer you. I don't believe it's a being, but I think you experience the aliveness of the universe in that moment.

STEPHEN: Which, of course, is God. The word I use is the *Divinity* or the *Divine*. What is God but the Divine?

RICHARD DREYFUSS

⁓

I met Richard Dreyfuss in the summer of 1974, while he was filming Jaws *on Cape Cod, and when he was on a break, he came to a clambake on the beach in front of my grandparents' house. I remember lobsters, daiquiris, and Hollywood gossip, but not much else.*

Jaws *made something of a splash, and Richard went on to star in* Close Encounters of the Third Kind *and* The Goodbye Girl. *At the age of twenty-nine, he won an Oscar for his role in* The Goodbye Girl—*the youngest Best Actor winner ever. (His record stood until 2003, when Adrien Brody won at age twenty-seven.) He also had a spectacular drug-related flameout, when he wrecked his car and nearly wrecked his career. But he got sober and went on to star in more great movies, including* Stand By Me, Tin Men, *and* Down and Out in Beverly Hills.

Thirty years after I met Richard, we worked together on a miniseries for PBS titled Cop Shop. *I remember everything about those three weeks. The man is relentless. His interests go way beyond acting—metaphysics, the right to privacy, shamanism, First Amendment rights, mental health, and, oh yeah, recovery, to name a few. When I asked him to participate in this book, he said yes immediately. He completely understood what I was trying to do and he was eager to help.*

I used to say that before I was twelve, I was the generic any-boy like everyone else and then when I turned twelve, I became me. I began to be more and more eccentric, I developed these passions, for acting and for civil rights, and I became one of two guys at my high school who smoked dope. I never went a day without it and I smoked it every day, in school and out of school, every day until 1969, when I'd been out of school about four years. I was in New York and I was rehearsing a play and I was in this really seedy hotel room and I had enough pot with me to last the whole time I would be there. I was smoking dope in my hotel room and the phone rang, and a voice said, "Hey, I'd like to buy some shit from you."

I said, "What?"

He said, "I want to buy some shit from you."

I said, "I don't know what you're talking about," hung up the phone, and I got so paranoid I put towels underneath the doors while I smoked my marijuana. And I remained paranoid. After that, every time I smoked marijuana I got paranoid. After a year I stopped. Then I proceeded to discover all kinds of things, uppers and downers and sidewaysers, psychedelics.

I have lived my whole life with drugs. I said to my sister once, not that long ago, "I wonder what I would have been like had I never taken drugs."

She said, "What are you talking about?" I said, "Well, when I was a kid, I was normal." She said, "No you weren't. Don't kid yourself. You were nuts before you took drugs, and if anything, they helped you." So the drugs were not the cause of my eccentricities.

A psychopharmacologist at UCLA once said to me that the moment man invented fire and gathered into groups, the next thing they did was to try to alter their minds. That was a spiritual experience for five hundred thousand years. The shaman would take the young away from the fire and give them mushrooms or whatever and offer them the opportunity to see the face of God. As a friend of mine, a doctor, once said, "Fifty people who have to take a painkiller will spit it out. Forty of the next fifty will take it because they have to. That last ten percent will put a bumper sticker on their car that says I Found It!" I am one of those 10 percent people.

Drugs have given me certain experiences that I really couldn't explain. One of them was, after two years of serious study, I took acid for the first time and it changed me. I sat on this rock in Malibu and I watched everything simplify. My image was of Einstein, trying to get down to the quantum theory. I was getting everything down to one simple statement, and that statement was "No more war." So I went to the draft board, tore up my student deferment, and filed as a conscientious objector.

That led to me working at the L.A. County Hospital. I was a file clerk in the basement, because this was my alternate service. I quickly sussed out that I was the one white guy among about thirty-five black guys, most of whom were working two jobs and raising families. I volunteered immediately for permanent night and weekend duty, which gave them a chance to be with their families and me a chance to be alone.

My job during the week was to set up the next day's appointments for the clinics, getting these huge files and putting them in carts and taking them underneath the L.A. County. That's what I did every night, except for Friday and Saturday. Those days, there were no clinical appointments the next day and I would go to the library. Until then I had never read outside of my discipline. I never read a book which I didn't already know I would enjoy. At the hospital, I used to go to the library and just take a whole shelf of books. Then I'd go back and get a coffee, put my feet up, and read. I read things I never thought I would read, like this book called *The Firmament of Time*. It was all a search for what was wrong with me, because I always knew something was wrong with me.

One night I was working the midnight shift and someone came in and said, "Anyone need anything to stay up?" and I said, "What?" He said, "Do you need this pill to stay up?" and I said, "Well, yeah." I took this little mini Benzedrine tablet and went back to work, and about twenty minutes later I went "BONG!" I just stood straight up in the air, because for the first time in my life, all sixteen of my personalities had become one. It was a spiritual experience, and no one was going to tell me otherwise. It allowed me to see something that otherwise I couldn't see, like a myth turned into reality.

At first I was taking one Benzedrine a day and then two and then four and then six, and by 1971 I was twenty-one years old and I was appearing with Henry Fonda at the Kennedy Center in a play, and I was taking thirty-two minibennies a day and drinking. I had never had a drink when I was a teenager, never wanted to. In my family the little liquor cabinet had cob-webs on it and the only alcohol that was served was on New Year's Day at the champagne party that my parents threw every year. But I was way into drinking by now, and into my bennies, and I remember making a very vivid entrance in front of thirteen hundred people.

I felt my sanity go flying right out of my arms, and I could hear me but I couldn't hear anyone else, and I had tunnel vision, and the other actors were all looming in front of me. I decided if at the end of the act they come and take me away, I'll know that I'm crazy. If at the end of the act they *don't* come and take me away, I'll just know I'm giving the worst per-formance in history. So when the play ended, which felt like a year later, I shuffled offstage. I was afraid to take my feet off the earth and so I shuf-fled out of the theater, through the Watergate Hotel, up to the Howard Johnson's, up to my room, and I took the bottle of minibennies that I had and I flushed them down the toilet. That was on a Sunday night and Mon-day was off, so the next performance was Tuesday. I cold-turkeyed in my room and showed up on Tuesday like everything was fine and then dis-covered that on Sunday I had given the worst performance in history.

That didn't stop me. I just decided bennies were no good and asked myself, "What else should I take?"

By 1982, I had won an Academy Award and there had been times when I was sober those years, but mostly I wasn't. By November of that year, I may not have been the founder but I was certainly a board member and probably chairman of admissions for the Assholes Center. I remember go-ing to the home of Sherry Lansing, who ran Paramount, and I was yelling at her, I mean I was *yelling* in her face, and I left her home at about ten thirty or eleven o'clock. I was drunk, I was loaded, I was enraged, and ev-eryone was an asshole. I got into my little convertible Mercedes and roared down the street. Never put a safety belt on. Why do I need one?

The next thing I knew the car was on top of me. The whole car was on top of me, and I was in my seat strapped in by a safety belt I don't remem-ber putting on. It was intensely quiet. My head was on the pavement and my body was dangling upside down, and it was very, very quiet. I knew that my life had changed, but I didn't know exactly how. I knew that I was either dead or about to die or I was permanently injured. At the very least I was looking at a DUI and an arrest for possession because I had a great deal of drugs in that car and on my person.

Finally a guy came up to the car—tap, tap, tap—put his head down, and according to him I said, "My name is Richard Dreyfuss. I'm a movie star." I always tell that version first because I don't remember saying it. Then I do remember saying, "Please help me."

So then there is a jumble of noise and I was taken to the hospital. I remember being at the emergency ward and having my dick stuck with a catheter, which as you know is the most painful thing in the world, while the police were going, "DO YOU KNOW YOUR NAME? DO YOU KNOW YOUR NAME? YOU ARE UNDER ARREST. DO YOU UNDERSTAND THAT? DO YOU?"

"Yes, I do."

"Who's the governor of California?"

"AHHHH!"

I woke up the next day in my hospital room knowing that downstairs there would be chaos. Of course the first phone call I made was to my dealer. My doctor came, my brother came, my dealer came. He was telling me that the news was all over the country, don't turn on the television. As we were talking in this private room I began to be aware of an image in my mind, an image of a little girl. I couldn't shake this image. I didn't know who she was. She was about eight years old. That's all I knew about her.

So the next day I woke up in the same room and I had the same little girl sitting there waiting for me, and this time I could see her a little bit more clearly and she was wearing horn-rimmed glasses and she had a pink-and-white dress on, and no matter what I said or thought about during that day she was there.

Of course when the lawyers started to come in I had to go down to the Beverly Hills Court—*that* was a zoo—and be arrested for DUI and for possession, possession of three or five Percodan tablets and less than a quarter of a gram of coke. So after I left the police and the court, I went to my lawyer's office and I said, "I have to tell you some bad news," and they said, "Oh, really?"

"The police are holding out on us."

"What do you mean? They have no reason to hold out on you."

I said, "I had just bought that day a transparent tube container of five hundred or a thousand Percodan. It was this big, and you could see through it. It was in my car."

They all looked at one another like "Oh, fuck," because they knew that had I been arrested for that—totally different ball game. They tried to talk amongst themselves as to why they wouldn't have been notified of this, but they couldn't figure it out.

I then embarked on about ten days of absolute denial. The only part of reality that I did check in with was I didn't drive. I hired a driver, but I tried to really drown myself in drugs and alcohol and behavior as much as I could because I knew everything was going to come out and I was going to bad places with bad people.

One of the first of God's little great subtle moments was that first day, after the hospital, I got into a limo to go to a party and realized that the driver was an actor I'd competed with and who was now reduced to driving a limo as opposed to costarring with me. I was in the back loaded, and he was driving the car.

Then I'm on my way to an orgy, and then I'm on my way to another one, and that's all I did for ten days in November 1982. And the little girl never left. Every day she was there, and every day I knew a little more about her. First she was just eight, then she was eight with glasses, then she was eight in a pink-and-white dress, then she was dressed in a pink-and-white dress with a crinoline and patent leather shoes, and I'm still thinking to myself there was no girl in my life. There was no little girl, I wasn't married, had no kids.

Meanwhile, one of my friends, Mandy Patinkin, had walked up Amsterdam Avenue in New York and seen from half a block away the *New York Post* headline that said, "Dreyfuss Busted," and puked. God only knows what my parents were thinking.

On the tenth day after the arrest I got into this limo in L.A. and I went out to Malibu to an orgy, to a coke night, with about three or four guys and five or six girls. To me, cocaine was demonic. It was like, "What shall I do today? I'll be anxious and insecure and hateful and disgusting—I'll take some cocaine." It just didn't make any sense, and I did it anyway.

Anyway, I'm at this orgy, and these girls were all beautiful, they were all laughing, and I saw in the eyes of one girl this glimpse of how desperately she didn't want to be there. I'd been around people like this for years. We all knew this game. We all knew that they were there for coke, they were coke whores, and they would do anything for that experience. There was still this little girl in the back of my head, just sitting there, and I looked at that girl at the orgy, and all of a sudden I just left. I was filled with such self-loathing and such revulsion for myself that I walked out that door, to the driveway, where my driver was standing.

As I got into the backseat of the car, I knew that little girl very simply was either the little girl that I didn't kill that night I completely lost control of my car, or she was the girl, the daughter I hadn't had yet. I knew that as a certain fact. And the moment I figured out who she was, she disappeared.

I went home that night and ritualistically poured everything out, and I went the next night to my first serious recovery meeting. During those ten days I had gone to a couple of meetings at Cedars-Sinai, loaded out of my head. This time I went and I was sober and that was the end.

I sobered up on November 19, 1982. My daughter was born November 19, 1983. My daughter wears horn-rimmed glasses. She wouldn't be caught dead in a pink dress, but it was my daughter, and the older she gets the more I see it.

But that's not the end of the story.

After I ended up in my car upside down, I said to my doctor, "You've got to test me, because there is something wrong here." The end result was that I was diagnosed as manic-depressive, and I went to therapists and I went to meetings. But I am Richard, and that means that if I'm going to be a drug addict, I want to know everything there is to know about drug addiction.

I just read my brains out, and then I began to look at the doctors I was dealing with, and I realized that there was only one thing they could successfully, confidently predict about what they would be saying about these things fifty years from now, which was "Boy, were we stupid fifty years ago." That's the history of medicine, all medicine about anything. I realized they didn't understand addiction any more than I did, and I was still an addict.

Then one day I ran into a psychiatrist in the Valley and I was telling him about how I hadn't been without drugs since I'm sixteen, and he said to me, "Richard, there is a faucet in your brain that is dripping either too slowly or too quickly, and we can help you." It was as if this weight lifted off my shoulders. I mean it was the first time anyone had ever empathized with my situation. So we embarked on a journey to find the right chemical balance, and that chemical balance includes everything. I don't make any distinction. When people say, "You know, you're still using. You should go to recovery meetings," I say, "You are a jerk." We are all here for one thing, and that is the attempt to alter our heads. One group does it this way, one group does it that way, but the end result, the goal, is the same.

I have a chemical formula. I take them every morning and sometimes during the day, and I am the nicest guy in the world. I am the nicest husband, I am the best father, I have the temperament of a prince. I am a pro. I spend the effort making sure that when you work on a movie, you are surrounded by creativity and relaxation and fun, and if there is any brouhaha on the movie, it's taken care of right away. Because life is too short, and I know that because when I got divorced and my wife kicked me out, I got so depressed. I was on a plane, and I picked up this magazine article all about depression amongst CEOs. It had a list: "If you have four of any of the next eleven or the next fourteen things, you are depressed." I had them all, I had every single one of them. I got off the plane and I called my doctor from the L.A. airport and I said, "Okay, we have to take this seriously. If you can't help me within a given amount of time, there is no reason on earth for me to live." And so what had been a kind of on-again, off-again attempt became a real search. "Let's try this . . . Okay, that doesn't work, so let's try *that*."

I was looking for what everyone looks for and no one ever finds. I was looking for inner harmony and contentment and an absence of anxiety and I was looking for what Buddha got.

Since then, I've found out a lot about it, and I've had moments of it. I don't know a lot of people who really are able to look at their own lives, their own mistakes, their own victories and defeats, their own processes, and learn from all that. I do. I'm a better person now than I was then. I realized a long time ago that the pursuit of my goal is far more fun than the achievement of that goal. The night I won the Academy Award, I took the award and turned it around and just stared at it. I had just won the Best Actor Award at age twenty-nine and I did not know or give a shit about anyone in that audience, and I was alone. I'm not alone like that anymore.

DAVID JAMES ELLIOTT

David dropped out of high school to be a rock star, but he soon wised up, got his diploma, and went on to Ryerson University in Toronto. That's where he got the acting bug, and after graduation he moved to L.A. He got roles in lots of movies and TV series, including Street Legal, Knots Landing, *and* Melrose Place. *I met him around this time, showing up for casting calls. He ended up getting the lead role on* JAG, *which ran for ten years, while I got . . . well, not that. At some point I noticed that he'd become part of the recovery community and I got to know him a little better. Even so, when I asked him to take part in this book, I thought of him as a long shot. Instead, he said yes instantly.*

This story breaks the pattern a little. Most of the time, I've cut out the places where the interviewee talks directly to me, but with this one, I left that in because it turns out I had a role in his recovery. I had no idea. I've included this not to blow my own horn—I'm just the guy that picked up the phone—but to show the nature of recovery. If you keep asking for help, you'll get it.

I lost my brother two years ago to addiction. He was the closest person to me my entire life, and I lost him to this disease because he was incapable of being honest with himself. That's ultimately what it took for me. I was afraid. It was way too big for me and it was killing me. I was hiding from it, and it just got heavier and heavier every day, because the more I hid from it, the more I tried to hide from myself, which is an impossible task. You just create more damage and more wreckage. I got to the point that it was life or death for me, and I hit bottom, thinking, "I'm just not going to make it."

I put together ninety days of sobriety five times before I finally really got it. I did the first five times because people were on my back and they wouldn't get off my back, and I did it to shut them up. Finally I had a moment of clarity after a night of debauchery—a *week* of debauchery—in the Bahamas. It was the next morning after a long night in a long week, a long night hiding in the grass on the beach, alone, hearing people whispering my name, scared to death, realizing that I had a problem that was completely out of control. I finally reached a point where I knew that if I didn't do something, if somebody didn't help me, I was going to die.

That was the first time I ever realized that. I'd been in tight spots before. You know, the next day I'd shake it off and I'd be okay for a while, I'd find some way to manage my problem. Or I'd find some people to tell me that I didn't have a problem, and there are certainly enough of them around, people who are in the disease with you. "Oh, probably you just had a bad night, man. Everyone has a couple of those." But that night on the beach, I hit that point when I really had to see I couldn't drink normally, I couldn't recreationally take drugs. I had to see that once I started, I couldn't stop.

Up until that point, giving it up was never an option, because I was taught my whole life that to surrender was to fail. But I finally realized, "You know what, I'm done if I don't surrender. I'm not going to have anything anyway." Not that I really had much. I didn't own anything. I had these suits, these two suits that I never wore, but they were like everything to me. I was so afraid that I'd lose these two suits that I had, that I would get in an argument with my girlfriend and she'd cut the suits up. That was my biggest fear. I had to persevere for fear of losing these two cheap suits that I never even wore. It was like they were all I had, the only things that proved I was a success or a grown-up or something.

But finally I just knew I was done. I had no control, I couldn't stop, I was afraid, and I didn't have anybody to tell me that it was going to be okay. I was afraid for a long time. I came into recovery and I was still afraid, but I thought, "Okay, these guys tell me that there is a way that I can be relieved of this obsession that's killing me." I showed up and I went to the meetings and I heard stories that spoke to me. I heard people saying things that were very familiar to me, things that I could relate to. Slowly things started getting better. The longer I stayed and the more I worked, the better things got. They started off as little miracles, because when you're first sober, you're pretty raw, and little things can set you off. You get a parking spot and you're sure God picked it out for you. Then I did the "fearless and searching moral inventory." I went through and I searched my soul. I put everything down, which was really scary, and I hid it. It was a big thick volume of all this trash—my fears and my resentments and my misdeeds and my sexual conduct and everything. My biggest fear was that revealing all this would define me as a person. I would be stuck in a box.

This guy I was working with in recovery told me to come over, and I was all set to read it to him. We're out in his backyard, and he kept getting interrupted with phone calls and stuff. I'd read a paragraph and he'd say, "Oh, can you hold on a second?" He was a big business guy. After half an hour, he came back after one of his phone calls and he said, "Okay, that's good for today. Come back next Saturday and we'll read some more." I'm like, "My God. This is going to take eight months at this pace."

I called another guy, and he was outraged by it. "What an asshole! Fire this guy. Call him up right now, fire him, and come over here. You can read it to me." So I went over there, so incredibly grateful and so incredibly scared. I remember every inch of the drive over with that book that I'd written, that thing that I just was so afraid to hand over. It was like the sound track of *Jaws* was playing. And then I showed up and, well, you know this, Chris, it was you. You were really there for me.

We went out and sat on the side of a hill, and I read through it. At the end of it, I was drenched in sweat. I mean, I couldn't even believe it. Some of the stuff as I was reading it, I almost wanted to hold back. But you know what, I walked through the fear. I was so afraid that you would judge me, and you didn't. In fact you still spoke to me a couple of days later, and it didn't seem to color your attitude toward me at all, all of this stuff that I felt that was just further proof of what a piece of shit I was. It was so incredible to have crossed that threshold. And after it was over, it really wasn't that big of a deal. It really wasn't. I just felt like more of a human being. I felt whole for the first time in my life, really. It was like the first time I got drunk, when I thought, "I suddenly don't care anymore what everybody is thinking"—it was a very similar moment to that. I didn't have to be afraid anymore.

I was with my brother Mike a few days before he died. I was about to do a movie, and I hadn't seen him in a long time. He sounded so great. When you're talking to someone, you know if they're living a program of honesty in life. I mean you just hear it in their voice, and I heard that in his voice. I just couldn't believe it. I really felt like I'd got my brother back. Then I saw him on the morning of the day he died, and he was a little weird. I said something about it, and he brushed it off and he went off on his way. He was going to see Mom. He died that night. She found him.

It was hard. I had to start working the next day, carrying this. It was a very difficult period for me, but I had to stop my feelings. It's just something you do. I think as a result of being sober, I'm able to do what I need to do, to suit up and show up and take care of business. I can feel the pain and not be afraid of feeling it, and not feel like I have to stuff something into my body so that I don't feel it. And the pain is pretty horrible. When Mike died, the pain was just unbelievable. At the same time, I was told, and I believe this, that if you feel the feelings, they'll go away, but if you don't feel them, they're not going anywhere. They're just going to manifest in some other way. I did the movie, and when I was done, I knew that I hadn't grieved for him, and so I took the time to do that. I did it in my way, and I'm probably still doing it. I still think about him a lot. I had a little trouble with my faith afterward, because I prayed for him all the time. I thought, "If there is a God, then why was Mike allowed to die this way?" I mean I prayed. Every night I prayed for him. And he died anyway.

I talked to somebody, and he said, "Maybe your prayers were answered. Maybe when he died, he didn't have to hang around in limbo, for lack of a better word. He was able to pass on and get going to the next incarnation or whatever's next." That was cool. That was something that I could believe in. I'm not a religious zealot. I don't profess to follow any one particular training of God. I just find stuff that I can believe. I know that God's working in my life—I've seen the miracles happen.

It's really hard to live in the moment when you're always focused on the future or the past. But I have these things that can bring me back to being right here with God. So none of the things that happened were as scary and as horrible and as severe as I had imagined them to be. They really wound up being nothing. Or they were transcendent gifts. Things got better because of them.

When I was first getting sober, I was up for a big role. This seemed like the thing that I needed. This was going to change everything, finally. I went to a meeting early in the day, and I was told by a friend in recovery to put up my hand and share about this big screen test. I put up my hand to share and the guy wouldn't pick me. This one guy in this meeting would never pick me—I don't know what it was. And finally, about three quarters of the way through the meeting, I felt an enormous resentment. I got up and I stormed out and I went home.

In my mailbox was this letter from a guy who was my best friend at the time, telling me I was a piece of crap. He was mad about something that really hadn't happened. So I'm armed with the major resentment that I got at that recovery meeting, and my best friend in the world never wants to speak to me again, and now I've got to go to this screen test. I'm driving there, and a car made an illegal left turn and t-boned me. Just came out of nowhere and destroyed my car, the only car that I had. And I've still got to get to this screen test. I call a cab, because the car was totaled. I don't have a job. I don't have a car. I'm at the edge of financial disaster. I finally get to the audition and I walk in there and I look around, and there's about twenty-five suits staring at me. I start to read, and I just completely fall apart.

The next day, my agent calls and said, "The casting people want you to come and see them now. They want to talk to you. You didn't get the job, but they want to see you." So I drive over there, I go in the room, and there are these big high-powered casting people. They said, "What the hell happened to you? That was your job going in and you blew it. You embarrassed us. You embarrassed yourself. You're finished."

I left. I thought, "How much worse can it be? I turned my will and my life over to you, God, and you grind me into your boot heel." But by some miracle, I stayed sober. I went to another recovery meeting. I talked to some people. I really had nowhere else to go. I knew even in that insanity that drinking wasn't an option. But in the back of my mind—and I had to admit it to myself—I'd had plans. I'd been thinking that if I got that job, the first thing I was going to do was get rid of these people who were a pain in the ass. I was going to leave my girlfriend. I was going to get high. And it didn't happen, and I didn't work for a while.

Around this time I started working with someone new on my recovery and he started telling me stuff like "Don't worry about believing. Don't let that get in your way. I'll believe for you." I remember him telling me that, and I only hung in to prove him wrong. "I'll fucking show you, man. You are so wrong. I'll wait it out here, because it's not going to get better, and then I'm going to go out and get high and prove that you are wrong." And he was right about it. Absolutely.

Nothing is ever perfect. Nothing is ever absolutely perfect. But it's such a relief to not have to orchestrate anymore. My arms were getting tired.

TOM ARNOLD

❧

Tom got his first big break when Roseanne Barr spotted him doing stand-up and hired him as a writer for the Roseanne *show. Anyone who read a magazine in the early nineties knows how that turned out. Since then, Tom has played Arnold Schwarzenegger's sidekick in* True Lies, *hosted Fox's Best Damn Sports Show Period, and written a very funny autobiography,* How I Lost 5 Pounds in 6 Years. *I met him when we were both hanging around L.A., begging for acting jobs, and he's become a friend, as well as a powerful example of how to stay sober and sane in the nutty world of show business—through service and not taking yourself too seriously. When I asked Tom how he wanted to be described, he said, "Just say I'm a recovering alcoholic and addict. I mean, I also act and write and stuff, but that's the thing I have to remember first."*

My mother was an alcoholic. She left when I was four. When I was ten my dad married the next-door neighbor. She had kids and I was the oldest, and we did not have a good relationship. It was hard. I remember when I was fourteen, I said, "I'm moving in with my mom and her sixth husband." Because she would let me do whatever I wanted, basically.

I had my boxes packed and my dad picked me up. He was putting them in the car, and he said, "I just want you to know that I love you." And I don't know if we'd had that conversation before, but when my dad said that, I knew he meant it, because he fought for us. I mean he *fought;* he was there. I mean how many twenty-two-year-old guys have three kids and fight for them in court? I mean this is in 1963 or something and the mother *always* got the kids. They went to court, and the last day they were going to have me testify, which was basically a four-year-old boy having to say who he loved more, his mother or his father, and my dad said, "Forget it, I can't do that to him." So he gave up and let it go. The very next day my mom came to his office and said, "Here's the keys to the house. The kids are there with a babysitter, and they're yours."

So anyway, I remember going right to my mom's house and the first thing she says is—I'm fourteen—she says, "There's beer in the fridge. If you want to bring your girlfriend over here and screw her, she can stay all night. I'll see you in a couple of days." I just remember thinking, "I just made a big mistake." I mean this is what I supposedly wanted, but it felt so bad.

Leading up to my moment, I'd been up for five days, doing a lot of coke, and I was driving home. I was driving my blue Taurus, and I'm surprised it ran, because like two days before, I'd pulled all the wires out from under the dash, thinking the car was bugged. In our house we had fabric walls, and I actually believed that I was being secretly filmed for a documentary on drug abuse. I would talk to the mirror. I was that crazy.

Our code on the gate was my birthday, and I couldn't remember what it was. At that time you couldn't get a signal over on Mulholland, so I couldn't call the house. I had to flag a car down and say, "Would you call this number and have whoever answers let me into the gate?"

I just remember Roseanne drove her car down our long driveway and opened the gate. She got out of her car and started walking toward me. I pulled my car over, and I thought, "Well, she's gonna lose it, as always. She's gonna freak out, hit me, whatever. And okay, maybe I deserve it, but I'm not gonna take it."

Instead, she hugged me and said, "I just want you to come home."

And as messed up as I was, I felt it. I felt this compassion from her and that was, I think, God working through her, and it just broke through my BS. Somebody who knew the truth still cared—that threw me off completely. I was ready to defend myself, to fight back, and I didn't have to. That was a real spiritual moment that I take with me to this day.

I asked Roseanne about it later and she said she was mad and then all of a sudden, walking toward me, she said that it just went away, all that rage went away. She said she just realized that I was sick and, you know, that it wasn't personal. That I wasn't *trying* to make her miserable. You know, that's a good thing for me to remember too.

That moment, it was a feeling of unconditional love, and I don't remember ever feeling anything like it before. I can't really explain it, but it sobered me up. I felt it. And I really hadn't felt anything except self-hate and contempt for myself and defensiveness and just living the lie and being in survival mode for so long, and it was a very peaceful, warm feeling, which led to me finally breaking down and being honest for the first time. I told her, "I can't stop. I know I always said I'd stop using drugs, but I tried, and I just can't." And it was the first time I was able to admit that.

I felt like the biggest weight in the world was lifted off my shoulders. It was so hard to live that lie and maintain it. I worked hard at it. I mean telling you now that I'm an addict and capable of being addicted to anything and that I still need to work on myself—that's freeing to me. But *that* particular moment, I felt that if anybody really knew how bad I was, really how bad I was, then they couldn't possibly love me. That turned out not to be true at all. I'm still amazed sometimes at the generosity and the compassion and support of other people. That moment and all the moments like that—to me, it's everything I didn't get from my mother.

Roseanne and I had been through the whole rehab thing about seven months before. I started hemorrhaging blood from my nose and I couldn't even stand up. Roseanne took me to this place, and I talked my way out after four days. I said, "I'll go to recovery meetings, it'll be fine." But soon enough, I was back at it. I mean it was so quick. I found some cocaine at home and just did it. I mean after all that. I think a lot of us are very manipulative in protecting our disease and lying to people that care about us the most and pushing them away and hiding—just doing these things that make us feel worse about ourselves.

So I was back to living the lie, and after I admitted all this, she did the right thing and said, "You know what? You can't be here. I've got kids. I want you to get help, but you have to do it." So I made the calls myself and got in a cab.

My second time in rehab, my roommate was a guy with AIDS. This is 1989, and AIDS was basically a death sentence. I just remember after three or four days sort of coming around and talking to him and saying, "Oh my God. You know, honestly, if I had a broken arm, that'd be an excuse to get out. But you have AIDS, and you're here, and you want to be sober?" And the guy said, "I want to die sober. I know I'm going to die, but I want to die sober." That hit me.

Then, on the eighth day, I looked around the room at the people in my group from all different places, all struggling and fighting for this sobriety thing—I mean Jesus. So that all added up. I had never even considered doing it for myself, and then it just hit me . . . that's what I have to do, but I hated the guy in the mirror. But strangely, when I was packing for rehab I accidentally threw in with my papers a picture of myself when I was four. That's when my mom left, and I loved and had compassion for that little kid. I decided to get sober for him—the little Tommy—because he didn't deserve to die.

That's the thing I have to remember—that it's worth staying sober. Not for anyone else, for me. That's something I had never considered—never for one moment—and I feel that that was my real spiritual awakening.

Hopelessness is knowing that you can't control yourself. You feel alone; you feel that you're not worthy of asking for help. You're not worthy of being alive, basically. You have nothing to offer. You know you're a drug addict, you know you're an alcoholic, and you hate the person in the mirror. I really felt that before I got sober. But on the eighth day of that second rehab, when I thought of myself as that four-year-old boy, I decided to stay for myself—not to get people to like me, not to get my fiancée back, not to keep my job, whatever. I decided that just maybe there was the possibility that I wasn't a piece of crap and maybe I deserved a better life.

Even in sobriety, I've had divorces and failures and those feelings that creep up on you if you isolate, if you don't reach out. That's why I try to be of service as much as I can. I think when your mother leaves when you are young, there's always something inside of you that feels unworthy. It's something I work on in therapy. The more I'm left to my own devices and my own thinking, the more the hopelessness creeps in. But when I reach out, and it's hard sometimes, but when I reach out to someone else, it's always worth it. I get out there and hear other people's stories and get out of my own head.

I just got back from this camp I have for kids who've had heart transplants, out on Catalina Island. There's no air-conditioning, it's dirty, there are bugs, it's not the Four Seasons in Maui. And yet it was really the greatest experience of my life, because I truly cannot think of myself there. Every day I was there, I tried to think of myself—I tried to worry about work, I tried to worry about money, I tried to worry about me—and I just couldn't, because you're around these kids that are living life today because they have to. They know what it's like to not be sure you'll wake up tomorrow.

VELVET MANGAN

Velvet has turned her experience with addiction into her life's work. I first heard her story at an addiction conference, and I was so impressed by how much she's accomplished, just surviving what she did. Then, during her own recovery, she realized that there weren't nearly enough places for women, especially women with children, to get the treatment they needed. With no money, no experience, nothing but the awareness of the need, she started Safe Harbor, which has helped thousands of women find their way to recovery. She talks about that here, and it's one of those examples of how taking one step after another on the right path leads you to amazing places.

I think of the path I've traveled and I think of the people that have traveled it with me, and it's kind of like that Verizon commercial where you turn around and all those people are there behind you. Every day, I remember every person that has come into my life, has held out that hand to get me where I am today. And I think of the miracle of God and the grace of God. I know that when I do spend that quality time, when I do keep up my relationship with my higher power, I am so awake to the world. And I just want to be awake for all of it, even the scary moments of it. I just want to be awake.

My dad died when I was fourteen, and then my mom tried to commit suicide, so they institutionalized her. That was how I ended up homeless. The foster care wanted to come, but I ran because I'd heard horror stories about living in the foster homes and I just didn't want to end up there, so I ran.

The only thing that my dad left was a car, and so I took off in that, which is how I ended up homeless living in a 1970 Buick, doing a lot of cocaine and sleeping with a guy that was about forty. He was helping me out with my habit, and we were drinking a lot. And I was so depressed that I just wanted to die most of every day. The hopelessness of my life . . . I was illiterate and hungry and alone. Every once in a while my friends' mothers would let me stay on their couches and I'd kind of get a reprieve, but for the most part it was a dark, dark time.

I remember going to visit my mom and driving away from her feeling like I had no other option except to take my life, because the addiction and the depression were just so great, I had no way out. I got as much drug paraphernalia as I could, and I was kind of planning my suicide. It was dark, and it was real late at night. I was in this car parked by the road, and I'd been up on coke for days. I just couldn't make the pain go away, and the fear that my life was going to look like this forever was just too much. I didn't think I could live through another second of this unbearable pain. I was so desperate and my soul was so empty. I didn't have a mustard seed of hope.

The only thing I could do was remember my Aunt Eleanor. She was a reverend, and she had told me that sometimes it helped her to write to God, and so I thought, "Well, I don't have much to lose." I wrote this letter to God, and I just said, "God, if you exist, can you help me? I don't know what to do anymore. I don't know what my life is supposed to look like. I don't know how to get help. I don't know who to call." That was it, and I still stayed up tweaking on drugs into the next day.

Then I thought I would go to my high school to tell my coach good-bye. I was in special education classes, and there was this football coach named Coach White who taught the special education kids. He showed interest in me, like he cared for me, and he'd ask me how I was doing after my dad died. I didn't show up at school very much, but the times I did, this coach was kind to me. He was just an amazing guy, so I wanted to say good-bye to him and thank him before I killed myself.

I weighed about 98 pounds, I had black eyes, I'd been up on coke for days so my body looked horrific. I mean the drugs were starting to really take their toll on me and my daily health. He saw me, and he still says he doesn't know what happened to him, but something in him took over. He grabbed me by the shirt and he said, "You know what? You're going to get help and you're going to get help today. I'm calling the authorities and I'm going to get you put away. I mean if you can't help yourself, this is just not going to work." There was no way that he was going to let me walk out the door.

He dragged me, physically dragged me, through the campus of the school. I was crying and screaming. I mean that was the last thing I thought was going to happen. That was not the plan. He's dragging me through this campus and he opens this door. There's this little lady with this little bob cut, and her name is Jane. She was at this place called the Stop-In Center, and it was something that they had developed in my school that I didn't know anything about because I was hardly ever there. He opens up the door and interrupts a meeting that they were doing on campus that day. He says, "Jane, if she leaves here, I want you to call the police. We need to get her some help, *today*." I was just stunned and completely out of it. I couldn't have been any more shocked. I sit down, and there's my friend Shannon and my friend Judd. Judd said, "You know, Velvet, you can stay with us. There's this young people's recovery support group on Tuesdays. You could sleep at my house."

I said all right. He was a good friend of mine. And then Shannon said, "Whatever you need. Just name it." I don't remember much. I remember kind of waking up to that Tuesday meeting and feeling just a glimpse of hope that there was maybe something that could happen. Maybe there could be some other plan for me, because all of a sudden people cared. All of a sudden somebody said, "We care about you and we don't want to see you kill yourself." I thought, "How did they know I was going to kill myself?" I didn't know that this was a common feeling of depression and anxiety that all of us felt. That day, I felt myself relaxing. An ease came over me. I don't even remember what I heard in that first meeting, but I was interested. I was interested, and they promised me a place I could go.

Before the second meeting, I crashed because I'd been up on coke, so they just put me on a couch, and when I woke up the next morning, there were all these young people talking about being clean and sober. I never really heard that before. I mean my uncle was an alcoholic and so he'd take me sometimes to this recovery meeting, but they were all, you know, old guys. They didn't look like me.

When Judd and Shannon took me to this other meeting, it was like all of a sudden everyone did look like me, and they all seemed to have a good time. Everybody was laughing. All of a sudden I felt warmth. I didn't feel all the anxiety I always had. It was like somebody put their arms around me and said, "It's going to be all right." I didn't fight it. That was as close to a feeling of comfort and ease that I had felt in a very, very long time.

I know it was God and it was grace, because I didn't even give myself time to think myself out of it. I just let it all carry me. It carried me into one more day and then to another day, and then I was introduced to a recovery club. And that's where I met another saving grace, my friend Dave, who was like the Marlboro man. This man was just amazing, and he believed in me. He didn't believe that I was this hopeless little kid. He made sure I got a home, and he made sure I was fed. It wasn't like they just said, "Go to meetings." It was like they knew that wouldn't be enough. They said, "Come with me, Velvet." It was a group effort, and I just think it was kind of a moment for all of us.

Up until that point, I had nobody I could go to, nobody who I thought could save me. Nobody outside of me could help me, and I couldn't do anything to help myself. As a human being I felt, "I'm illiterate. My family doesn't love me. What can I become? Obviously I don't matter." My body, mind, and soul had been so emotionally and spiritually abused, just looking for someone to love me, just looking for someone to tell me I'd be okay.

The only way out was simple surrender. Blind faith. I mean they told me early on, "Just keep it simple. Sweep the parking lot and pray for a miracle." Okay. I sat at the coffee bar at the club and ate Top Ramen and pickled eggs every day. That was the best I could do. I just trusted these people, these strangers. I trusted that they saw something in me, and I think God was carrying me through the whole thing, and now I know why it all happened. I think I had to see it all in hindsight, because at that point I really, really believed that I was unworthy and that I was unlovable, that even my mother didn't think I mattered enough to stay alive for.

I know now my mom did love me, she just didn't have it in her to take care of me. That didn't mean that I wasn't worth living for. When you're a teenager, you're fighting everybody and everything. That's just what you do. So I had to fight everybody and everything, and then pretty soon I was just in the dark, fighting nobody. There was nobody there to fight, nobody but me. Then I had to ask myself: Do I really choose to be this? Do I want to be a drug addict for the rest of my life, living like this? I had to go through that struggle, knowing that I was just fighting the dark and losing, knowing that I was done. Surrendering to pain. It was that pain that got me to that new place.

I got sober and my life was beyond my wildest dreams. I got married, I had kids, but there was still a voice in my head telling me I'm not enough. I didn't do the healing work that I needed to do with my God and myself. You know, you get married for better or for worse, for sickness and health, but nobody ever tells you to take yourself in the same value. Nobody ever says that. Even in your sobriety, they say find someone in recovery that you want to be like, but how about becoming who you want to be? How about loving you the way you are and the way you're not?

I couldn't allow myself to be a work in progress, I wasn't willing to grow in public anymore. So I started to internalize the grief of daily living, and that's when I started to make mistakes. Then I went bankrupt at twelve years sober, and I was very embarrassed about that. I made bad decisions, almost like I was getting high. I felt a lot of shame and embarrassment and I didn't know where to go with it. I got filled with resentment and self-pity. I thought, "I have all these years. I've earned my right to have my grievances." Then I got so depressed that I created this really painful disease in my body. They thought I had cancer because my muscles would seize up so hard, based on fear and restriction.

I know I'm a spiritual person, and I know the only way a girl like me lives is through my relationship to God, by being close to my higher power. I know that's my nature, I know that's my purpose, and I got far, far away from that. The pain of sobriety, the pain of being in my own skin, became too much to me. I internalized that pain, and so I got this body disease, and then I got so fearful I got agoraphobic. I mean I just created this suffering in my life, in sobriety, because one more time I was rejecting myself. Who I was wasn't good enough, and so I couldn't get close to God anymore. I just felt so shut down.

After about nine months of suffering, the doctor said, "Why don't you just take some Soma?" I took this Soma, and within four months I was completely strung out. I was strung out on fentanyl patches, morphine, liquid morphine, Dilaudid, I mean I had a box full of every pharmaceutical thing I could get. Every day I lay in this bed, and there I was again in the dark, totally suicidal, and I completely knew what I had done. The voice in me was low, but I could hear it, saying, "You relapsed, and you gave up a lot, but you know what you have to do." But there was that bigger part of me, the ego part that had taken over, that said, "No, you're sick, and screw recovery and screw all those people, because they screwed you over." All that sick demented thinking comes and takes over. That went on for about four months.

I was lying in my room, wanting to take my life again. My little seven-year-old son comes in, and he lies down on my bed and he starts to sob. He says, "Mama, when you believed in God you were healthy, and as soon as you stopped believing in God you got sick." And it was like . . . all those clouds, everything that I was trying to convince myself was there, all that went away. I could not question the truth when it came from him.

I got up from my bed, I gave him a hug, and I told him, "I love you, son, and I'm going to get better." I walked down the hall and I asked my husband, "Is it time for me to take my fentanyl patches off?" He said, "Yeah, baby, it's time." And so I took off my fentanyl patches and detoxed like you can't even imagine. It was that moment of my little boy saying that to me: "You weren't sick when you believed in God." I mean that moment couldn't have been any more clear. I couldn't question it.

I was going to have to go to the recovery group that I had been going to for all these years and raise my hand as a newcomer and be willing to give up everything that I thought I was or that I wasn't. I did it because I wanted my relationship with God. I knew happiness, I knew freedom, I knew that when I did pray for a miracle and swept that parking lot, my life was comforted. I just wanted that simplicity again. I wanted to go back to the hope and the freedom of knowing that just being sober *today* was good enough. Just being happy and smiling and laughing with my friends on the back porch was enough. Being a mother to my child, where we could hold hands through Disneyland and I could be present, was enough. I just wanted that again.

And here I am again. What I know is that I turned my back on God. God never turned his back on me. I did it myself. I turned my back on love, I turned my back on faith, I turned my back on the simplest things. I let my ego get the best of me and suffocate that beauty and that peace that God gave me. For fun and for free, God gave me a life beyond my wildest dreams. I didn't do much to get it. I just swept the parking lot and prayed for a miracle every day.

I think a lot of times we just adopt everything our parents thought, everything our family of origin thought. Violence was a big one for me. I was beat up a lot when I was a little girl. I was taught to be violent. That was the only thing I was ever good at. I was completely empowered by being able to go up to the craziest person there was in school and fight a fair fight, and be known as somebody that was good at that. That was a big thing that I had to learn, that I didn't need to physically protect myself anymore.

And my mom, bless her heart, she was an addict, and so her life was nothing but violence. People beat up on her, so she did the same to me. Or my dad, who was married to another woman and had his own family—he just got my mom pregnant. So I come from a lot of shame. I had to get rid of a lot of ideas I had about me, and I did that through people lovingly teaching me different ways of coping.

And then—not knowing how to read and write, and being told that I could and believing that I could. One of my counselors at the club took me to the Department of Rehabilitation and I learned how to read and write with all the immigrants. To me, it looked like it was way too big, but each little step with them holding me . . . I was able to get past a lot of these root beliefs about myself. At the department, they did an aptitude test and they said I should be a factory worker. Basically, the world said I was hopeless, but the people in recovery said that was bullshit, just bullshit. I liked those people so much that I believed what they said about me.

The second time was more about committing to *me*. Like saying to myself, "I'm done rejecting you. Yeah, everybody rejected you and you kind of kept that going. But no more." I kept abandoning me, looking for someone to save me. I wanted somebody to tell me that I'm enough, that I've made it and that I'm good enough. I just came to a place where it was like, "You know, God made you the way that you are. You are enough. You're way more than enough." I committed to not letting my head go on and on and on about what it is that I don't have or what it is I'm not.

I've really worked on training my mind to believe in higher things and to live in a place that's the highest good for everybody. If I could inspire one human being and love one human being a tenth as much as the way I've been loved and inspired—that is all I want to do. So I'm committed to loving God, loving my fellow man, but first loving me. If I make mistakes or I don't achieve what I want to achieve . . . well, you know, tomorrow is another day. I'm learning to just be gentle with myself. I'm learning to really know that God is love and that if I love, that's enough. That's the commitment that I've made to myself.

But I had to go back to recovery and learn that. You don't get thirteen years sober, and then relapse, with *newcomers* saying to you "Keep coming back" without . . . I mean that's going to hurt. That's going to require a lot of faith in God, a real relationship with God. Some of my friends who relapsed never made it back. Some of them are dead. This guy, he had seventeen years and he lost them. He relapsed and he came back in and he said to me, "You know, Velvet, your value is not how many days you've been sober. Your value is your experience, strength, and hope." Because he told me that and other people told me that, it made it feel like it was not a race, that I hadn't lost. I had just forgotten, and so I was able to come back and not be so ashamed.

In 1993 I was serving on the board of directors of the Costa Mesa Alano Club and there was an epidemic of girls that were being violated and there was just nowhere for women to go that was affordable and safe. Sober-living homes didn't exist for women. I kept trying to get somebody with money to open something up, because I didn't have money. My husband was a cable man, I'm a failed hairdresser with two little kids, so it's not me, it's got to be somebody else. I'm begging people to do something for these young girls, get them off the streets and give them a safe place to go. Everybody is like, "No, no, there's no money in it. It's high maintenance. You know, girls are just too much trouble." I was so disheartened.

But God kept giving me these visions, like this dining room table with six girls sitting at it, and they're smiling and they're healthy and they look put together, like they're ready to go to work or go to school. I could not shake the vision. I knew that I had to do something, I just didn't know how I was going to do it. I just kept asking God what would He have me do, how can I help, and one day my thought was to open up the newspaper and kind of look around. I found this two-bedroom house for rent, and it was right around the corner from the Alano Club so I knew that if the girls didn't have cars they could walk. I thought, "Okay, I'll just call this person who's renting the house." I told him about my vision, everything about what I wanted to do. I figured the worst thing that can happen is he'll think I'm crazy, so I just went fully with it. I just told him my whole plan. The guy goes, "Velvet, I really would love to support you in this. I think what you want to do is great. I can waive the deposit. You just come up with eight hundred dollars to start." And I was like, "Well, thank you so much," because eight hundred dollars was like a million dollars for me. I could barely pay my rent.

My husband comes home from work and I tell him about what I did and he goes, "You're not going to believe it, honey. Today, a guy offered me eight hundred dollars for my van so he can go on the road with his band. I believe in you. I know that you're supposed to do this. I see the way you help women, I see what you do and your commitment, and I want to help you. I want you to do this."

So he fearlessly sold his van, and by the end of the week, there were six girls in this beautifully furnished house. People heard about what I had done and what was happening, and they completely helped me. That was the beginning of Safe Harbor. And now Safe Harbor is one of the most respected women's programs in the country. I get referrals from the greatest of the greats, and we've had thousands of success stories. I was twenty-three years old when I started that house. It's an amazing story of what the mind of God can do if you just step out of yourself to help somebody else.

The thing I've always been most afraid of was to be alone and rejected and disliked. In my second life in sobriety, I had to make a commitment that it didn't matter what the outside world said. I was so pleased with pleasing others in my first sobriety because I'd never pleased anybody before. I was so excited about that, and it became what I did. That's why I didn't allow myself to talk anymore. That's why I didn't allow myself to be ugly or have anger or any of these feelings that didn't appear to be likable. I repressed, and then I suffered, and then of course that repression becomes outward and physical, and then . . . it's just that whole cycle.

But I learned I could survive the thing I was most afraid of, and if you don't learn that, you're never going to make it. You're haunted. Those thirteen years, I was never ever in my truest place as I am right here, right now, today. Because when I got up this morning, I did my daily reprieve. I said, "God, this is your deal. And yeah, I'm scared, but let me serve, get my ego out of the way so that I can best serve, serve and keep my desire to be liked out of the way. Let me be of my greatest use."

JAMIE LEE CURTIS

❧

When I was a kid, I was friends with Kelly Curtis, and Jamie Lee was just her little sister. Of course, she's considerably more than that. On screen, she's been everything from a teen scream queen to a sexy leading lady to a hilarious comic (and still sexy) lead. In the past few years, she's moved behind the camera, producing films and TV specials, and she's written several bestselling children's books. Jamie herself puts it like this: "I would say that I am a recovering drug addict and alcoholic, that I am the mother of two—I have a daughter in college, I have a son in grade school—I am married for twenty-three years to the same man, I write books for children, and I used to be in show-off business a lot and I am not in it so much anymore." Jamie is such a private person, yet she tells her story with such passion and intensity, as if her life depended on getting her message across. Which it does, in a way. We both cried when I was interviewing her, and I still cry every time I read this.

Hopelessness is a problem that has no solution. There's no hope for salvation or serenity or some end to that terrible, terrible feeling. In my case, hopelessness was the fact that I was hopelessly addicted to Vicodin and alcohol and I couldn't stop even though I tried everything I knew to do to stop.

What is most profound to me is that the Serenity Prayer and the recovery program both include the word *change*. Jung said, "only that which changes remains true," and when I do public speaking, I talk about that quote all the time because hopelessness is the state of no change. Change equals hope, so you can't escape hopelessness without change. I think that change is an absolute necessity, for any sort of salvation.

I knew that I was addicted to drugs and alcohol for a very, very long time. I was able to manage the cocaine craze with very few consequences. I did seek professional help and got it for a brief moment. I always knew that alcohol was a problem for me, as it was in my family, and there was one point where I actually went cold turkey. I just said, "I don't drink anymore," and I did that for four years.

However, in the process of that, I found painkillers, and that's when my addiction to Vicodin began. I just replaced alcohol with Vicodin and found myself on a very long ten-year path of always looking for Vicodin. I tell you that background because it lets you know that I started and stopped, I accelerated and pulled back many times in the acceptance that I had a real problem. I kept it hidden because I had everything that anybody would want. All the wealth, property, prestige, fame, attention—I only got it more and more.

My bottom, if you will, was what I refer to as an Everest bottom because there was nothing that would show an outside person that I had a problem. It was a secret, and it was *my* secret. No one in my close purview knew that I was a Vicodin addict. No one. Not my family and none of my friends. After I started drinking again, my husband knew that, and he noticed when I started drinking more because there was evidence of that, but he did not know that I was a secret Vicodin addict. No one in my family knew, none of my friends knew.

One woman knew. I got sober in February, and the December before that, she was with me in my vacation place. She is Brazilian and a shaman, she is a healer and funny as hell. She saw me when I thought no one saw me. I was preparing dinner and I poured a glass of wine, and out of my pocket I take four or five Vicodin to take with my glass of wine. And from behind me I hear this voice, with this heavy, heavy Brazilian accent: "You know, Jamie, I see you with your little pills. You think nobody sees you, but *I* see you. I am telling you, you are dead. You are a dead woman. You may think you are alive right now, but you are *dead*. You are killing yourself every day.

You can continue to do this and I will not tell anybody, but I am telling you, you are dead, and I love you and I do not want you to be dead." That was in December 1998.

On New Year's Eve, I went to a friend's house and we decided that we would all get together on the millennium, a year later. What we decided to do is, we would all write five things that we wished for ourselves and five things we wished for others. We would write them on a piece of paper, roll them up, put them in a bottle, and seal it. Then the next year, we would have a big party on the millennium and open the bottles and see if we had held this idea of hope for ourselves into the millennium. And that's what we did.

So I have just gone through Christmas, my friend giving me that very clear message about seeing me dead, and then on New Year's Eve, thinking about this millennium, this idea of hope. Whatever else happened in January I don't remember, but I clearly remember that I woke up many mornings feeling sick and tired and *being* sick and tired of being sick and tired. There were many, many more moments in that month where my will-power, my strength, my belief that I was more powerful than this drug, failed me one more time, and I woke up filled with shame, private shame. No public humiliations, no paparazzi pictures of me scoring drugs. No public humiliation at all, but private humiliation that one more day, I had said that morning, "I am not going to do it again," and when that afternoon rolled around I had to find drugs, I had to find something.

That was January.

I was so terrified. I was terrified of the public side of the surrender to my addiction. I couldn't go to a treatment center because I had a young child, a little boy, he was two years old then. I couldn't not be with him for a month—impossible, impossible. Which is why I now support places where women bring their children. Had I known then that there was a place I could go with my little boy, that might have made me think, "I can do this." I was terrified of the public shame. That fear actually kept me in check during my using years, kept me from really behaving badly or driving badly or whatever. It was the fear that I would get caught. That was too big for me, I was too proud of myself. I would not have been able to suffer that.

After January was over, I remembered that a girlfriend of mine, an actress, had been in rehab and I called her. I had reconnected with her through another channel and she had a child of my son's age. I thought, "Oh, I should call her because she will be safe for me because she's a public figure. She'll help me, she'll know how to help me." Our kids had a play date and I went over, and while we were standing and watching them play on a trampoline, I turned to her and said, "I am addicted to Vicodin and alcohol."

She looked at me and said, "Me too. Isn't it the greatest thing? I couldn't live my life without it." At that moment I looked at her and went, "Wow!" Then she said, "And I have a doctor who will give us Vicodin."

Prior to that, finding Vicodin had been an ongoing problem. I had stolen them, talked my way into them, occasionally befriended an injured person. Honestly, I befriended a lot of injured people. I was drawn to people on crutches. I might show up bringing flowers or fruit, and then I'd use their bathroom and go through their medicine cabinet. I never had a dealer. I had been on a movie where, through a stunt person, I was able to get a number of Vicodin at once, which lasted me for a very long time because I only used during my cocktail hour. I would never use during the day, ever. I was an unbelievably controlled drug addict/alcoholic. I never would drink in the beginning of a day *ever*. I'd save it for cocktail hour.

So I'd never had more than maybe thirty Vicodin, except for that one time on a movie, and now I was being told that there was a steady stream. By the way, this was before drugs were available on the Internet. If they had been available like that, I think I would be dead today. My friend actually gave me the name of that doctor and gave me some of what she had, so I drove home thinking that God was really looking out for me. We had children of the same age, so we could see each other socially, and now I had an open stream to this drug, and I thought that God had completely answered my problems.

The next morning I woke up and I knew that my friend was going to be dead and I was going to be standing at her funeral with her children in the front row, and I would look at them and I would know that I killed her, that I had her blood on my hands. Or I would be dead and she would be at my funeral with my kids weeping in the front row and she would be standing there knowing that she had my blood on her hands. I haven't had a drug or drink since that moment.

That was my moment of clarity—between connecting with a friend, a *compadre*, a colleague, to the next morning realizing that one of us was going to be dead. My Brazilian friend's prophecy was going to come true, and we would die from this. There was no question, because I knew what an open stream of this drug would do to me. I knew.

That day I called the only sober person I knew. We had ended up spending a lot of time together, taking care of a friend who was very ill, and I had shared with him that I had a problem with Vicodin. All he would ever say to me is "There is a solution. If you ever need me, I'm here." No proselytizing. I called him and I said, "I'm terrified," and he said, "I understand." I said, "I feel like I need someone in my profession to help me walk in there. I don't think I can walk in just on my own." He said, "Stay where you are," and five minutes later the phone rang. It was an actress friend of his, and she said, "I'm so-and-so, and I heard you'd like to be a guest in the meeting tonight." I sat in back with her, and I don't think I heard the message that night, but I sat there. Then the next day I got someone to work with me in recovery, and that's how I got sober.

The thing is, that moment was just as invisible from the outside as my problem was. See, I'm a creature of habits, many habits. I wear the exact same clothing every day. I eat the exact same thing every day. I go about my day in the same manner every day. I wear my hair the exact same way every day. If I love a certain blue shirt, I have ten of them in my closet and nothing else, and when one gets dirty, I get another one. So that morning I woke up in the exact same room that I woke up in every day, with the exact same sheets, and ate the exact same thing for breakfast, and had the exact same cup of coffee the exact same temperature, the way I like it. I read the exact same paper at the exact same time.

The only thing that had changed was my certainty that I was going to die from this, and that I would hurt my family, the very thing I loved most in the world. Prior to that, I didn't think about my family suffering from this. In fact, I thought that I was doing this to make me function better, that I deserved this because I did so much for everybody, so this was my reward. But that morning, the idea, the clarity that it was going to kill me was the crystalline moment. It cut through everything.

What I felt after I made that phone call was immediate relief, immediate surrender. It was that fast, because the secret was out. And then I dove into my own recovery, dove into it, couldn't wait to continue, because I'm an action girl. You give me something to do and I'll do it, so all I had to have was some direction. And my recovery is the single greatest, most important thing I will ever do in my life. I have had all sorts of accolades, and they are irrelevant to me. The single most important thing I would ever do in my life is to have arrested this addiction, this family trait, this family history, this family link—to say that the buck stops with me. That is the single greatest thing I will do, bar none.

I was in an interview about the book I was promoting, a book about self-esteem, and so the whole conversation with the writer from this women's magazine was, well, how do you account for your good self-esteem? My daughter was at the table with me, and I was talking about this and that, and as I sat there, I looked at this woman and I looked at my daughter, and I took a big breath and I went, "I think that the biggest reason that I'm feeling so great is that I've been sober for two years." She said, "Gee, I didn't know that!" Yeah, well . . . nobody knew. But I knew what I was doing in that moment. I knew exactly what I was doing, because what I wanted was to connect the word *recovery* with a positive change.

She, of course, was like, "Well, let's talk about that! What was your addiction?" and I said, "I am not prepared to talk about that. The addiction is not what's important here. What's important is the reason I told you about it. When you asked about positive influence, positive change in my life, to not include that would be a complete omission of something extremely positive."

That was the beginning of my public discussion of addiction. That was how I entered the public debate, in that interview, in that moment. That, of course, became the banner headline of the article and I knew it would.

Then I took it to work with me. What I did was, I put up a sign by the lunch trailer that said, "Recovery meeting in Jamie's trailer at lunch." We ended up having a disparate group of men and women, young and old, very sober and newly sober, who sat together every other day at lunch and talked. One of those men, recently sober but passionate, said, "When I wake up in the morning and I look in the mirror, I am looking at the problem."

See, before that, I was in the victim/blame world, because that is the deluded mind's favorite couplet. You are the victim and everybody else is to blame. It's the perfect little sandwich. I now know, when I wake up in the morning and I look in the mirror, that the problem exists from here to here, between my ears. The perceptions that go on in this head, *they* are the problem. I am the problem, and I have a solution for that problem. It's not you, it's not my husband, it's not my kids, it's not my coworkers, it's not anything outside my own head.

Taking it into my work was another way of saying I want it around me always. I don't want it to be hidden; I don't want it to be closeted away. By putting that sign up, that was my way of letting go of the secret within my work environment, and that gave me the chance to have support at work. I've told people, if you can get an ally at work, get some support at work, do it. Because it will save you.

My fear was public humiliation. Now the first question I have when I work with someone new to recovery is, "Did you get a DUI?" And often they go, "Yeah," and I'm like, "Great! Did you get a picture?" They're like, "Yeah," and I say, "Oh, fabulous! First thing you get to do is go get it." They're like, "What are you *talking* about?" I say, "Go to the police department, thank them for arresting you, and ask would it be possible to get a copy of your mug shot. Then frame it and put it in your kitchen, put it in your bathroom, put it next to your liquor. Every time you see it, remember that that's what your better thinking got you."

I am not a deep spiritual being, but I know that there is some acceptance of God in my life, without a religion attached to it, without a face or a look. I couldn't do this before, and now I can, and I don't know why. To me, it's the process of elimination. It's like, "Well, what changed?" and I believe my answer was God. See, I don't *know* what changed. I can look at the perfect-storm elements. I can look at my yearning to change, my openness to the possibility of change, and then this potential stream of the drug, which I knew was dangerous somehow—all of that is included. But I still can't tell you why one day I didn't call this guy, the one sober guy I knew, and why the next day I did. I believe that that's where God showed up. I don't have a picture of him, her, it . . . whatever. I just know something changed. I'm a different person today.

It's New Year's Eve 1999. I go back to the same place for the holiday. I am now ten months sober. We all get together and we open the bottle and we pull out all the little scrolls of paper we'd written the year before that had our names on them—"Jamie, here's yours." I was thinking, "Oh, this will be interesting." Of the five things that I wished for myself, the first thing I wished for was sobriety.

I have that on my desk. I don't have a mug shot. I don't have a letter from my husband saying, "Sweetheart, I love you but I am leaving." I don't have a letter from my child saying, "Mummy, why are you killing yourself?" I have what I wished for myself.

So it was already in my head. I knew I wanted it, I just didn't think I could get it. You have to remember, that was December thirty-first. I still went six more weeks of being sick and tired of being sick and tired. It's there in black and white, that's what I hoped for in the New Year. It wasn't even a resolution, it was a hope. A resolution is white-knuckling your way through not drinking. Hope is the possibility of change.

EARL HIGHTOWER

❧

Like Velvet Mangan, Earl has made recovery into his life's work. He's an in-
spiring speaker and a skilled and sensitive interventionist, as well as a gener-
ous presence in the L.A. recovery community. I've known Earl for years, but
until we sat down for this interview, I'd never heard the details of his story. I
was moved by the cataclysmic events he survived on his journey, and the
thoughtfulness with which he revealed them.

When you're an addict, there's a shroud of denial that's persis-
tent and ongoing, an inability to be aware of other very via-
ble options. A kind of not-knowing. I'd been an alcoholic for
sixteen years, I was close to dying, and I had just tried to kill someone
when I got to the end of my not-knowing. It was the blink of an eye, coming out of that blackout. Just a quick scan of the horizon and starting with
the not-knowing—"It's not my alcoholism, it's not my addiction, it's not
my heroin, it's not my cocaine, it's not my barbiturates . . ."—and then
surrendering to the knowing—"Oh yeah? It *is*. It's all of those things."
There it is, and that's that.

Suddenly a consciousness beyond my own has entered into my life, in
this moment, and I've been offered a choice. I can continue to attempt to
blot out the intolerable nature of my existence. Or I can accept this new-
found consciousness—which is really an unavoidable truth. I call it the
"bitch of enlightenment."

This is what nobody tells you. Once you use that stuff, you're stuck
with it. There's no going back; once you know, you can't *not*-know anymore. You can load up the syringe, or uncork the bottle, or chop up the

lines, but it's no good. "Will this work?" "No. That got disqualified already, remember?" "Is *this* going to work?" "No, that's not going to work either." "Shall we try that other one again?" "You can if you want, but it still isn't going to work. And you know it."

I got sobered up in 1980; I pretty much missed the seventies. I had no anchors, nothing that required me to hold tight to the reality of my youth. I had no family; my family was dead. I had no friends, I had no career, I didn't have a wife or children, I didn't have any goals or aspirations, I was just a flat-out crazy addict. I was in flight, and I'd been in flight since I was twelve years old. I'd been alone so long that I didn't even know I was lonely. Madness kind of creeps up on you. The drunken lunacy, the violence, the acting out was *way* above the radar. Having to be detained, the police being called regularly, the ambulances coming.

The day I had my moment of clarity was a Thursday, and the last thing I remembered was the Monday before, but I'd gotten used to Monday immediately becoming Thursday. I was standing at the corner of Twenty-eighth Avenue and Ocean Front Walk in Venice, California, in a parking area just off the boardwalk. It was during the day, there were lots of people scurrying around. I was coming out of a blackout, so I was unaware of what had come before, but there's a commotion, an intensity in the air. There's the police, there's an ambulance, there's emergency medical technicians. The girl I was living with at the time, she was there but I can't recall her name. There was this older Jewish man too, his name was David Luboff, and I gathered from the conversation around me that I had just tried to beat him to death.

People were deciding what to do, and I understood immediately that I was not included in the decision-making process. Apparently I had already said my piece, so I just sat there with my broken hands. The police were deciding whether to arrest me and charge me with attempted murder, or just let the ambulance take me to the hospital, because they could tell I was dying. My thyroid had shut down, my heart, my kidneys were shot, my liver was really angry. . . . Just standard, run-of-the-mill, late-stage alcoholism.

Finally they decided to throw me in the ambulance, because it wasn't a case the DA was going to file. They just said, "Let the ambulance take him to the hospital so he can die there instead of in jail." As I'm being strapped into the gurney, David Luboff—the guy that I had tried to kill, for no apparent reason—screams at me, "You don't understand the ramifications of the situation!"

I remember thinking, "You know, he's right. I don't. I don't understand." It was just a blink of an eye, a heartbeat, and I thought, "I'm here as a direct result of my drinking." That consciousness could not be denied any longer; it asserted itself. I felt an overriding sense of calm, and the calm was the surrender.

I had no idea that was coming. For sixteen years, from age twelve to twenty-eight, I had fought, wrestled, attempted to control and to manage, battled my demons, did what I could, and then there was that moment when I opened my eyes. You don't *decide* to have that moment; it just happens, and you're done. All that was left for me to do was acknowledge it.

Could I have drunk again? I don't know. All I know is that I haven't; for twenty-six years, I haven't had a drink, I haven't used a drug. I've been absolutely clean and sober and have had no desire to drink the entire time.

I'm thinking of a moment I had years ago, when what I perceived at the time as clarity was really a series of interpretations, or decisions, born of my emotional condition. I got shipped off to boarding school at age twelve, and I'm the youngest and smallest kid there among two hundred and fifty boys from all over the world. They've scoured the earth to find the brightest, most disturbed young men they could find, and I'm the youngest and the smallest. I'm fodder. I'm fighting all through the first week, and at the end of the week I call my mother. I'm a twelve-year-old boy, a child, calling my mommy and saying, trying to say, "Get me out of this. You couldn't have possibly meant to send me here. If you knew what was here, you would rush to my aid immediately and get me out of here." And I hear my father in the background saying, "Hang up. He's fine."

I felt such a sense of abandonment, a sense of betrayal. . . . My family, who knew me better than anybody in the world, had thrown me away, and I didn't know why. What did I do? And something shut down inside of me, my ability to trust, my ability to connect to other people, a willingness to try. I thought at that time, and for years afterward, that *that* was my moment of clarity: "You don't get any help in the world; it's every man for himself. So steel yourself and get to it." Not the kind of thinking you want to encourage in a twelve-year-old child, but there it was.

Forty-two years later, at fifty-four years of age, I look back on that twelve-year-old, and I go, "You know? He was right, and he was wrong." *Was* it a moment of clarity? For the boy . . . yes, absolutely. Did it impact my entire youth? Yes. But I can also look back on that moment and say, "Well, I understand . . . but I'm not going to act anymore based on the decisions of that twelve-year-old boy. I have a lot more experience; I have had other moments along the way. I can leave that one behind."

That's one of the great gifts of recovery for me, the knowledge that if I feel confused, undecided, lost, unsure—if I use my meditation, my ability to be still and to quiet the mind, the answers will come. If my own house is in order, if I'm available and open for it, then I can tap into consciousness beyond my own in any given moment.

Before that moment of clarity, the thing I was most desperately afraid of was love. I was afraid of loving, I was afraid of being loved, I was terribly afraid of losing love. I was in a plane crash in 1974 and I lay there on a mountain in Mexico and watched my mother and then my father and then my little sister bleed to death right in front of me. Right then I renounced God. Any god that would let my little sister die like that . . . I had no interest in a god like that. Now I see that that's such an incredibly limited view of God. God in my own image, ruled by my emotion. Is it God up there going, "Okay, kill that one . . . save that one"? I don't think so.

Then some guys scavenged the wreck, took my money, and left me there to die, so I renounced any connection to other human beings. After that, I was out of the game. I was broken in every way: physically, emotionally, spiritually . . . just a shattered human being. I'd already been an addict for ten years, and I came out of the hospital in Santa Monica in late 1974, early 1975, renouncing God, renouncing any connection to other people, absolutely certain that life is nothing but pain and suffering. Later I discovered that this really isn't far off the mark, but the question is, what do you do with that? The Buddhists' first noble truth is "All life is suffering"—once you accept that, then being in pain doesn't mean something is wrong. *That* allows you to define the path toward happiness. I'm a firm believer in that.

We live in a country that very, very methodically goes about the business of ignoring the fact that we're all going to die. "Don't talk about that. Just consume effectively, and you'll be fine." It's lunacy. No, you won't be fine. You're still going to die.

I had one guy say to me, "I have enough money to live like a king for a hundred years"—and believe me, he wasn't exaggerating—"and the idea of getting up and getting dressed and going out into the world today is more than I can bear." I was there because the people around him knew his life wasn't working for him, that he was on the point of ending it. It's interesting to tell a guy, "Okay, you have hundreds of millions of dollars, you are a captain of several industries, you're famous, all the world's illusions have been made available to you—so how are you feeling?" And he just starts crying, because there is the illusion and there is the real world, and his real world is a mess.

In situations like that, I go in and try to help bring them to a consciousness beyond their own, which might work or it might not. You can create environments within which people can come to these things. But all you can do is make space for it. You help them let go of stuff that doesn't work. The rest is up to them.

People say to me, "How can you know this stuff? Where did you get this?" I just tell them I've been clean for twenty-six years now and I can guarantee that anything of value in that twenty-six years has absolutely nothing to do with "as Earl sees it." There's none of Earl's best thinking in it. That's the beauty of it. All my information—all of it—is from others who walked there before me. I embrace that, and I constantly place myself in the company of those who walk ahead of me, and I listen. They create little voids in me, they create little opportunities for that consciousness to come in. The poet Robert Sward said that "God is in the cracks." God is in the fissures. Right on, man! That's such a beautifully poetic way of saying it. When I heard that I went, "Yeah, give me that. I'm going to put that in the bag."

Thich Nhat Hanh, the Vietnamese monk, is such a profound teacher and he says things so simply. He talks about spherical things in a way that linear people can hear it. He has a book, *The Miracle of Mindfulness,* that makes you gasp when you read it. He doesn't talk about peace, he talks about being *in* peace. He talks about taming the tiger within—not getting *rid* of the tiger, embracing the tiger. Thich Nhat Hanh is like one big giant moment of clarity who's walking around, blowing people's minds.

And I love the guys I see all the time who are just so enthusiastic, they want you to have this information, this insight—"Check this out!" They start tripping on these concepts and ideas, tripping on life and the living of it. Then, two years later, I'll be at a conference and I run into that guy, I go over to him and say, "So good to see you! Remember two years ago, you were talking about this stuff, and it was just really an interesting perspective for me." And he goes, "Yeah, yeah, yeah . . . never mind that, check *this* out!" I love that thinking, like the excitement of a child. We're all trying to get back to that wonderment, to be able to marvel in the ordinary.

I've completely accepted death; occasionally I'm mildly curious—what's it going to look like? But I'll just wait and see, because I'm not fully cooked, you know what I mean? There are still pieces of me that need work, places I fall down, but I know how to deal with that now. Pick the spots, man. Pick the spots. Where's the hotbed of opportunity? Not to get your thoughts and your ideas in, not to spread the gospel according to Earl—but to just simply, effectively, consciously interact. Participate, be a part of it. Connect.

I'm an elder now. That was a shocker, the first time I realized that. "Me? I've never been an elder at anything." And when people say, "Dude, how did you do that?" I know they're going to hate the answer. I say, "You already know. One day at a time, man. It's true. Just one day at a time."

What's beautiful is, "one day at a time" means one thing at ninety days and something profoundly different at twenty-five, twenty-six years. And that guy asking the question, he just might find that out. It's possible. It's always possible.

CHRIS MECHAM

&

The Internet has created new ways for people to connect with other peo-
ple, put their thoughts and feelings out in the world, get support and
encouragement—in other words, build a community. I don't think blogs and
chat rooms can replace face-to-face relationships, but they do seem to be a
good way for people in recovery to find additional sources of support. That's
been the case for Chris, and I'm glad because it gave me the chance to find
him and his story. I found his blog, The Last Chance Texaco, when I was
looking for people with interesting stories to tell. I admired Chris's honesty in
talking about the difficult issues we all face—loneliness, feeling isolated,
worries about money and jobs. When I asked him to participate, he was
newly sober, and I have to admit, that made me pause. But I decided that his
voice and his story were both unusual and universal enough to include. Since
then, I'm glad to say Chris has continued to walk the recovery road, one step
and one day at a time.

I've always loved Patty Griffin's music, and I happened to get sober on
Martin Luther King Day, so her song "Up to the Mountain" is especially meaningful to me. This particular song is about having a mission and being called to that mission by a power greater than yourself.
When I think I can't do it anymore, I remember that it's not about me. It's
about performing God's will in the world.

I'm the last guy most people would ever suspect would have a problem
with drugs or alcohol. There's a family picture taken in probably 1971 and
I swear my little sister and I look like we're sitting in the laps of the most

optimistic young couple in America. We were LDS—Mormons—living in Idaho and Utah. I earned money delivering the newspaper, mowing lawns, and shoveling snow. I got reasonable grades, though my test scores indicated that I should have done much better. I was an Eagle Scout.

I was also hopelessly unhappy, terminally unique, and, I see now, doomed to look for a solution outside myself to the problems I had inside. Everything worked to a degree. I liked pot. I liked to drink. I smoked crack one time and knew I had better never use it again because I could see it becoming a problem. And then I did a line of crystal meth.

I knew immediately that something terrible had happened. I knew it because for the first time in my life I felt okay inside my skin. I knew it because the very next thought I had was that nothing had better *ever* come between me and getting more crystal.

By the end of 2006, beginning of 2007, my life was falling completely apart. It hadn't occurred to me that things weren't normal, in spite of the fact that I hadn't really been employable or employed for years. I had a relationship with somebody who was only using me for drugs, and I was unable to see that for what it was. I was evicted from my apartment, and in the process of moving, I managed to lose most of my material possessions. I wasn't working, I was rapidly running out of friends, I was out of money, and I was quickly losing any hope that it was ever going to be any different.

It was my birthday, and this person I was dating said he'd take me out. He was seven hours late, and I decided to try and hunt him down at the places where I knew he might be. Not only did I not find him, I found nobody home at all. At this point it was about three o'clock in the morning. I was in a nice older neighborhood with Christmas lights and decorated trees in the windows and everybody asleep, and the snow has just begun to fall. It was cold, and I didn't even have an adequate coat because I hadn't expected to be out there for so long. I was standing under a street lamp, and I remember the particular sensation of little snowflakes against my face.

It was very cold and I was very tired and I sat down against the light post and cried. I didn't believe that it was possible for things to get any worse, and I didn't think that it was possible for things to get any better. I could see a light on in one of the houses, and I couldn't figure out how those people got there, just having normal, happy lives.

I was smart, I knew I was smart, but apparently having some smarts wasn't enough to give me the things that other people had. It wasn't enough to make me happy. How come these people had managed to end up secure and happy, and I, with all the same advantages, had managed to let that slip through my fingers? I knew there must be something wrong with me, something fundamentally defective, and that's why I was so miserable. And I had no idea how to change that. I couldn't even identify what exactly it was that was wrong with me. I knew that meth was part of the problem, but I didn't know how to live without meth.

I was sitting there, with the snow falling, with all this turmoil and all this noise inside my head, all this pain. I just kept asking whatever power was out there, "What is wrong with me?" Then everything just got incredibly quiet. All the noise in my head stopped, and all the pain in my heart stopped, and I could breathe again, and I could see that if anything was going to change, I had to start changing what I was doing. For the first time, I felt like I was being given the opportunity and the strength to follow that through, that the path would open for me if I just started walking. I could feel the calm settle down on me, like the light from the street lamp. I felt so quiet, so at peace, and I hadn't felt like that since I was a little kid.

I walked back to the place where I was staying and I went to bed, and the next morning I got up and contacted some friends in the recovery community and arranged to go to a sober-living house, and I stayed there until I got into an in-patient treatment program. When I made those phone calls that morning, part of me still didn't believe that there were people who stayed sober permanently. I still didn't believe that I was going to have to practice complete abstinence, forever. That just was incomprehensible to me. But I knew the path forward was to start reaching out to people who seemed to have the answer I was looking for.

As I've gone down that road, obviously my views have developed and my willingness to be completely abstinent has developed. But all that began with that one moment, that first step, and I think that was a gift of my

Creator. I don't think it's something we can work for or will into existence. I think of addiction as a box, and at any given moment, I think a lot of people are trying to beat their way out of whatever box they're in, and they're too busy and making too much noise to stop and listen to somebody who's reading the instructions from the outside. I simply reached a place and time and a level of brokenness where there was nothing I could do but stop and listen.

For the first time I was completely out of answers. I was always so sure I could think my way out of everything, but I couldn't. I'd managed to keep a pretty sophisticated denial mechanism in place for years and years and years, and it just all stopped working.

Those first few weeks—oh my God, I was angry. I don't think I realized it, but going back and looking at stuff, I can see how angry I was. I managed to place myself in the care of a few friends who were actually sober, and then in places where I knew I wasn't going to be around people who would influence whether or not I used. But all that was complicated to arrange, and there were money issues to deal with. I was in a lot of pain physically and a lot of pain emotionally. And suddenly there were these demands placed on me for certain levels of behavior. I didn't want to be told where to go, or what to do, or how to do it, or who I should talk to, or what to eat and when, or what voluntary work I was supposed to do. I was so tired and hungry. Starving, really. When you get off crystal meth and start eating again, you're really hungry.

But I managed to get through that. I just plugged away and made sure that I was in a place that was at least somewhat safe. I burned all my meth bridges. I closed all of those doors and just threw myself on the mercy of people who were sober. I did not want to continue doing what I was doing, but I knew that left to my own devices, I would have relapsed. So I made sure I wasn't left to my own devices.

I think of that moment, with the snow falling on my face, all the time. I still live in that same neighborhood, so the visual cues are never really very far away, and some of the people that I used with have made their way into the same kind of recovery that I'm following. There are always little things to remind me, so when I need to connect with that moment in a profound way, it's not very hard. Anytime I'm working with somebody who's new, anytime I'm offering my phone number to someone who has just a few days clean, wondering how the hell they are going to do it, I can see in their faces exactly where I was.

I resisted a program of recovery because I kept telling myself that I could think my way out of my problems, that I'm smarter than your average bear, that relying on something outside yourself means you're stupid. And with so much of my sexual identity tied up in my use of crystal meth, I was sure that I'd never have sex again. That has turned out to be true so far. I still don't know how to be intimate with people and be sober. It's probably going to take a while more, but right now, that doesn't seem to matter as much anymore. I thought that sexual intimacy and love were the same thing, and I no longer think that. Now I see that there are lots of people who love me in ways that are far more significant than a physical relationship.

Those were the big fears. I thought that I wouldn't be smart anymore, I thought I'd never have any energy anymore, I thought I was so broken that I should just give up. None of those things turned out to be true.

Of course I can't say that everything has suddenly become wonderful in my life. I still don't have a boyfriend, and it's hard to meet other sober gay guys here. I'm still dealing with the consequences of my bad decisions, and that causes job problems, legal problems, money problems. Some days my head, my disease, tells me that the price I'm paying is too high, that the world is unfair, that I'm being punished for being biologically defective.

That insane idea is as much a part of the problem as anything else, and luckily there's a set of simple instructions I can follow to try and override it. I don't always follow those instructions right away. I seem to have to reach a certain level of misery before I understand that the only effective solution to my worst problems is the same solution I've learned to apply to my drug and alcohol problem. I don't know why, but it seems to take me a while to get there.

I don't think I earned that moment of peace, the moment when I knew I could change. The trauma didn't earn me that gift; it just came when it came. If I could talk to that pre-moment self, I'd say, "How much longer are you going to put me through this?" And even if I could go back and say that, I'm not sure it would have made any difference. I was absolutely helpless to effect any change on my own, and I was absolutely incapable of asking for help. I don't think there's anything anybody could have said that would have changed things. I was just completely off on my own, and goddamn anybody who tried to stand in my way.

I remember that when I see someone who's struggling. I let them know that I'm there, but I allow them to be the one to reach out. I don't do anything except try to live by example and remain open. There was nothing that my friends or family could have said to me to change what I was doing, but at the time I was able to reach out for help, I was really glad they were there.

Everybody comes to it in their own time, and that time might be never. All we can do is wait and hope for them to get there.

KARL FLEMING

❧

*As Newsweek's civil rights correspondent, Karl covered most of the pivotal
moments of the civil rights movement: James Meredith's integration of the
University of Mississippi; the murders of three civil rights workers in Philadelphia, Mississippi; the Watts riots, where he was badly beaten. He recently
wrote a terrific memoir,* Son of the Rough South. *I interviewed Karl at his
home, and it was a humbling experience to sit in his office, surrounded by his
personal photographs from that time. Karl's an imposing figure, the epitome
of a man's man, and I admire his courage, revealing his secrets. As I was
leaving, he pointed to a photo of Dr. King and said, "Martin Luther King
taught me everything I needed to know about being a man."*

When someone asks for help, I say, "You know, I was about as
hopeless and lowdown as a human being can get, and here I
am today. And here's what I did, and if you want to try this,
I'll be glad to help you." I don't judge them. How can I? I'm one of them,
still. All I do is just try to be honest, to show up and be who I am. You
know the great thing about me now? My insides are exactly like my out-
sides. Exactly. You may not like me. That's fine. Sometimes I don't like
myself either. But I am a completely authentic human being now. There's
no pretense. I don't have to pretend anything, and everybody who knows
me knows everything about me. I don't care. And that's just a fabulous
feeling of liberation.

I was born down in the tobacco lands of eastern North Carolina during
the Depression. My father died of a heart attack when I was five months
old. He was fifty-four. My mother was younger, she was twenty-eight. She

struggled to take care of me, without much success—tried to sell dishes door-to-door at one point. Finally, in desperation, she married my father's best friend, also a much older man. We moved to a tenant shack, down on a swamp, and soon he got ill and died. My mother sank into bad health herself, and we struggled along until finally, when I was eight, she put me into an institution in Raleigh, North Carolina, called the Methodist Orphanage.

You know, I grew up hearing all about this loving Jesus who took care of children, a God who was, according to all the advertising, kind and loving and embracing. I went into this orphanage with a sense of being betrayed by my father, by my mother, by God, and by Jesus. I had such a sense of shame, of being just a piece of trash. And a big part of this shame was something I couldn't even talk about at all. When I was five, I was surrounded by a bunch of older kids and forced into a garage and forced to my knees and forced to commit a sexual act on this kid, and then they laughed at me. I went home and was in the bathroom crying and my mother said, "What's wrong?" I said, "Nothing." I spoke not one word of that secret until I was sixty years old, but it ruled my life in a way.

So I was in this orphanage, which was a very harsh place, and that was when I began to develop hostility toward religion, toward authority. The matron of the cottage I was in was a kind woman, but she was no protection against bullying, and I was bullied a lot. My nickname was Pretty Boy, and there was a kid named Fatty Clark who beat me up every day. You know, I look back now, and if you're a kid named Fatty Clark and there's a kid called Pretty Boy, you are going to beat him up.

I became a very withdrawn kid who found refuge in books. I read every book in this orphanage's library, about three thousand of them, and I lived in this fantasy world. But I soon learned that I had to be a tough guy if I was going to survive this experience. I became just as rebellious and pugnacious and ready to fight as the others were, and I ran away from there when I was seventeen and joined the navy.

The superintendent of the orphanage was this towering figure, this Somerset Maugham character who preached about the evils of sex and particularly the evils of drink. You take one drink and you're on the certain road to hell—he preached that over and over and over again. So naturally, on my first boot camp leave, I went with two buddies down to Baltimore to a strip joint, a burlesque house. We proceeded to have some drinks, and I got very sick and threw up on the side of the highway, and the highway patrol threw me in jail. The first drink I ever had, I got put in jail. You would think an intelligent person would get some sort of message from that. But obviously, I didn't. It was part of the southern tradition: tough guys drink. Also, all my literary heroes were big drinkers: Hemingway, Damon Runyon, Somerset Maugham, Fitzgerald. They were all big drinkers, and these were my heroes, the people who rebelled against convention, who more or less told the church and society to stick it. And I became one of them.

I got a job on a newspaper, and I became your typical rebellious young reporter. Reporting was a craft, not a calling. I was cynical about authority and contemptuous of people who made money as a way of life. And I drank a lot, even though nothing good ever happened when I drank. I got in fights. I threw up. I came to work with hangovers every day. That's the way my early life unfolded.

After my first job as a reporter, I got a job on a bigger newspaper in Durham, North Carolina, with a bunch of hard-bitten, hard-drinking guys, all of whom wanted to be novelists. We'd rent a hotel room and drink all night and play poker. I never drank during working hours. Then I moved up to Asheville, where Thomas Wolfe, the writer, had thumbed his nose at society. *You Can't Go Home Again. Look Homeward, Angel.* I drank a lot up there, then I wandered on and got a job on the *Atlanta Constitution,* and I continued to drink really hard. I still never drank during working hours. I did my job.

Around 1960, when the civil rights movement was just kicking in, *Newsweek* magazine hired me, and I covered all the major events in the civil rights movement—the Birmingham church bombings, the marches in Birmingham with Bull Conner and the police dogs and fire hoses, Selma, Montgomery. Jackson, Mississippi, and the assassination of Medgar Evers. Philadelphia, Mississippi, with three civil rights workers assassinated by the Klan. James Meredith and the violence when he integrated the University of Mississippi. I covered all that stuff, and by this time I was 210 pounds of swaggering, crew-cut, cigar-smoking, hard-drinking, cynical tough guy. Again, I never drank during working hours, so I never really thought I had a drinking problem. It was part of the culture. That's what newspaper guys did, what southern tough guys did.

I came out to California in 1965, just in time to get almost killed by black people after the whole Watts riots got going. I got my head opened up and I was beaten and stomped nearly to death by a bunch of black guys—which was a tremendous psychic shock, because I had been very much committed to the black civil rights cause. I lay in the hospital, thinking about how I'd nearly died, and I thought, "You know what? I should stop drinking." And I did.

Then I went up to San Francisco. This was '67 or '68 and the Vietnam War protest was beginning to get really strong. I went up to San Francisco to cover a peace march in Golden Gate Park, and I got into marijuana. It was fabulous. The food was great. The sex was great. The colors were great. The music was great. I had a great time. For the next twenty years, I didn't have one drink. I just smoked marijuana.

During this period, I left *Newsweek*. I got divorced. I rented an apartment on the beach out in Malibu. And I fell in love with Anne, my wife now of thirty-seven years. I started a newspaper here with the help of a wealthy backer, which lasted about a year before the guy jerked out his money and left me stranded. The newspaper died. All the talented young people I had hired lost their jobs. Then I got involved in a very humiliating event. I was caught in the middle of a con game, which caused me tremendous personal embarrassment, with my name in the *New York Times,* subjected to public humiliation. I was taking a lot of steroids for asthma, which kicked up after I got hurt in the riots. That affected my judgment.

I was still smoking a lot of marijuana, suffering from a lot of hubris and then a lot of humiliation. I began on this absolute downward slide. For over a year, I lay on a sofa in my office, hoping I would die. I thought my life was over. I wanted it to be over. I was a failure and a counterfeit and a phony. Finally, I had a complete breakdown. I ended up in a nut house, lying in a straitjacket on the gurney, trying to choke myself with the sheet.

I got out of that place by strength of will, and I began to get back on my feet. An old colleague came to L.A. to be the general manager of the CBS affiliate station, and he hired me to be managing editor, and then an on-air reporter. At the height of my insanity, I had a '65 Mustang convertible. I would go out to the CBS parking lot and smoke a joint and go on the air live with Connie Chung, stoned out of my mind. I mean I was really nuts. And then, on my sixtieth birthday, I decided that I would quit smoking marijuana. And I did. I got a big sixtieth birthday party, and I made a vow I was not going to do this anymore.

I had tried and tried and tried and tried to quit before, but I could never make it past 10 A.M. The pain was too great. I just wanted to be novocained from the shame and the pain and the humiliation—not just being fired and losing my newspaper but the old shame from the sexual humiliation and growing up in this orphanage and not having much education. But I decided to quit, and I did.

About Christmastime, we went to a friend's house one night, and—mind you, I had not had a drink in twenty years—I opened the freezer and there sits a bottle of frozen vodka. I reached in without a thought and took a couple slugs. And I was off again.

There's a classic definition of an alcoholic: when an alcoholic takes a drink, you cannot predict what's going to happen. And that was me, big time. After I got sober, my oldest son—who's also now very much sober—said he used to be able to tell what kind of evening it was going to be by the way my car door slammed when I got home. I would have been up at the Cock and Bull drinking after work, and some nights I would be just fine, and some nights I'd walk into the house an angry and volatile guy. If we went out to dinner, I would be perfectly fine, or I would get on the waiter's case, and my children would just cringe and want to hide under the table. It was completely unpredictable, and I had a clear recognition of that because all that time I was smoking marijuana, none of that happened. The instant I started drinking, the bad behavior came back. I had a really bad period of about eight days, and I can't remember exactly what happened, but one particular night, at my wife's birthday party, I turned into a monster. I ruined the birthday party.

I got up the next morning, and that was my moment of clarity. I was embarrassed. I knew what I had done. It was the symbolic thing of ruining my wife's birthday, who had been so loyal to me during all of my bad times. She had taken in my children, been a friend, really, to my four sons from my first marriage. She had stood loyally by me, and I had just treated her like dirt. I was just so ashamed. I'd never done anything as stark as that before. I woke up and I immediately knew this was not going to be a good day. I had ruined my wife's birthday party. She was extremely angry, just gave me a cold look and went off to the kitchen. What was I going to say? I had no defense. There was no justification for my behavior. I was facing the stark reality that I hadn't had a drink for twenty years—and after a few days of drinking I was right back where I had been. I thought, "You know what? I'm an alcoholic. I'm sick. And I got to do something." If I was going to live—and apparently I was, because I didn't have the guts to kill myself—I was going to have to do something.

Mary is a friend of mine who'd been in recovery for a long time. I called her, and she took me to a mutual support group meeting that day—January 4, 1988. There were twenty-six sobriety birthdays that day. By the end of that meeting, I wanted to take an AK-47 and kill everybody in the room. I didn't want to have anything to do with these people and all this talk about God. I had nothing but contempt for God and for organized religion. I was definitely not a joiner. I had been an individualist my whole life. I had learned, because of the cumulative evidence, that I had to take care of myself. Nobody else was going to do it. I had "friends"—a lot of friends, compatriots, admirers—but I never let anybody get close to me at all. Of course, part of it was the secrets I was holding on to, that I had never uttered one word about to anybody. I was invulnerable. But then I was not able to hold on to this facade I had created to protect myself, you know, the tough guy. I had destroyed my own image of myself, so there was nothing left. Who was I? Nobody.

After that first meeting, I thought I'd never go back, but I did. Still, I was angry. So angry. I went to this men's recovery meeting, and people would literally get up and move away from me. That's the literal truth. I radiated such anger, and anger all comes from hurt, and I didn't know that. I had no understanding that I was just a hurt and frightened little boy who just wanted somebody to love me and to be able to love other people. I had no inkling of that.

It's like William James, *The Varieties of Religious Experience*. Some people have this incandescent awakening. For me, it was very slow. Very slow. I saw a tiny ray of hope, something that I could hold on to. I saw all these other people and I heard their stories and heard that they had gone through the same stuff I had or worse, and it worked for them. That meant something to me. I'm a very practical guy. Don't tell me about faith and some guy up there in the sky; show me the evidence. And I could look around and see these people from all walks of life who'd come from circumstances much more desperate than mine. And it had worked for them.

Also, an old-timer said something to me. . . . I was saying, "I don't want to be hearing this God crap." He said, "I don't believe in the same God you don't believe in." I thought that was a great line, and it helped me understand that I could pick anything to be a higher power, whatever worked for me. It was a recognition that my self-will had done nothing but get me in trouble and make me unhappy.

I had achieved all this tremendous professional success, and I had four wonderful children and a fabulous life and a nice house in the richest part of Los Angeles, a mile from a beautiful ocean, and the sun shone every day. I cleaned up pretty good, and I could spread about fifteen minutes of charm, but underneath I was just so unhappy, with no clue as to how I could change that. But then I began to change a little bit after I spilled that first secret. I began to feel a little of the dirt go away. I always felt so dirty inside, and then I started to feel clean inside all the time. Even when I do screw up, I can see it and say, "Okay, there's the five-year-old boy. But I'm not that little boy anymore."

About a month ago, I was hitting golf balls, just practicing, and up walks the psychiatrist that I went to during the period that I had that breakdown. He asked what I was up to, and I said I was going to make a commencement speech, not trying to preach to the kids, just tell them a few things that transformed me from being an abjectly depressed and unhappy person into being a happy guy, give them four or five rules that worked for me.

He said, "Well, that's kind of funny. I'm putting out a disc, my ten commandments for being happy. What's on your list?"

I said, "Well, the first thing is get rid of your secrets. That worked for me. Is that on your list?"

He said, "No." This was the guy who I had gone to all that time, but I never breathed one word about the sexual molestation that had ruined my life. Not a word. I had no chance of getting well with him, because I never told him my secret.

I had always had this sense of forced independence. If I was going to make it, I had to make it on my own, because nobody had ever helped me. I had never allowed anybody to help me because I was so distrustful of making myself vulnerable. And I didn't want anyone to discover the shame and the guilt I felt. Now I know—what do I have to be afraid of? I'm completely happy today without having to prove anything to anybody. I can be the authentic Karl, and what a relief. All those years, I had to prove that I'm a man, I had to prove that I'm a big shot. That's over. I'm just a guy who has found a way to be happy. I don't know why we're put on this earth, but I know enough to know that that would be a good start.

LARRY KUDLOW

A conservative economist, Larry hosts the CNBC show Kudlow & Company *and is the economics editor of* National Review Online. *He also runs his own consulting firm, Kudlow & Company. During Reagan's first term, he served in the Office of Management and Budget, and later became a senior managing director at Bear, Stearns & Company, until his addictions got totally out of control. He's not somebody you'd necessarily expect to see in this book, which is why I'm glad he's here. I asked him how he wanted to be described, and his words apply to me and just about everybody else I know in recovery: "I'm a guy who still works to stay sober a day at a time. My principal line of work is sobriety, and that's what I do. That's my main mission."*

W ell, the great news for me is that hopelessness is something in the past. I am hopeful and optimistic. In fact, people in my professional life are staggered at how optimistic I always am about things. What they don't understand is that I know all about hopelessness. My whole experience as a drunk and a cocaine abuser—until I surrendered finally, on my knees, having lost everything except my wife—those were the hopeless days. I held a prominent Wall Street job for many years and I made a name for myself, and I drank and snorted myself out of that job.

Toward the end I was invited out to a lodge in beautiful Pebble Beach, California, to give a speech. Fantastic! They gave us this magnificent room, where you look out on the Pacific Ocean and the golf course and all that gorgeous weather, and I will never forget this. We were there a couple of days, and all I saw was a black shade being pulled down. I did not see the beautiful ocean. I did not see the beautiful sunshine. I did not see the eighteenth hole or whatever. All I saw was a dark black shade pulled down.

That metaphor was with me for quite some time; I'm sure there are a million meanings to that, but I think it had a lot to do with hopelessness. My life was coming to an end, and I could not stop. That was my hopelessness bout, which probably lasted for at least a year and maybe more than that, back in the early nineties.

Then I got sober and I spent six months in Hazelden, and when I got out, the only job offer I had was from a very dear friend of mine outside of San Diego. But I was hopeful. In Hazelden I developed hope and a certain amount of optimism, and I think the key to all of that was faith. At that time, the faith was not manifested in a particularly religious God. It was just faith in the spiritual program. Now, I am a full-fledged card-carrying member of the optimists' club. I figure, any life, any country, that gives me this kind of second chance, puts me on the air for an hour or so a day—it has got to be just the greatest life, the greatest country in the world. So I am very hopeful and very optimistic, but I do always remember the black shade being pulled down.

I think my moment of clarity came near the end, and it was my growing recognition that I was not in my right mind. The only thing in what mind I had left was how far I had fallen, how awful it was, how low my bottom was, and how close I was to being a homeless bum on the street. I was staggered by that. Staggered by how bad it had gotten. I had a Wall Street partnership, and that was gone. Then I was a senior magazine editor, and that was gone. I had a lot of television work as a commentator, and the trouble with TV is if you don't show up, they put somebody else on. They do not wait for you, and that is a handicap for an alcoholic and a drug addict. That was gone, it was all gone.

I would go out on a binge for many days at a time. I'd walk around, wearing a nice pinstriped suit, but I'd be wearing it for three, four, five days at a time. And I remember actually having homeless people looking at me like I was weird and looking back at them and realizing, "That could be me," or at least that's where I was headed. That was pretty scary, and I do not pretend that I understood it at all.

But it was occurring to me that this had gone so much further than I ever thought it could. I had been in and out of recovery programs. I used to go out and then come back in, so I thought I knew the limits. I just had no idea how far it could go. That was my first burning bush, when I realized that this was really serious and really a problem. I was failing, I was dying, I was gone. There was no more Larry Kudlow.

When I went away to Hazelden, which was a godsend, the first few weeks I was angry at myself, at the world, at everybody else for what had happened. I began to realize through some mentoring and tutelage that if you take your will back every time, if you exercise these selfish actions every time, then you are the problem. I was the problem, not you or her or Wall Street or *The McLaughlin Group*. I was the problem. These were self-inflicted wounds.

I look back with the benefit of a decent sober mind-set, and I believe God saved me. I believe that. I absolutely believe that. I have no idea how, nor do I know why, but He kept me alive and He eventually led me to a point where I surrendered to Him, to Hazelden, and to a program of recovery. I am a Catholic convert, which is different from my recovery experience. I have adopted that religious faith as well as my spiritual program faith. I have no idea why He led me there. I just know He did it. It was His design, not mine. Faith is a mystery. How it was that I finally surrendered is a mystery. This whole thing is a mystery to me.

If someone comes to me for help, I help them. Or I try to. I give them advice, but I am not a proselytizer. You know what they say, "When the pupil is ready, the teacher appears." Down through the years, I've worked with a bunch of men in recovery. Some have worked out and others have not.

Outside of the fellowship of recovery, I get a lot of letters and e-mails from people who are aware of me or know my story of recovery. They ask things, and I almost always tell them that I go to a mutual support group and they should too. I do not really give any advice other than "Go to a meeting and keep your ears open." People may come up to me, as they often do, maybe on the street or after I have spoken someplace. They come up to me and they know my story and this and that: "Oh my God, look what you did." I just douse that claim as soon as it pops up. I am not a hero. I am just a guy that went through bloody hell and then started climbing back, literally one step at a time. I avoid giving advice, I avoid prospecting, I avoid congressional hearings. But I try to be there for people.

That's one of the cool things about recovery. You get knocked around so much that you kind of learn to deal with up, deal with down. Life is up and down. You can't obsess about it. I am a hard worker and I show up, but my whole career has changed in sobriety. I'm a professional broadcaster now, and I write a column or two. That is totally different from what I used to do. I worry periodically about X, Y, and Z, but I don't fight it. I always accept it. Do you guys want to fire me or push me aside? Okay, it will be what it will be. Whenever something is off center, when there's something worrisome creeping in, I pick up my meeting schedule and pick up my phone call schedule and pick up my reading schedule; I retreat deeper into recovery. That is what I do. I just do it. It is my instinct now, and it serves me very well. I have come to believe that the recovery fellowship saves me from myself because self is the problem. Things still go wrong—quarrels, uncertainties, jobs, people knifing me behind my back. Let's get real, broadcasting is not your most laid-back business. But whenever stuff gets to me, I go deeper into my recovery, increase the meetings, increase the phone calls. More prayer. Faith really sustains me.

LOU GOSSETT JR.

Lou's first acting job was in the film A Raisin in the Sun, *with Sidney Poitier, after he decided to ditch the chance to play pro basketball. That was in 1961, and he's worked steadily ever since. He was one of the stars of the huge mini-series* Roots, *and he won an Academy Award for his work in* An Officer and a Gentleman. *Lou is one of those people who has tremendous presence—not just his physical stature (the guy is big!) but his energy too. When I asked him to participate in this book, he said yes right away and welcomed me into his home, where he had hit bottom and his life was transformed.*

I was afraid that I was inadequate as a man. I was afraid that once I got sober, I would not be hip enough. If I got sober, the fun would be over. I would be out of the mix. In fact, it is the opposite. You are in the mix, maybe because God is in charge now. Everywhere I go, when people are doing something halfway decent in music, in movies, in sports, in businesses, they seem to be going through a spiritual shift. Maybe it is the planets, but there are more of us than there are of them. Numbers cannot be taken advantage of.

My biggest moment of clarity before the *true* moment of clarity was when I was in Capetown, South Africa. I had been offered movies in South Africa for different reasons, but I would not go during apartheid. As soon as I heard that Mandela was out of jail, that changed. I coproduced a film called *Inside,* about the Truth and Reconciliation Commission (formed in an attempt to heal the wounds after apartheid).

I was cold sober at the time, but it was very new. What happens when you are recently sober is what they call the "pink cloud"—everything is wonderful and you're doing missions and you're saving people's lives. On top of that, everybody was celebrating because Mandela came out. I meet Mandela, meet all of these people, and I am in this great spiritual mood. At the same time, I came into sobriety with a package, with resentment against racism, and that resentment was kind of strong. I am going through my life and all the lives of all the black people who died before fifty, including my father, who drank so much. I have come there to play this character who had to have the same resentment, and so I had opened up those wounds, to prepare, and I was really in a terrible state.

I was looking out at Robben Island, where Mandela spent twenty-seven years in prison, and I burst into tears, because there is absolutely nothing that ever happened in my life to compare to what that man went through and what his people went through. I said, "What am I doing? I should be very grateful." It was a clear day, a blistering day, and I must have spent a couple of hours there reflecting on what had happened on this land, how much blood was shed because of apartheid and how much this man had lost—the prime of his life, in a cell, beaten, starved. Nothing like that ever happened to me, and I started thinking about the drinking and the drugs, and the resentment. "What the hell am I doing? Why did I get to the point of abusing myself? I did worse to myself than any person, white or black, did to me." Then I felt a kind of calm, and the resentment eased, and I just got rid of it.

Now my life is devoted to those people who are caught in the same trap, who want to prove how tough they are by basically shooting themselves in the head—which is what drugs were in my life. For me it was the resentment of knowing that somebody did something very bad to me, and I was so pissed off I took drugs and some more drugs to show them how bad I was, how mad I was—I mean it's insane. It does not make you feel better, but the insanity makes you think that you have won over on them. Every thought is a resentful thought, every thought was a fucking thought—"fuck this, fuck that." And then came that moment of looking out at Robben Island, the moment that led me to understanding the anger and made it go away.

Fade out and fade in ten years later. Ten years of sobriety and I am getting tired. I have gotten every award you can win as an actor, but I still have not gotten a million dollars for any movie. There was a lot of respect, but still people were pointing their fingers at me: "You still have got to behave yourself, be a role model." I saw all of my white contemporaries going back to what they were doing, using and all, and they were making millions of dollars, and I was sitting there, starting to say, "Well, fuck it" again, like before that moment in South Africa. And then the doctor tells me, "You are not doing too well. You're going to die in six months." And I said, "Well, why be sober? Why help somebody else?" I lined out all the stuff that I got high on. I got the best I could find. If I was going to die, I was going to do it high.

Nothing happened, just a mess on the table. I was not high, I was not stoned, and I was not sober, I was just very sick. I was too sick to get up. Absolutely nothing happened. I sat for about ten days, getting weaker and weaker. I sat and I watched the TV. The electricity went out, and the TV went off. I did not have any food, and I couldn't go out the doors looking terrible.

I was 167 pounds and I was looking dead. I called my son and said, "I gotta go back to rehab." So that was another moment of clarity. I had to have that slip. I really desperately needed to reach the worst part of my life to have the best time of my life today.

Through those ten days, I didn't want to give up my best friend, the drugs and alcohol. It's almost worse than a divorce when you know it is all over. No more fun! No more calling the girls in. No more of the giggles. It is a terribly tragic feeling—now what? But the fact is, it hadn't been fun and giggles for a while. And then you go from there to maybe the third week of that thirty days in rehab and the family is there—everybody's family is there—and people start breaking down. I just broke down, especially to my son. I said, "I am sorry," and I was.

In some sense, every black person in America is carrying the yoke of the Africans, carrying the yoke of the African Americans like Jackie Robinson, Martin Luther King. But I've learned that in order to be of any value, I have to carry my own burden, I have to look at my own self and deal with that. I say it in my autobiography, the worst resentment that an addict or an alcoholic can ever have is one that he feels justified to keep.

That is the worst poison in anybody's system, whether alcoholic or not. It closes all the doors, wears you down. I don't know what it is or where it comes from, but it seems to be happening all over the world today. People are blowing themselves up to make a point. I almost did. It doesn't make any sense.

God looks like everything I see. God is the way you are looking at me. God is my cat. God is the alpha and the omega, and I see him in everybody and everything I see. He sends somebody to look like Jesus or Allah or Buddha or Muhammad. I hang out with a lot of rock and rollers in some meetings, and they're always talking, "Gee, I wonder what God really looks like, what Jesus looks like." They'll say, "I think He looks like a combination of Jim Morrison and Bob Dylan, what do you think, Lou?" So I look at them with a smile and I say, "Well, the last time I looked at things, She looks like Tina Turner."

I ask God every morning, "What do I do?" There is a moment of clarity every morning now. I am not in charge. I thought I was in charge before; I never really was. That is a big yoke off my neck. God is in charge always. He was in charge before I was alive, He is in charge while I am alive, and He will be in charge after I am gone. The Saint Francis Prayer is my prayer on a daily basis. Where there is darkness, you bring light. Where there is sadness, you bring joy. Where there is hatred, you bring love.

MALACHY MCCOURT

$\backsim$

I feel connected to Malachy on so many levels: the Irishness, the love of acting and story-telling, the dark history with drinking and drugging. He also makes it easy to connect with him because he's so open. He's written several books, including two memoirs; he's appeared in many movies and TV series and soap operas, including a recurring role as Father Clarence, who dispenses wise holiday-season advice to the citizens of All My Children's *Pine Valley. I've always known him to speak his mind, so I knew his story would be worth reading.*

It's all simple, you know. That's the great thing—this getting sober is so simple. It isn't that there's nothing to it, it's not easy, but it is *simple*. You're perfectly safe doing what you need to do, and it is okay to be selfish, in a sense. Take care of yourself, because you can do fuck-all for anybody else if you don't take care of yourself. The more you begin to realize it's a disease, you begin to realize the lunacy of it, the insanity of it—"Oh, I did all of that, yes, I did that, I did *that*"—and then you learn about making amends and how you can go about that. And it's all right if you're not forgiven. Some people will not forgive you. I always thought you have to be forgiven, otherwise you haven't done the right thing. But the right thing is always the right thing.

I wish I hadn't gone through all of that, I wish I hadn't done such damage to my first wife and my children then, and to other people over the years. I wish I hadn't, but I'm trying to make amends as best I can. At least I know I ought not to be damaging people, doing damage to them or to myself. Doing damage to people—particularly children—does terrible damage to yourself. I found that out. Did I *have* to go through that to reach the point of healing? I mean it's the old joke about knocking your head against the wall. Why are you doing that? Because it's so nice when you stop. Was it necessary I go through all of that? Well, then the question arises—if you're not carrying a burden, would you know the relief of putting it down?

We all get sober and clean eventually, but it's best to do it while we are alive. It's much more fun.

I was born in Brooklyn, and due to a set of sort of tragic events in the family, including the death of a sister, we took off to Ireland, and that's where I grew up. It was a very poor neighborhood—it wasn't poor, it was poverty-stricken, really. I was a reasonably good-looking kid, but with a terrible low self-esteem, very stupid in school. I couldn't comprehend what it was they were on about there at all—I failed everything—and so I left and went to work at a bunch of menial jobs in England and Ireland. I came back to America when I was twenty-one. I worked at the usual again, on the docks and so on, and then got my sails for a while, got into the theater and by remarkable accident became an actor. I became a bartender and then became a bar owner and got married, divorced, became an alcoholic, was an alcoholic, two children through that marriage, and what else did I do? I got on the radio, continued the acting, continued the saloon business, got married again, and took up writing when I was fifty-four, and I've published eight books since then.

And I would say that out of all of this, the greatest achievement was finding self-worth. That's the greatest thing, finding out that I really deserve to live. That is very important to me. If I could say something to that twenty-one-year-old boy, I would tell him, "If you have felt like one of life's discards, if you have felt unloved and you have felt disrespected—you don't have to go through that. All you need to do is keep control of your senses. Do not drink or drug, because you can't handle it. Do not damage your health with cigarettes. Realize that you're a talented and lovable human being, and start off by giving yourself a big hug, an embrace. Just do the right thing, tell the truth, and be what you are in-side, a human."

I say this quite consciously and clearly, that the organized Catholic Church in Ireland was very cruel if you didn't have money or if you weren't of a certain class. You eventually become the thing you hate the most, and so many of the Irish became imitators of the snobbery that was the way the English treated the Irish. I still think that the English are my superiors intellectually, morally, and educationally. I was abused sexually by three priests at various times, not very seriously but enough to make me feel dirty and ashamed of myself because I thought it must be me, I had done something wrong. When I realized it was their fault, it wasn't me, that turned me off organized religion totally.

School was more brutal than anything. There was no love of learning. It was inculcation by the fist and by the stick and by ridicule of children. There was *no* love of learning. The only thing that saved me then was reading. I was an omnivorous reader, but I failed everything. There is an exam that one takes in Ireland at the age of twelve, which is the primary examination. You can't go on to high school or secondary school without it. My scores were not good enough for that, so I left school when I was thirteen. Here I am without a spiritual life, without a formal education, a shameful situation at home with the poverty and my mother sleeping with this guy and my father gone and all this kind of stuff. It was a total wreckage.

At the same time, I became a very cunning guy. I realized that the way I was going to make my way was by charm, so that's how I got through, by charming people. My brother Frank was short-tempered, he glared and shouted at people, "fuck them" and all that, so he was considered the odd one, where I was more the peacemaker, the charmer.

The sequence here is quite clear in my head because it had to do with coming to America and finding a certain amount of respect. People would say, "You're funny," or "You're very bright," people would pay me compliments. I wouldn't quite believe them, but it began to seep in. Frank and myself, we wrote this play, *A Couple of Blaggards*, and we had done it here in New York. By then I had been reasonably successful in the saloon business and on the stage, doing television and that sort of thing—no great success but it was okay. Far more than I thought I could expect coming from the slums of Limerick.

Then we decided to take this play of ours to Limerick, and in my head there was this idea: "I am going to show these fuckers, all these institutions that have failed us, the church, the schools, the charitable institutions, and the educational system—I am going to show them all what I have done." We went back there and did this play, and I'm expecting people to say, "We're sorry for what we did to you" and all—but there was nobody left to say it. No representatives of these institutions ever came up and bowed down and said, "We're sorry for what we did." Of course it's totally unrealistic to expect that kind of thing, but I did expect it and it didn't happen. I got more and more frustrated, and drank more and drank angrily, and got more and more depressed.

I came back from there in July of 1965 in a terrible state. I felt wretched, I felt awful, I felt physically and mentally ill, and spiritually I felt absolutely destroyed. I didn't know why. I went to a physician I knew and he examined me pretty thoroughly and he said, "I can find nothing wrong with you organically, but I can tell you this. I know that you are drinking too much, you are smoking too much, and you are eating too much, and that's the diagnosis." I said, "And the cure? What are you going to give me for that?" He said, "I'll give you two things. I'll give you a boot in the ass and I'll give you a bill if you don't fuck off out of here, because you know what to do. You're a very bright man, McCourt, you know what to do."

I left that office thinking it out like this. "The drinking is no problem," said I to myself, "and then you can't have a drink without a cigarette, so I know what it is, it's fucking food is the problem." I started searching out what I would do, and the truth is that my entry into recovery was a program for overeaters. I'm looking at these charts there, and all the sayings, it all has to do with alcohol, but they just substitute food. So then I decided to stop drinking, but the thing is, you can eat some but you can't drink some, so I was thoroughly confused by this. I realized, "You're fooling yourself there, kiddo. Drop it, stop the denial, and go for it. Go to a recovery meeting." I decided I would go, but I'm not going to accept this God crap that they have. I was always going around saying, "I'm an atheist, thank God," that was my mantra.

The first meeting I was told, "You don't have to drink anymore." You don't have to be anything you don't want to be, you don't have to pretend anymore, you don't have to put on a show, you don't have to be charming or witty or anything. You can just be honest, and that was fantastic. Then somebody said, "You are in the safest place you can be." I looked around and the guy said, "Nothing can assault you here, nothing can attack you here, and nobody will attack you here." I found myself saying, "Oh really, that's nice." I felt my shoulders ease, no more tension; my shoulders weren't up around my ears. I felt that portion of the body between the eyes relax. I found my jaw relaxing, the teeth weren't grinding together, and I had that lovely feeling of "Ahh, I'm at ease." All I need to do now is just do my best. I always remembered what Mark Twain said: "In case of doubt, tell the truth," and I have amended that to "In case of doubt, do the right thing." That has been my guide ever since.

I'm fairly certain that addiction comes with being born. Just like our head comes with our body, addiction comes with us. I'm convinced of this. I think that as little children, when we get our buckets to play with, the ordinary normal child would fill up these buckets with sand and make sand castles, you see, and we—the addicted, the alcoholic—we fill ours up with shit. Somebody says, "Your buckets are full of shit!" so you put down the buckets and get two bigger buckets and fill them up with more shit. We go through life filling up our buckets with shit, and we struggle. People tell us to put down the shit, and we say, "No, I can't. It doesn't matter, I'm used to it." And then we get to a point where we are told, "Look, what you ought to do is, there's this higher power that has a huge cold storage facility for shit, and you can hand in your buckets, get a receipt, and you can have your shit back any time you want, hot or cold." Now that it's in storage, the less you're going to want it, but putting your shit down is the real key, because it opens your hands. You can't give or receive the grace of God or Allah or whoever with your hands closed tight around the handles of your buckets of shit. So you open your hands, you open your mind, you open your heart, you can open your nostrils because you don't have to be breathing stink, you can open everything, just be open to what is great and good in this world, and you'll be able to hand over what is not.

Diana, my wife, gave me a thing to hang in my office which says, "Good morning. This is God. I will be handling all your affairs today, and I will not need your help. Have a nice day." Isn't that great? That has helped me a lot. So yes, I believe in the power, the greater power, the higher power. To me, it's an amorphous, mysterious power that I don't understand, but I don't have to. My understanding is, there's a power greater than myself, and I can invoke that power, ask its help. It may come and it may not, but that's not my business. All I can do is do what I need to do on a daily basis. I feel like I'm sublimely devoid of knowledge. What I am is a conveyor of divinity, and that's all I am.

I guess the operative phrase for me was "You're in a safe place." Immediately I relaxed. And actually, when I think about it, I'm in a safe place anywhere I go so long as I don't drink. That was the moment for me, hearing that man tell me, "You're in a safe place."

Growing up in a slum, growing up in poverty, leaves you with that same residue that alcohol leaves you with, the residue of shame and fear. Shame takes care of the past, turns it into something terrible that's been done to you or something you've done or thought about doing. That's shame. Fear is firmly rooted in the future and it makes sure to ruin that for you too. The shame says, "Look what you did, look what you are, you'll never be anybody." Fear says, "Don't come up here, don't even attempt to come up here, to make yourself any better, because you're a piece of shit, just look at your past." You have to dismiss the two of them and say, "I'm living in the present, I have the gift of the present." *Present, gift*—the words are so similar. I stay *here,* in the moment, I don't get into the future.

Mike Judge, who was my brother in recovery, was a Franciscan priest, killed on 9/11. He said to me once, "What are you worrying about?" I said, "I'm worried about the future. I'm old and washed-up and going nowhere. I don't know how to make any money, I'm deeply in debt," and on and on. And he said, "Well, the God I believe in, the God I've asked to look after you too—that God is very busy, so busy He has not yet made tomorrow, that future which you're so worried about." I said, "Yeah?" And Mike said, "He doesn't know what's going to happen tomorrow because it ain't here yet, and you can't tell a future that's not made. So as all-powerful and all-knowing as He is, He doesn't know. So who the fuck do you think you are?"

So I don't attempt that. I listen. I listen to my kids, listen to Diana. She had a serious operation, and I stayed at the hospital with her for six nights and it was very tense because I just thought, "Oh my God, what if I lose her?" and I just kept telling myself that tomorrow wasn't here yet. The lads in recovery were great. They called me and they told me they were thinking about her and me. They became such good friends, all of them, and a lot of them I don't even know their last names. I'm so blessed, so blessed to be sober. The decency of it, the generosity of sobriety is astounding. It's the way, it's the path, that's what it is. I know it's a long road, as long as I've got.

Alcoholism is about loss, primarily loss of love—that which we cannot live without. In a program of recovery I found out about love and am empowered to be able to open my whole being to the love offered by my friend and spouse, Diana. She also taught me to return that love to all my family, to be honest, to stick to the program, and that we can surrender without being defeated and that we can be elevated without getting above ourselves.

The God that I believe in is totally merciful, gives us totally unconditional love, and would not condemn anything or anybody to an eternity of hell. It would never do that, couldn't do that. If it created us, then it knows what we are, so it wouldn't fuck around with us. Why do that? We attribute things to God that are just human. We attribute anger to God. Why would God get angry? Anger is losing control. A perfect, pure being loses control? That kind of thing annoys me.

Where is my higher power? It's here, it's in books, there's yourself, there's your voice. It's an aura that surrounds me, and it's almost like a spiritual sustenance I can take in. Breath, the act of breathing ... for seventy-five years I have not stopped breathing or my heart has not stopped beating. For seventy-five years, *bump, bump, bump, bump*. Isn't that amazing? Isn't that a miracle?

GREG BEHRENDT

Greg says he's tall. "Unusually tall. Unexpectedly tall, for a guy who's five ten and a half." He started out in stand-up comedy, part of a circle of San Francisco comics that included Patton Oswalt, Margaret Cho, and David Cross. He still does stand-up, but he's also the author of two bestsellers: He's Just Not That Into You and It's Called a Breakup Because It's Broken. The success of his first book led to a cable talk show, and while I was promoting Symptoms, he invited me on to talk about relationships. I proceeded to humiliate myself in front of a large group of women. It's funny, thinking about his story now, there's a certain amount of humiliation there too—which is true of most recovery stories.

Hopelessness is when you feel like you've turned over every stone and you found nothing. You just cannot find the answers, because you've been searching so far outside of yourself that you're totally lost. And that's where I was before I quit drinking.

A week before, it was business as usual. I had this routine pattern of being fucked up. It was very ritualized. Throughout all of my drinking, I still managed to lift weights and go to the gym and run, and at five o'clock I'd get fucked up beyond belief and not remember where I was and wake up the next day and not have a job and go do an open mike and start over. I would quit drinking and then not quit and then bargain with myself and tell myself I was going to have a drink. But it was repetitive. It was really the same. It was lots and lots and lots of the same. There's a phrase called "routine misery," where you're not aware of it because it's business as usual. I didn't realize how fucked-up and how sad I was till weeks, months, even years later when I finally got some perspective on it.

The one thing I do remember is a couple of days before I got sober, I met a girl and we went to have coffee. She asked me, "How much do you drink?" And I couldn't answer the question. "Not a lot. I mean, more than . . . it depends." I just couldn't get it out. So then I asked, "Why do you want to know?" And she goes, "One of the things that I really don't like is when somebody is all fucked up and calls me in the middle of the night. I hate that. It's like my pet peeve." And I was like, "Oh yeah, I get that. That sucks."

And then three nights later, I got super fucked-up and called her at two o'clock in the morning. I liked her because she was sober and had this bright light burning inside of her and her friends were sober and she was funny and fun. I guess I wanted to fuck that up so that she would go away. I was constantly doing the one thing I knew I shouldn't be doing.

I woke up sweaty and fat, belly distended, midmorning, at an apartment that I shared with another comic. On my futon. And my first thought was "Fuck, I am so fat." My belly was really distended, and I could feel it. I could feel my belly sticking out. And I remember thinking, "I'm just fat. I'm fat. I got so fat." And then that just sort of broke the dam of "How the fuck did I end up like this?" Truly, that was my first thought. How did I end up like this? And then the next thought was, "This was not the plan for you. This is not what your parents had hoped for you. This is not what you had hoped for you. You need to make some changes pronto." That was it. "You're fucked up. You need to fix this." I'd heard this voice before, but it was always a quiet voice. I'd heard it since high school, since the first time I threw up in my parents' bar sink—"This is not good for you." But I just ignored it until finally the quiet voice got real loud and finally it just fucking won.

You have to understand. I grew up with wealthy and loving parents who gave me everything. I'd never done for myself. I didn't earn shit. My roommate was a guy who didn't grow up with as much. Grew up a Jewish kid in the South, and he fucking earned everything. He had his own TV show, and I had zero. I was like, "This is just not how this is supposed to work out. I can't be done at thirty-three." But I had no career. I had no girl. I had nothing.

A couple months before that, I'd run into a friend I drank with, and he looked fantastic. I said, "What's been going on? Haven't seen you in a while." And he goes, "Yeah, I quit drinking like six months ago. I started going to this mutual support group." And I thought about him and I thought, "I'm going to call." So I just fucking picked up the phone and called 411. Got the group's number, called, said, "Here's where I live. Where's the nearest meeting?" There was one in an hour, down the street. So I went, and then I went to an audition, because I was acting at that time. I had the shakes, and I was totally ill-prepared and whatever, but I didn't care because I'd been to a meeting.

I go to this audition, and I was terrible. An ant crawled out onto my arm. My shirt was dirty, and it had been on the floor, and there was an ant in it, and it crawled out from underneath my arm during the audition. It was bad. The casting lady said, "Why would you come in if that's how you were going to read? That was terrible." I know, lady. But I just quit drinking today and I don't know what I'm doing.

That was the last time I ever worried about it. After that, it was just "Go to the group," and I went to the group. "Listen to the people at the group and do what they say." Literally. It was not my decision. I didn't feel like I was controlling things. Every time I'd quit before, I would just say, "I'm going to quit. I'm not drinking." Just willpower, and that never worked. I had no tools. I had no guidance. I had zero spirituality, no faith in anything. I'd go to a meeting, but I never actually made a commitment. I'd go to one and then I'd not go back. I'd go to another one and then never go back. They would bring up God or some foreign concept, and I would just find some reason to leave. "I don't believe in that. I'll just go to the gym."

But this time, I had no willpower. I just went to the recovery meetings, and very quickly I lost the desire to drink. At first I didn't want to drink because I was so fucking sick, liver all swollen and everything. Then there was a period of "What am I going to do with my time? How am I going to socialize?" But I didn't want to go back to drinking, to all of that, to being completely and utterly fucking miserable and hopeless, to feeling like it would be okay if I was hit by a bus. I was thinking, "There has to be something better than this, because I would like to die, and I'm not a guy that likes to die." I'm chemically fortunate. My body chemistry allows me to be happy most of the time, my outlook is generally pretty sunny. But there was nothing happy, nothing sunny then. My mom drank until she died, and I'm thinking, "That's where I'm going. The path has been set. I'm going to be that person, miserable and unable to find happiness. She was a good mom, a nice person. But she was miserable. So I guess I'm going to be shitty and miserable and unhappy for the rest of my life." And I was like, "That just can't be. There has got to be some other answer."

I got rescued from oblivion. I had all of these warnings, and none of them meant anything to me, not even when I had a doctor tell me my liver was going, and all that shit. I had all those warnings, and none of that did it. I just woke up one shitty morning and I'm like, "Okay. Enough is enough. I have another purpose." I finally listened to that voice saying, "You need to get your shit together." And I wouldn't have anything I have now otherwise. There's no way I'd have my wife or my kids or anything. None of that.

About three months after I started going to that mutual support group, I met God. I was at home visiting my father and stepmother and I was out for a run, and all I can say is, for the first time, I really got the whole God thing. There was a voice, for lack of a better description, that said, "I've always been here." And then I'm like, "Right. Of course." And all I had to do was turn it over—turn over my life, my will. Just "You show me the fucking way and I'll do whatever you say." And I did. I went to meetings, but I didn't share for the whole first year. I just listened, because I like to talk. I like to tell my story because it's far more interesting than yours. So I shut up and I listened.

I called my dad and said, "You have to stop funding my excess. You have to stop. It's not your fault, but I can't fucking tie my shoes. When I call you and I'm in tears about some bullshit, you got to go tough. You got to fucking bring the hammer, dude. I have no job skills, I have no life, I have nothing going on. I've never built or made anything for myself. I've never earned anything myself. I've got just nothing, and I've got to get something on my own."

Then I called the IRS and I said, "I owe you an enormous amount of money and I don't have it. And we have to figure something out." And they're like, "All right. Well, let's get on a plan."

And then I called a friend and I said, "I need to get a job. Any job." He said, "They're hiring at this show." So I went down there, and within a couple of weeks I got this job. I said to my roommate, "Look, I don't have money to pay rent right now. But I'll be, for lack of a better word, the houseboy. I'll clean and I'll make food and I'll bake and I'll do shit until I have money, and then I'll pay you. If you're cool with that." And he was fine with it. I worked on his show a couple of times in cameos to earn a day's pay and then paid him.

I'd done everything my way the whole time and it wasn't working, so I was going to do it like everybody else does. Get a fucking job. Earn my own money. I just went for it. It was time. A year later I got an HBO special, and it sort of just went up from there, so I knew right away. The change was so quick, once I finally connected to the spiritual side of things, that I was like, "Oh, *this* is what's been missing the whole time."

I think about that friend of mine, the one I ran into who'd turned his life around. He didn't say anything to me about going into recovery or about not drinking, nothing. But he looked great, and happy, and I wanted that. So I try to be that guy for other people. I try and live an exemplary life and hope they ask me about it.

When I quit drinking, I gave up an entire social life. I gave up the only way that I knew how to meet women. I gave all that shit up. At first I was bound and determined to keep my old friends. I wanted my *lifestyle,* I just wasn't going to drink. And then I'd hang out with my old friends and think, "Fuck, I hate this."

I think the thing I was most afraid of, the thing that made me want to hang on to those people, was sex and women, because it never worked any other way. That was the only thing I was really scared of, that I wasn't going to be able to meet anybody. What are sober women going to be like? I don't want to meet someone that doesn't want to fuck. And we'll have to do it sober. That's gonna be weird. Like how is that going to be?

I think my drinking and my fucking was always a search for the spiritual. I was always looking for something, but I was doing it my way. And eventually I said, "I want to do it your way, because I don't fucking know what to do anymore. I don't know how to do it. I'm going to die if I keep trying to do it my way." But I was always trying to find something. We had no religion growing up, and I wanted it. I wanted some kind of god. But I was such a cynic that I didn't want to have anything to do with churches. I just had this built-in cynicism about spirituality, and yet all I wanted was to be spiritually sound. So I think God just came and said, "Get off your futon and go to a recovery meeting. Meet me there. Go find me. I'm here, but you have to go find me." That's the best way I could describe it.

I'm not looking for that giant rush anymore. I had it. I had the dramatic moments, those TV moments, and they were all short-term things. Now I want sustainability. I want something that lasts. That's what God is. That's what life is. It's not heroin. It's not *whoosh*. *Whoosh* doesn't last.

MARIE MORNING-GLORY

❧

I heard Marie speak at a recovery mutual support group two years ago, and I never forgot the grace and clarity she shared that morning. I called her and asked if she would be willing to tell her story in this book. She said yes, and we met at the recovery house she runs with her husband called Miracle House, established in 1995 to provide an environment for living without the use of alcohol or drugs.

I'm Native American, a full-blooded Apache, and I grew up on the reservation in Arizona. Once, when I was about ten years old, I was standing on top of a mountain and I looked down and saw a light in this old burned-down church. I'd never seen a light there before, so I walked down the trail to the church. I went inside, and there was a man sitting in a broken pew. I walked up to him and I said, "Are you okay?"

He stood up, and he was a Franciscan priest, in the robes. I looked up at him and I asked him again, "Are you okay?" And he said, "Oh, yes, Marie." I said, "How do you know my name?" He didn't answer. He said, "You're going to be okay. Don't worry, you're going to be fine." And he put his hand on my shoulder and he walked with me outside.

I went to my church on the reservation and I told the priest that there was a priest at this old church, all by himself, and he needed a place to stay. We went over to the old church, and by now it was dark. Nobody was there.

The priest called me a liar. He said I was making it up to get attention. I said, "No, look, he walked me outside and you can see the footprints." He said, "Those are from somebody else that you brought down here."

He didn't believe me, so I just shrugged it off. I forgot it, and I didn't remember it until years and years later.

I went to prison at the age of thirteen and a half for killing my cousin. My grandma had made some liquor, and I drank two jars and I don't remember what happened, but my cousin was dead and I was covered with blood. I was tried and convicted and I went to prison. I was just a little girl, and they did things to me in prison that little girls don't deserve.

I had an aunt there who got me a job in the kitchen, and I drank vanilla extract every day because it has alcohol in it. I drank shoe polish. We had a smoke, tea with crushed aspirins in it. I just wanted oblivion, because I had killed my cousin in a blackout.

The good things I got out of prison were my GED and a certificate that said I was a cosmetologist. The bad thing was, I left with the disease of alcoholism even worse in me. I left with the attitude of "I'm going to show them." I hated everyone and I was going to get even with everybody. I got home and I just started partying.

One night I met the man who was going to take me away from everything, and he turned out to be an alcoholic like me but even worse, and a heroin addict. He was a musician, and he did take me places and show me things, but once I got pregnant, I didn't go anywhere. I stayed at home and I drank at home.

We were married for twelve years, and we had four boys. We fought all the time. I had this ugly mouth. I wanted to get back at everybody through him, and he put me in the hospital more than once. The last time he sent me to the hospital, they put me in traction for the broken bones and they wired my broken jaw. I figured I couldn't do this anymore. When I got out of the hospital I found a new place to live. On December the fourth, we moved in and I put my kids to bed and I told them that I loved them. I always told my kids that I loved them and I always hugged them, because I never got that from my mother. I never had a mother's love, as far back as I can remember.

Anyway, I put my kids to bed and I drank my bottle, because that's what I did to put myself to sleep every night. My husband came during the night and burned down my house. I lost my four boys, and I nearly died. I wound up in a catatonic state and I was in the hospital about eleven months. The first thought that came into my mind was, I didn't get to kiss them good-bye.

I decided this was God's punishment for what I did when I was thirteen and a half, killing my cousin. That's the thought I had, and I said, "I don't want God. I hate God." I hated everybody. Mostly I hated myself.

I got a job at the VA hospital, and that's where I met my second husband. First I thought he was a cuckoo bird. He said he recognized me, that he knew me. He didn't know me, he was just talking. A week later I moved in with him. We got married on Thanksgiving and I always said, "I married a turkey, a real turkey." He was sober and he went to recovery meetings. I thought, "Well, I'll go to those meetings too." I'd stick my head in the door and then go to the bar across the street.

By this time I was working at Lockheed, and I had a good job paying fifteen dollars an hour. Back in the late seventies that was a lot of money. My apartment was only $235 a month. My husband wasn't working and I was supporting him, so I moved out.

I went to a lot of places, those last five years of drinking. I went to a lot of places, not just in my head, but physically I went places that I thought I would never go. One night I smoked a supercool, at Griffith Park. That's where we'd go on Thursday nights, after we got paid. I smoked the supercool, and next thing I know, I'm in a van, naked. I banged on the door and I asked the guy, "Hey, what happened to me?" He said, "Don't worry, baby, nobody touched you. You took all your clothes off and got on the merry-go-round. It took eight guys to get you off that horse."

I got tired of that and I quit. I was sober nineteen months. In April 1982, I called my aunt in Arizona to wish her a happy Easter. She said, "How come you didn't come to your mother's burial?" That's how I found out my mother had died. My family back in Arizona had my number and my address, but they never told me.

I said to my aunt, "I didn't know my mom was dead." She said, "Well, you should have been here," and I said, "I didn't know." I hung up the phone and sat there for the rest of the day.

A few days later I was driving around Burbank like a nut. I had this beer between my legs and I am drinking it and then I just threw it out the window. I didn't know it was going to be my last drink, but a voice inside my head told me, "You don't have to do this anymore." It was a soft voice, it didn't sound like me. It was the same voice I heard in that church when I was ten years old. It was that same voice telling me, "You're going to be okay." My life was going to be good. I drove home and I went to sleep.

That week went by, and Mother's Day was coming up. That Friday I was on my way to a retreat up in Redlands, and I was like a caged lion. This priest said to me, "What's wrong, Marie?" and I said, "Nothing," thinking I'm tough.

He said again, "What's wrong, Marie?" and his voice was so soft. I started to cry and I told him, "I don't know." So I told him my whole story. I told him about my kids dying and how I missed them every day. I went home after the retreat, and the next morning I went to wash my face. That's when I saw the reflection of God looking back at me through my eyes.

I never looked into my eyes, ever, but that day I caught my eyes in the mirror and I said, "You are an alcoholic." I called that priest, and the priest suggested I go to a meeting. I went. I did what he said and raised my hand and now I'm here.

I don't believe in what I used to believe in. I don't believe in my thinking anymore, for one thing. My thinking gets me in trouble.

A few years ago, when I was seventeen years sober, I was at a women's retreat, one I was running, and I was supposed to speak at another women's retreat too, but I was contemplating suicide. My head was telling me, "You don't deserve a good life. You don't deserve the good things that you have, because your kids aren't with you. Why should you enjoy life when your kids didn't get to enjoy it?"

Saturday morning when I woke up at the first retreat, I went into the dining room to get my coffee, and my sponsor, Angie, was there. She said, "Sit here and talk to me." I looked at her and I said, "Just because you have a lot of time, that doesn't mean that you can order me around." I went and got my coffee and I was walking out and Angie said, "Marie, you want to talk to me. Let's go to my room." I said, "No, I don't want to talk to you," and I went back to my room. When I'd finished blow-drying my hair, I came out and Angie was sitting out there at my door. She said, "Why do you want to kill yourself?"

I started crying. I told her, "I don't want to speak tomorrow. How can I give the Sunday morning feature speech when I want to die? I don't deserve the life I'm living. I need to be with my kids."

She said, "What makes you think that if you kill yourself you're going to be with your kids?" And I started crying even more.

She handed me a hankie and she said, "I am going to help you embrace that pain. We are going to do it together. I'm telling you, you're going to be okay. This morning I saw in you what I saw in myself almost twenty years ago, when I had eighteen years of sobriety. I got through it with help, and now I'm helping you, and you'll be able help someone else when you see it in that person."

I believe God does for me what I can't do for myself.

What I'm afraid of is disappointing myself, because I've done that all my life. I've been a loser all my life before I came into recovery. My mother always told me, "You're worthless, you're good for nothing, you'll never amount to anything." I was at Portland, Oregon, speaking in front of thirty-eight hundred women. I got up there and the first thing that came into my mind was "What if my mama could see me now?"

I did become something. First I became an alcoholic, and then I became someone who helps other alcoholics. And that's what keeps me going. That day in Portland, women were coming up to me and hugging me and thanking me for my honesty and for my courage. I kept thinking, "You don't know how I feel inside. I don't have courage." I don't. Sometimes I give in to my thinking. I am human. I make mistakes. I am guilty of a lot of things. But I don't drink, no matter what. That's the bottom line.

Miracle House is a place for addicts and alcoholics to live without drugs or alcohol. People come here from prison, from the street, from other recovery places. I work with the women and they call me Mom. That feels good. It feels really good.

I encourage them to do things that are positive. I encourage them to do it for themselves, not for their kids, even though it's good for the kids too. Their recovery has to belong to them. I encourage them to learn to be good mothers and good daughters and good friends. I tell them that life is too short. I've seen a lot of women die, I've seen a lot of men die from this disease, and it's not a pretty sight.

After I heard that voice—"You don't have to do this anymore"—and I threw out that beer, I didn't know what I was going to do. I was so empty. I was so empty inside that I felt hollow. I was walking around, and I had to touch my heart a couple of times to see if it was beating. I didn't know what was happening to me. All I knew was, there was something I was looking for. I was looking for love, and like the song says, I was looking in all the wrong places, but love was always here. I didn't know that.

I know it now. Love is here with my husband, and we've been together for over twenty-six years now. Love is here with the women at Miracle House, with people in recovery all over the world. I live a good life, and that's something beyond my wildest drunken dreams.

THOMAS HENDERSON

❧

Thomas has had a colorful life. From 1975 to 1979, he was an outstanding linebacker for the Dallas Cowboys, as well known for his outlandish behavior as for his incredible speed. (He wasn't nicknamed "Hollywood" for nothing.) By 1980, his football career was over and his life rapidly spiraled out of control. He says, "Hollywood died on November 8, 1983," after an arrest on drug and assault charges. He maintained his sobriety through two years in prison, and became a dynamic, inspiring, in-your-face motivational speaker. In 2000 he won the Texas state lottery and used part of the money to start East Side Youth Services and Street Outreach to help at-risk youth in his hometown, Austin, Texas.

Telling his story, Thomas talks about crying—not just in sorrow but also in gratitude. In his interview and all the others, any time two alcoholics connect in recovery, there's an enormous sense of gratitude for the way our lives have been transformed.

I saw too much as a kid. I'm a little bit of everybody I've ever met, and I met too many people. I'm talking about pimps, whores, drug addicts, and heroin users, and that messed me up. But I have to tell you something. For twenty-something years now, my pain has been the greatest library of sharing. I can go a lot of places deep down in my pain, in my shame, and find something that's useful to another human being. That's the gift of this thing I'm in, this recovery.

In 1983 I was in Long Beach, California, living near the beach. I was working for a construction company as a foreman, and basically my days were spent working six to seven hours a day and the rest of the time I was smoking crack. I had lost my football career because of a neck injury, so I ended up in California. I was going to be an actor. I had O. J. Simpson's agent, and I was his only other African-American client. I went on some interviews with network television executives, and my agent got me into this acting school. But I was smoking crack at such a crazy rate that I couldn't even make appointments. I couldn't go to auditions and I couldn't show up for the classes because I was too busy smoking crack.

At the end of October, I called the Long Beach Fire Department because I was convinced there was a bomb under my car. Here comes three fire trucks, the bomb squad, and twenty police officers to my address. I'm lying on the ground, on top of all these rocks and the asphalt, and I'm showing this fireman and this cop this wire under my Mercedes-Benz, and it *has* to be a bomb. And of course, it wasn't true. I was completely paranoid. Mentally, physically, and spiritually . . . I was completely annihilated by crack cocaine.

You know, different drugs have their different tortures, but the torture of crack cocaine use is extreme paranoia. You think people are looking for you, out to get you. You think there's somebody in the bushes and the weeds, on the roof and in the light sockets. It took me a long time to get this, but now I know who was really looking for me when I was torturing myself smoking crack, and that was death. Death was looking for me, and death just about found me. Everything I was doing every minute was killing me. That's the crack experience. You think there's somebody out there looking for you. You peep out the window, you think you see a shadow, and you wonder, "Who is that?" It's death.

A week after the bomb squad came, there was a scene that had happened with me a hundred times, at least, with a gal or a couple of gals— some cocaine and some sex. That's pretty much all I thought it was. I was accused of threatening these two girls, waving a gun at them, but that's not what I saw then. In that cocaine culture, the deal was, I bring the cocaine and the girls bring the sex. Who says no?

Of course, that's not the culture everywhere, not in the moral society, not in the normal world. But in the dope-addict world, that *is* normal, unfortunately.

People who have been to jail know that you'd rather be in prison than city jail, but there I was, in city jail. I'm sick and I'm humiliated. I remember standing over a sink, which is right over the toilet. The sink is dirty, the toilet is dirty, the mirror is dirty, everything around me is dirty . . . and I catch a glimpse of my soul. I'm looking in this mirror and I think, "Who the fuck are you, and what have you done with Thomas?" I saw a stranger that I didn't recognize, the stranger I had become.

But then I got out on bail and I was back at that Long Beach apartment. I had a check, so the first thing I did, I cashed it and I went and bought more cocaine. This is *after* being arrested. This is *after* putting up my Super Bowl ring for my bond. This is *after* looking into that mirror.

The next few days are a blur of crack annihilation. I mean just sucking it into my lungs, brain, and spirit, all day and all night. Then a friend came to the house. I think he heard about my arrest on the news. Anyway, he showed up, and he literally had to pry the pipe out of my hand. He got me in his car and took me out to Orange, California, to the care unit.

I don't recall much about that day. I know I didn't have insurance. I had no money by then. But this little doctor took me in, Dr. Joseph Pursch. After my assessment, he looked directly at me and said the words I needed to hear: "Thomas Henderson, anything is possible if you stay sober. Nothing is possible if you ever drink or drug again."

It was that statement that gave me a choice. That was my moment of clarity. I understood what I had to do, I understood what my choices were, and thus began my introduction to treatment and to halfway houses and all of that.

I'm in the treatment facility a week, two weeks, and I'm still trying to get my hands around this depression, this suicidal thinking, this constant noise of "I can't do this. I can't fix this. What are people thinking about me?" in my head. I can't defend myself. How do you explain "Oh, I've been doing this for years. You know, I give girls coke for sexual favors. It was just a misunderstanding." How does that make it any better?

So I did not know how I was going to handle this. I was thirty years old, I'd never been arrested for anything, never even been accused of any kind of sexual force. Yeah, I did a lot of drugs, I got in trouble with coaches, but this stuff . . . I'm just thinking, "That isn't Thomas." Well, then . . . who did it? And where did Thomas go?

I'm going through the program and I'm saying, "Oh, this is finally good." But in my soul, I'm not feeling so good. I'm feeling hopelessness and helplessness. My esteem is negative-something. My self-worth is nowhere. All those things that keep you sane and alive—I was on empty. I had nothing.

And then I got a phone call. The lady says, "A Roger Staubach called you and wants you to call him back." Well, Roger Staubach was the Cowboys' quarterback when I was linebacker, but that's not even . . . Roger Staubach is a Naval Academy guy, Heisman Trophy winner, Super Bowl champion, All-Pro, a man of God, a man of family, just one of the greatest human beings that I have ever known, as a man and as a friend.

I pick up the phone but I can't call Roger. I just didn't know how to speak to him, so I didn't call him that day. But I finally did call, and he picked up the phone. If there's a moment when I thought maybe I was going to make it, that maybe it was going to be okay, that was the moment.

The conversation basically goes like this. "Hey Thomas, how are you doing?"

"Well, not so good."

And he said, "Thomas, let me tell you something. You are a good guy. You have always been a good guy."

I have to tell you, at that point I did not know I was a good guy. But if Roger Staubach says that I'm a good guy . . . at that moment in time, that was enough for me. I was at zero and he says, "You're a good guy." I've got nothing and he gives me something to build on.

Roger says, "Now, you've screwed up. Get it straight. Pay your dues. Get the consequences out of the way. But you are a good guy."

And that saved my life.

When I was a boy, we were poor. Not starving, but poor. I'd come home from school or get up in the morning and go to have some cereal, and there'd be no milk. Or we'd have milk but no cereal. I'd take walks and talk to God. I'd scream at God, crying. That little boy said, "I am going to do better than this. When I grow up, I'm going to college. I'm going to make lots of money and we're going to have lots of goddamn milk in the house, and we're going to have bread, and peanut butter and jelly, and eggs. And I'm going to take care of Mom and I'm going to buy her a car. I'll buy her *two* cars." I would tell God, "I do not want to live like this my whole life."

The strength of that eleven-year-old boy . . . That's who got me through high school and college. That's who got me to the Super Bowl and the World Championship, that determined little boy. That day in jail, when I looked in the mirror, I couldn't see him, and I didn't know if I'd ever see him again. That scared me so much I never forgot it. Then when Roger told me, "You are a good guy"—I went back to that spirit. I found that strong little boy in my darkest times.

I ended up getting twenty-eight months in prison, on a plea bargain. I mean I was guilty, so why torture anybody else, making them testify and so on. So I'm at Chino Prison, and my brother—I have a younger brother on my DNA-donor side. That's what I call the man who caused my life, my DNA donor, because he was no father to me. He had other children, and one of those boys was Allen, a great kid, good-looking kid. Allen was a correctional officer in New York, and he got busted for bringing in substances to work, and he goes home and he hangs himself.

I'm in prison, just about to start my sentence. I get this phone call and it's my Aunt Gwen, and she says, "Allen's dead. He committed suicide."

I hang up the phone and I start to walk down the corridor back to my cell, and this corridor looks like it's half a mile long, just concrete corridor as far as you could see. I take a few steps and then I fall out on the floor in this primal, guttural crying. I don't think I'd cried since I was twelve years old, about anything. *Anything*. And I know I'd never cried like this in my life. The sounds that are coming out of me—barking, screaming, wailing. The guards come and I am spasmatic, crying, crying, *crying*. It felt like an hour, but it was probably only two or three minutes of just the hardest crying you can imagine.

When I got back to my cell, my eyes are swollen, I'm clearing my throat, snot everywhere. Another moment of clarity. I wasn't crying for Allen. Not *just* him. I was crying for him, and for me, and for all the men who are hurting so bad and can't ask for help. I give talks to men's groups and I say, "There'll be times when you need to cry and you don't cry. But you can't keep that up forever. Sometimes you just *got* to cry, about all of it. All of us."

When I'm with somebody who's struggling, I tell them the truth. I have this ability to be honest about my own stuff, and I'm really not judgmental. But I have to speak the truth. I've had some success with people by just telling the truth. I think they know it *is* the truth, and not a lot of people are willing to tell the truth. That's the whole magic of this thing, that some of us get to live—live and tell the truth.

I read recently somewhere that 2 percent of recovering people get twenty years. And there goes the 1 percent at thirty years. It's not even measurable at forty. You go to enough recovery meetings and you'll run into that one guy in there with forty years.

So I'm really still humble in this. In November 1983, Roger Staubach said I was a good guy, and I've been trying to live up to that ever since. I'm still working on keeping the spirit of that eleven-year-old boy who didn't have any milk. 'Cause I don't want to see that *other* guy in the mirror again. Not ever.

MIKE EARLY

❧

Mike is the chief operating officer of the Caron Treatment Centers, and he's worked in the recovery field for thirty-five years—almost as long as he's been sober. Mike is the one who persuaded me to work with Caron, hitting the road to talk about addiction issues as public policy. He's one of the people we all look up to in the field, and a tremendous example of someone who's made recovery his life's work. He spent a while in the limbo of "not drinking but not sober," and his family was instrumental in getting him out of that limbo.

I fought getting sober because I was afraid of losing my best friend, the one that wiped out all my insecurities, all my problems. My fear was that I wouldn't be able to face life without that escape. Even after I was in recovery—and I use that term loosely—I wasn't willing to face my problems. When I finally recognized that things just weren't working my way, that's when I started the whole process of *learning how*.

Not long after that moment, I went to a dance and I thought, "I can start drinking again or I can learn how to dance, because I'm sick of not having any fun." I'd danced when I was drunk but after I got sober, I never danced because I was afraid of everybody laughing about how stupid I looked. So I asked a girl to dance and once we got out on the floor, I looked around to see how I was doing. I found out nobody was looking at me. Nobody cared how I danced. I was not the center of the universe. I started laughing because I realized how arrogant I'd been, how much I'd missed out on because I was so worried about how I'd look dancing. I remember that vividly.

When I was eighteen, I bought a brand-new 1969 Mustang. I bought it on a Saturday afternoon and two weeks later to the hour, at five o'clock in the afternoon, I totaled it. I was with a friend, both of us drunk, and I was driving 115 miles an hour when I tried to take a 25-mile-an-hour curve. Flipped over, bounced on both sides, ended up 180 feet away—just a total mess. The buddy who was with me ended up in the hospital, but I was just beaten up a little bit.

The cop on the scene comes to the hospital and tells me what he can get me for—drunk driving, minor in possession, all these things. Then he said, "But I think you've learned your lesson. You know you were driving too fast. You know you've got to stop your drinking." I told him, "I'll never do this again."

Two weeks after that, I woke up drunk, in my mother's car, sliding sideways down the hill on the wrong side of the road.

By the time I was nineteen, I was in the National Guard Reserve. This was the height of Vietnam and the whole reason I was in the Reserve was to avoid the draft, avoid being sent to Vietnam. I went to Fort Leonard Wood for basic training, and after that I manipulated my way into a five-day pass to go to Arizona, where my parents were vacationing. When I got to Phoenix, I decided to extend my five-day pass by two days, so by the time I got on the plane back, I was already AWOL. I got drunk as a skunk on the plane and when we landed in Kansas City, I decided to throw a party for myself and whoever was in the airport lounge.

I remember leaving the airport to catch a cab to the bus depot so I can get to Fort Leonard Wood, and then I wake up in a jail cell. After about half an hour, a guy with "MP" on his helmet walks by and I ask him where I am. He says, "Leonard Wood Penitentiary." I didn't know how I ended up there. It could be because I was AWOL, or it could be because I'd knocked off the cabbie. I was sitting in this cell thinking, "Drinking has gotten me into trouble." There's a Southern Baptist kid from Alabama in the cell next to me, and he and I got into Bible study in a serious way. I was praying like a son of a gun for a way out of this mess. I was afraid they were going to activate me and ship me to Vietnam. I was there three days before I found out what happened. I'd passed out in the cab so the cabdriver took me to the police station. The police searched me and found my military stuff and called Fort Leonard Wood. The MPs came and picked me up and took me to the base.

A few weeks later, I had my twentieth birthday and my buddies said, "We'll take you out for your birthday on one condition, that you don't drink." I said, "That's fine." We're at the pizza joint and I said, "A couple of beers with a pizza, that isn't going to hurt, right?" And they said, "No, a couple of beers is fine." So I drank a couple of beers. Then I got up to go to the men's room and I didn't come back. I went over to the other side of the bar where they couldn't see me, and I started drinking shots and hanging around with whoever was sitting at the bar. I ended up back at Fort Leonard Wood, in jail for being drunk and disorderly. The next morning, I met with the company commander and he said, "You can't handle your liquor, can you, son?" And I said, "No."

Did that stop me drinking? No.

I made it back home, without being sent to Vietnam, and I continued drinking and drugging on a daily basis, not sober a single day. I was working for my dad's plumbing and heating business, and one particular Thursday morning I left for work and I got as far as this little saloon. I drank all day and all night. Friday morning I headed out for work and I stopped at the same bar. I sent somebody in to get my paycheck.

Fast-forward to Sunday night. I started off at this big party on Sunday afternoon, about four or five buddies with me, and by Sunday night they were gone. I was sitting at a bar next to these close personal friends I'd met that night. I went to buy them a round and I had only ten bucks left in my wallet. I hadn't paid for groceries, I hadn't made my car payment, I hadn't paid rent, and my paycheck's all gone.

I came to the conclusion that I didn't get paid enough. I started bitching to these good friends of mine about the fact that my old man didn't recognize what a great plumbing-heating-insulation specialist I was, and how I should be running the company. I go on and on and on, bitching about my old man. They said, "Don't tell us, talk to the boss. Call your old man." So that's what I did. I walked over to the payphone and called him and told him to stick this job up his ass. He said, "Well, suit yourself," and hung up. I walked back to the bar and these good friends were gone.

I'm sitting there by myself with no money, no place to go, no job. I remembered being in jail at Fort Leonard Wood. I remembered my company commander who said, "You can't handle your liquor," the cop that said, "You can't drink and drive, you can't handle it." Those thoughts were constantly running through my brain.

I ended up walking out of there and going to my dad's sponsor's house. I pounded on his door and he opened it up and we sat and talked. He said, "Sleep it off and come and see me in the afternoon." Next afternoon, he had a meeting set up with me and my dad and him. They say, "We think you need to take treatment." I said, "Well, I could go watch the meetings." They said, "You need to get into treatment." I said, "I'll go to meetings." They said, "No, you *need* to go into treatment."

I went in on a twenty-one-day program, and I completed it in seven weeks. Fought it throughout, did everything I could to rewrite the program. Fought it for two years. Did *not* want to be a member of this community. Did not like the people, did not like the concept of being sober the rest of my life. But I didn't drink and I didn't drug. I went to lots of meetings and I tried to figure a way around the program.

A little over two years after I completed treatment, I walked into my parents' home, and my sister and a couple of my brothers were there. I got into an argument with one of my brothers and I punched him. He ran out of the house, got onto his bicycle, took off. That's when my sister said, "You used to be a drunken son of a bitch and now you're just a son of a bitch."

That was like a slap in the face. I knew she was right. I'm supposedly in this program of recovery, and I was the same angry, unhappy, depressed individual I had been when I was drinking and drugging.

That night, I spent a couple of hours chasing down my brother. When I finally did catch him, I told him I needed to talk to him, and he said, "The only thing I have to say to you is what a prick you are." I said, "Okay. I'm willing to listen to whatever you say." He sat down and for about two hours he told me what he thought of me. I sat and listened for the first time in my life. I finally listened.

Willingness . . . in a word, that's it. I became willing to look at alternative ways of dealing with my addiction and dealing with myself. I became willing to look at this program, willing to follow it. I had been in it but I hadn't been willing to participate. I hadn't been willing to be a part of it, to live it. The only thing I was willing to do was change it to my liking.

I recall that moment at my parents' house often. Almost forty years ago, and I remember it like a slap. When my sister said, "You were a drunken SOB, and now you're just an SOB"—yeah, I remember that.

I start my day thinking about the twenty-four hours ahead. I watch for selfishness, dishonesty, a self-seeking mood. On a daily basis, as long as I'm practicing my program, my recovery, it takes me back to that moment because I don't ever want to let go. I don't ever want to end up there again.

DENNY SEIWELL

When Denny was five years old, his dad put him behind a set of drums. From that minute, Denny knew exactly what he was supposed to do with his life. He's been a professional drummer since he was barely a teenager, and he's played with some of the best and the best-known acts in the world: Paul Mc-Cartney, Joe Cocker, The Who, Astrud Gilberto, Deniece Williams, and too many others to list. He's still in demand for studio and film score work, and he's a beloved teacher to aspiring musicians and recovering addicts alike. I heard him speak at a recovery meeting and was taken with the role resentment played in his addiction. Resentment is such a poisonous emotion, one of the major stumbling blocks to recovery. The irony is, recovery is the best way to get rid of resentment—just let it go.

"Mas Que Nada" is a Brazilian song that's intricate, free, moving, rhythmic, and just happy. It makes you feel good when you hear it. And to this day, I play in jazz clubs and when somebody knows that song and plays it, my heart sings. It's the deal. And that's my recovery.

I had one big problem in life, and I had no way of dealing with that problem other than pouring alcohol on it. The more alcohol I poured on it, the more the problem grew, and then I had more problems. Pretty soon it just fed into every area of my life. A typical day: I'd roll a joint in the morning, get high, get a burrito from Poquito Mas, have some beers in the morning, and at noon I'd start drinking Stolis. I just didn't want to feel what I was feeling. What I was feeling was resentment, because there was this big piece of work that I did years ago that I didn't get paid for, and I couldn't live with that. It should have taken care of my wife and me financially for the rest of our lives, and it just didn't happen that way. The only way I knew how to deal with that was to slam booze. Those days were just really horrible.

I lived in a nice but small one-bedroom apartment near Universal Studios. It was close enough to a bar that I could drive home one-eyed, which I did most of the time. My life was just sad. My wife was working, and all I could do was drink. I did get some calls to play music. I used to work for a buddy of mine up in the hills, doing TV commercials. He'd call me, and a couple of times a week I'd go up and record a commercial. Before they were done with me, I'd leave. I could not wait to get back to that bar. That was the only thing that gave me any solace. They knew where I was. They'd call the bar and they'd say, "Is Denny there?"

"Yeah. He just walked in."

"Well, tell him to get back here. We're not done with him yet." That was what my life was like. I was just medicating myself to the extreme.

Alcohol really had me by the short hairs. I tried acupuncture. I tried hypnosis. I tried everything that I could try. My wife is French, I lived in France, I drank like a gentleman for a couple of years. But when this problem hit me, it took away all of the pleasure that alcohol afforded me. The only way I could live my life was to just overdo everything, drugs, alcohol, anything and everything. And I was just miserable.

One day, I'm playing golf at Lakeside, I'm having a nice day, and all of a sudden my chest started hurting and the pressure wouldn't let up. I finished the round and then went into the clubhouse with the guys. I had a beer and the pressure went away. But then the next day I got up to move some drums around and go to work, and the chest pains came back. I saw my doctor, and he put me in the hospital. They did an emergency angioplasty on me. I died on the table that day. I was awake but really drugged up on the anesthesia, and I heard the nurse say, "He's going, he's going—he's gone."

The doctors never told me how long I was gone, but they paddled me back and they fixed me. That was probably one of the first moments of clarity that I had, because I realized that this was brought on by my drinking and my drug use. But on the way home from the hospital, I drank again.

The docs told me that a glass of white wine was good for circulation. So for the next five years, I drank like that. One toke off the joint, no cocaine, and one glass of white wine a day—that was my program.

The thing is, it wasn't scary when I died. I don't like to talk about it much because it was so beautiful. I realize there are a lot of people out there who want to take their lives, and I don't believe it's the same for everybody. But when I died, it just got really beautiful. I now know there's life after life. It got all warm and fuzzy and really, really nice. I think that was the day that I got my first little dose of spirituality.

The moment the resentment lifted . . . you know when that was? There's an old friend who allowed me to talk about my resentment and then he just said, "This is no longer yours. I want you to give this to your idea of a higher power. Let him deal with it, because if you touch it, you're going to screw it up. Every time you think about how you're going to deal with this, bless it and dismiss it and keep your hands off of it. Let the big guy take care of it for a while and see what happens." It took a little time, but when I learned how to do that, a miraculous thought came to me. I thought, "It's gone." And it was. That resentment was just gone.

Of course, it comes back now and then, but it's not the same. It doesn't take over like it did before. I know that I'm done with it because I'm just so happy to get back to the music and my life. That resentment kept me from enjoying my work as a drummer for quite a while. I'd gone so far off the track. That was the beauty of it, just getting back to what I started out to be. When I was nine years old, I knew I was destined to be a drummer. Forget school, I'm going to be a drummer. Get out of my way, here I come. That was my mind-set. It wasn't ego. It was just . . . I had the gift, and I knew it.

That was the easy part. Then at some point I realized I was off track. It's like taking a boat to Catalina, and you're three degrees off course, and all of a sudden you turn up in Brazil. That's what happened with me. Being able to get back on course and get my life back on track again was of the utmost importance.

God is everything and everywhere. I don't just have a picture of God. I talk to God anytime I want. He is in me; not out there somewhere amorphously in the sky. He's in everything I see.

MICHAEL GLASSER

Some people are born entrepreneurs, and Michael is one of those people. Early in his life, his business plan involved drugs and money laundering, but since then he's become a legitimate—and very successful—businessman, as one of the founders of the popular jeans company 7 For All Mankind. Michael's also one of my neighbors and a good friend. I'm grateful that he's agreed to share his story here, since his moment is one of the most dramatic I've ever heard.

The week before I got sober, I was living in a friend's apartment in North Hollywood. I weighed 240 pounds, I was unbathed and unshaved, and I had not brushed my teeth in six weeks. My life consisted of going to the market every morning and buying a quart bottle of Popov vodka and going back to my friend's apartment and taking the cold empty bottle of Stolichnaya out of the freezer and putting the Popov vodka into it, because I wanted to make sure that if somebody did come in they would think I had money. But no one ever came over. It was a lonely existence. My friend had a gun collection and I used to always tell him, "If I have enough balls, I am going to kill myself to get out of this misery." He kind of believed me.

One day he got some bootleg pills—I do not know what they were to this day—and he left them around. That next day, I get my normal Popov vodka and start taking those pills. I took twenty-five of whatever they were. When my roommate called, no one answered, and he called 911. The paramedics came over and found me dead.

Before they shocked me back, I was in the tunnel. I was halfway down to that white light. I remember the voice, it was so calming and so nice. It was seductive, but I remember saying, "No, I don't want to go." I didn't want to go wherever that voice was taking me, which was dead. So I made a conscious decision not to go.

I woke up in the ICU after a couple of days with all kinds of tubes in me, and I tried to figure out what had happened. I put some things together and then the thought came into my head, "There's something wrong with me and I need help." That was the very first time in my life that I looked at myself and not anybody else, that I recognized that there was something really wrong with me. So there was a significant change in my psyche.

I think I hit such an emotional rock bottom that, for the first time, I was egoless. Any agenda that I had was done. I had destroyed everything, and all that was left was the shell. And I had to own it for the first time.

From that moment on, I have been sober. I'll never forget that moment. I know I'm a very lucky guy.

I was twenty-seven days sober and I'd just come back from a recovery meeting and I was standing at my brother's house. There was a knock on the door, and FBI and DEA agents came in to arrest me for dealing and money laundering. I was in Terminal Island for two days. It was just before July Fourth, and they were about to shut down for the long weekend. I was able to make one phone call. I called my dad and he said, "The only thing that would prevent you from getting out is if you have any other warrants." Well, I had warrants because I never paid parking tickets and I never paid moving violations. But I got out. The guy at Terminal said, "The goddamn computer is down today so we're just going to let you out."

There's something that happens in recovery. You start to notice all these coincidences. You look and you say, "God really was carrying me on this thing. I know it now." You start seeing the connections. And that's what happened to me my first year and a half in recovery. It was a well-publicized case, and everybody in the program knew I was going to prison. They would get me through the day. I remember a couple of guys would go running with me and we'd run until my head stopped talking. We were going fourteen, sixteen, eighteen, twenty miles a day, all that period of time that I was facing this day of reckoning.

A friend in recovery told me to go and tell the U.S. attorney everything I'd done. I said, "No, I'm not going to do it." He said, "You got to do it." He made me go down, and I told the U.S. attorney that I started it. I dealt drugs, I was a high-volume money launderer, I put the whole drug ring together. He looked at me like I was crazy and he said, "Listen, we'll call you back by the weekend." When he called he said, "We checked it out and I can't believe it. No one has ever come to us and told us this much about themselves. Good for you. But you're going to prison, no matter what."

I just kept putting one foot in front of the other. I went to my recovery meetings. I went down to my probation officer. I went through this thing clean, not worrying and not lying.

The day of reckoning came, when all of us who'd been arrested, all twenty-five of us, were sentenced. It was August 1, 1983. A Monday at one thirty in the afternoon. I remember I had to wear a suit. There must have been fifty or seventy-five people from recovery down there, and many of them had written letters to the judge on my behalf. The courtroom was filled up with them, and reporters. The reporters were there because the case was such a huge case and so well publicized. It was the biggest money-laundering case in the history of California up until that time.

I sat there and I listened to the sentencing, and the judge was handing out sentences of fifteen years, twenty years, twenty-five years, fifteen years, and so on. Until that moment, I never got the depth of what I did. I never thought it was such a big deal. It never got to me inside until that day, when I started to hear everything. All the disasters that were happening around me, and the anguish and the pain that existed because of what I'd done. It dropped into my soul, and I realized what a despicable thing I had done.

Then they came to me. The U.S. attorney got up and he said, "Michael was trying to change his life before he got caught. He was cleaning himself up. He was in drug rehab, and he did not know we were investigating him." The place was stunned. Then I stand up before the judge, and the judge says, "This is the hardest sentence I have to hand out." I almost died. I don't know what he means, "the hardest sentence," after I've listened to all these people going away for a minimum of fifteen years. He said, "One of the reasons it's so hard is because I truly believe you're trying to change your life. Second, I've never read letters like the ones written for you since I have been a judge." Finally he said, "You have five years probation and a fine of five thousand dollars." This noise went through the place. I was stunned. All the reporters were stunned.

When we walked outside the courtroom, all the people in recovery stood around in a circle saying the Lord's Prayer. And Judy Ann, who was my counselor in rehab, nudged me and said to me, "Michael, never forget where that verdict came from. The judge just said the words, but that was God's verdict." That's when I found God. That was my moment of clarity.

That moment has never left me. I think about it every day. I will never forget how I felt. The power, the process that goes into that power, is amazing. All I did to get that was show up for the first time in my life. I was honest, I conducted myself in a humble manner. That moment has lived with me and has allowed me to take it into my life and look at a series of things and say, "Thank you!"

I wish I could sit here and tell you that Michael became perfect from that moment on, but that was not the case. How I have changed is that I know—down in the core of me—everything will be taken care of by a power that is far greater than me, that wants me to be happy and joyous and free. I know that if I live in absolute truth, then everything is always going to be okay. I can hear that voice, not my screaming voice but that quiet voice that always tells me the truth when I choose to listen to it.

I'd like to get to a place where I think about the pain my actions are going to cause others. That's another level of consciousness that I'm just really getting into after twenty-five years. It's not always about "I'll do this and pay the price." It's "That's going to pain that person, so I do not really want to do that." That's a shift.

When I was younger, I was afraid of girls; I was afraid that I wouldn't be good enough, I wouldn't know what to say, they wouldn't like me. And that fear continued with me a long time. When I was drunk and on drugs, that fear left me. In sobriety, what I've realized is that the mere fact that I own that fear—that makes it less powerful. I can work on it.

Does that fear still live inside of me? Yes. Is it something I spend a lot of time thinking about? No, but it is there. I know it. Because of this fear of rejection, I rejected myself. In high school I was captain of the basketball team, and maybe if I'd asked out one of the cheerleaders, she might have said yes, but I took myself out of the game. I didn't want somebody to say no to me.

I try to teach my son better. I say to him, "When you look across the room, there is nothing like the magic of seeing a special person for the first time. And if you don't try to introduce yourself, that's sad. It's sad for you. It might even be sad for that other person. It could have been a great connection. And the more you're able to do that, the more you're able to be at rest with yourself. Be vulnerable. Ask."

I'm sixty-five years old. I still worry about the girl, my actions toward the girl, and what will happen if I go over to her. But I know I have to try. I have to ask. The more you ask, the more you're going to receive and the more you're going to learn.

BOB TIMMONS

Anyone who spent any time at all in L.A.'s recovery community over the last twenty years knows who Bob Timmons was. Multiplatinum musician or teenage gangbanger, it didn't matter—if you were trying to get clean, Bob T. would do anything for you. That included calling you on your bullshit, as often as needed. Somehow he managed to do it with compassion.

Bob could connect with such a wide range of people because he himself had such a wide-ranging journey. His schizophrenic mother tried to kill him; he was put in foster care and ended up on the streets; he became a violent felon, in and out of prison. Yet by the time he turned forty, his entire life was devoted to helping others. Thirty years ago, he cofounded Impact House, a pioneering treatment center that combines support, confrontation, accountability, and counseling to help people deal with their addictions. He helped establish several other treatment and outreach organizations, including MusiCares, a part of the National Academy of Recording Arts and Sciences that helps musicians struggling with addiction.

In 2006 Bob was diagnosed with emphysema, and when I interviewed him he was showing the effects of the disease—yet that only made him more gentle, more empathetic, more willing to reach out. He died in spring 2008, and at his memorial service, everyone who spoke said they'd felt like they were Bob's best friend.

Somebody said to me the other day, "We thought you were done teaching, but you're teaching the greatest lesson you could ever give us, how to have courage and not be afraid of death." Because they're going through all of this with me, every inch of it. Good, bad, I don't hide it. And of course I am scared. For a couple of weeks now I haven't been able to sleep because in my little-boy mind, if I go to sleep, I won't wake up. Fighting sleep, like the boogeyman is going to get me. I'm starting to share all that with everybody because I'm human. But the Buddhism thing keeps me together, you know. They say death is just going into the next room. They celebrate death. And they say if you look any fear in the face, particularly fear of death, then it flees like an unwanted stranger. I've gone to the last chapter, where you're back to being a child. I'm like an eight-year-old, full of joy—and none of this makes sense.

I've got two choices. I can feel sorry for myself and be angry because I'm dying. Or I can let that go. And so I choose to be happy. Fifteen, twenty times a day, I just say, "Thank you." Laughing out loud—"Thank you."

I never would've come into the rooms unless Danny Trajo brought me. We were cellmates at San Quentin, and we got along really great because we both were full of rage and anger.

One time in a meeting, someone asked if we'd ever been in knife fights in prison, and both of us laughed. They said, "What's funny?" and we said, at the same time, "We'd never fight with a knife, that's too plain." Danny said, "Pipes, lead pipes, because—well, picture a watermelon being dropped from a height. That's much more dramatic than just a nice clean little knife wound." So both of us were soldiers for a well-known white-supremacy group. The way it worked, a Mexican guy could approach a black guy without him knowing it's a hit. It's not about let's have lunch or play dominoes. So this is the kind of person I am, and the kind of person Danny is.

Then Danny got out, and three, four years later, I paroled. He'd given me his mother's number, because where does any forty-year-old self-respecting convict stay? With Mom, of course. So I call his mother's house and she says, "He doesn't live here anymore," and gives me his number. I call and he says, "Where are you staying?" I said, "Well, I don't know—all I got is the Department of Corrections start-up kit," which is a bad suit and two hundred dollars. He said, "Well, hey, I'll come and get you and you stay with me for a couple of days until you figure out what you're going to do." So he comes and picks me up, takes me to the extra bedroom at his house.

I'd like to get a little money, you know, so I say, "Let's go do some things," and he tells me he's not doing that anymore because he's in a group, and he wants to take me to a meeting. I had no conception at all of what he's talking about. I mean I went there to do crime with him. But nothing else is going on, and I'm in between careers, so to speak, so I go to the meeting.

Danny, during the break, waves me over to where he's talking with this redheaded guy and he says, "Bob, this is Eddie. He's your recovery sponsor," and Eddie says, "Good to meet you, I'm glad to be your sponsor." This is contrary to the steps—you're supposed to choose your own sponsor—but Danny knew in his wisdom—well, he knew a couple of things. First, he had to pass me on right away like a hot potato because we had too much history together. And second, if I didn't get a sponsor and jump into recovery, I wasn't going to stay long enough to do anything. Eddie was my sponsor until the day he died, with forty-seven years sober. He was my main man, and Danny kind of made that marriage.

Anyway, I was about six months sober and clean, and Eddie asked me what my sobriety day was. I said, "I don't know," and he said, "Well, you're supposed to know," and I said, "Well, I didn't know I was going to stay in the program." I thought about it, I remembered it was cold and rainy, sometime in the fall, so I said, "Let's say October—October the sixteenth, because that's my birthday." So I decided I was going to stay.

And what happened then was, all the planets aligned or something. I knew I couldn't just take up space anymore. I'm not here and I'm not alive just to take up space and be selfish. I had a purpose, and I knew that my purpose was to save people. I didn't know exactly what that meant. Maybe I could have been a doctor or something, but it soon became clear to me that I'd be saving people through the program.

Looking back on it, I can see little things—I always knew, wherever I was, I wasn't where I was *supposed* to be. I mean my mother tried to kill me when I was nine years old. She's still alive, been locked up ever since—she's eighty-eight years old, in the state hospital, the *Cuckoo's Nest* place, paranoid schizophrenic. So then I stayed with my dad until I was twelve, and then—well, I used to say I ran away, but you know how the longer you're in recovery, the more willing you are to be gentle with yourself? So now I say, I left home because the streets were safer than my own home.

And then in prison, in my organization, a lot of the guys have tattoos all over their face, on their hands—I can show you pictures—and I got tattoos across my chest, my body, but for some reason I never got anything on my face or my hands, any place that really marks you, sets you apart for good. I said, "I'm not going to do that," even though everybody else was.

When I decided that I was going to stay in recovery, at that moment I knew I had a purpose. No burning bushes, but with every ounce of my being, I knew my life wasn't just a random thing. I was where I was supposed to be, ready to do what I was supposed to do. And it felt . . . it felt joyful.

Well, pretty soon I realized that there are no treatment centers for all these people trying to get clean in these horrible environments. I got a house—I had no money, but I found a house and got the owners to rent me the house for a dollar a year because it was abandoned and I promised to clean it up. And then I started bringing in people, and that became Impact House. I was seven months sober when I started Impact House. No education, a convict. But it was so clear. The need was there, and that was what I was supposed to do. So I did it. No education, no history of sobriety, no credentials at all—it shouldn't have worked, but it did. And the only reason it did was, I took myself out of it. I trusted that whatever it was that had brought me to that point wouldn't just dump me there and leave.

See, I know it's not me. I'm just the vehicle. I didn't get myself here. I got invited here. And if you're here for a purpose, you're not invested in win-lose. And so Impact House worked, for a lot of people. We brought a lot of people into sobriety, and it didn't matter where they came from, a million-dollar mansion or a flophouse on skid row.

One thing about working with stars, actors or rockers or whatever, it gives you resources, that network. You come across a kid, ten, ten and a half years old, selling heroin and coke at the park. The eighteen-year-olds give it to these kids because if they get busted it's just juvenile time, and the kid gets all his drugs for free, so he's got more track marks than a fifty-year-old junkie. I'm thinking of one little guy, brought to me by a cop. I don't know how many times they make the movie but it's always the same movie. Father died of a heroin overdose, two brothers killed in street-gang stuff, one other brother doing life, all the generations of the gang world, and that's who you are and that's what you do.

But this kid could make it, and I figure, well, you know, if he's going to have a chance, he has to be mentored. And so maybe I have a friend of mine take him to a Lakers game and they gave him a jersey that all of them signed, and it happened to be Shaq's jersey.

Or say the kid's interested in guitar. So he takes guitar lessons twice a week from West L.A. Music, and then whoever's in town, they might set up some tutoring. Santana's done some tutoring, and he's the same story, come up from selling Chiclets down the corner in Tijuana.

Or one of the guys I know, he set up a little business that made him a billionaire and he's currently the president of the USC alumni association. He can help get a kid a tutor, get his grades up, talk to the president about getting him into USC.

And then you know what? Whatever that kid does in life, he's going to be giving it back. An attorney advocating for poor people, an environmentalist . . . hell, even if he's just a guy who does a good job, he's a good friend, a good father, a good husband, he's giving it back.

So there's a lot of stories like that, and I appreciate that network. But the fact is—this is something Mick Jagger told me, it was 1991 in Paris, they'd just started a tour. We have lunch in his room, and I say, "Why do you keep touring? Obviously, you don't need any more money, you're getting older, what's enough?" And he didn't even hesitate, he said, "Bob, if I stop touring, I'll die. That's my narcotic, that's where I get my energy from. One thing I know, with all my wealth, my name, the fucking Stones— all of that combined won't give me one more day here on earth. And I'm afraid when the music stops, so will I." Now a lot of those guys live it—look at B. B. King. He comes out, they sit him on the stool, and he plays better than most of the kids half his age. But Jagger's the only one I've heard put words to it.

No matter what—no matter how many people we helped, how wonderful we are, what we got in the bank, who we know or don't know—none of that gets us two more hours here on earth. That's the equalizer.

You know, I do have sadness about not being here physically. I'm just not ready yet . . . just being a little selfish because I enjoy the same pleasures we all still get here. This a wonderful place.

A couple of days ago, a little baby hummingbird was down out of the nest, and I go get something to keep it warm and feed it, so focused on this little bird. And I just think about me in prison, and here I am. I got to laugh, this is what gets me off now, taking care of this little bird.

That's what I have to teach now, what it is to be human, what it is to face death. I'd like to be here, turning seventy or seventy-five, but at least I got some teaching left to do for a while yet. So when somebody asks "Why do you think this happened? Why did you get your moment?" I think it's because I was supposed to be a teacher.

RUDY TOMJANOVICH

❧

Rudy started his career in professional basketball in 1970 as the San Diego Rockets' first-round draft pick. The team relocated to Houston the following year, and Rudy played or coached for the Rockets for another thirty-two years. When he ended his playing days, in 1981, he was the team's third-leading scorer and a five-time NBA All-Star. After a few years as a scout and assistant coach, he took over as head coach for the 1992–93 season. The next two seasons, they won back-to-back championships. He's also a tough guy; I still remember seeing the punch Rudy took during an on-court brawl in December 1977. The blow shattered bones in his jaw and skull and nearly killed him, but five months later, he was back on the court. I had no idea he'd ever had substance abuse problems until a mutual friend suggested that I talk to Rudy for this book. When I met him, I realized he truly is a gentle giant: so humble, so soft-spoken, so nice. Like so many people I've talked to, it amazed me to hear that he could have achieved so much while dealing with such deep emotional torment—and that all those achievements didn't do a damn thing to relieve the torment.

I have a belief that—and I wish it wasn't this way—but in the formula of life, to get to the good stuff like recovery and the joy it brings, it just seems that you have to hit bottom and go through pain to get there. And the bottom can be financial ruin, the loss of a relationship, health problems, or any number of things that hurt like hell. Mine was emotional; I became depressed. I had a wonderful supportive wife, I had good money coming in, I had stature in the community, I was a local hero for helping bring two championships to our city, but I was not happy. I had no appreciation for the good things that were happening in my life, and really good things were happening. My owner liked the job I was doing and gave me a substantial raise without me asking for it, and we had found a great piece of property in one of the best neighborhoods in Houston. It didn't make sense that I had this black cloud hanging over me.

I thought I was living a pretty healthy life. I was eating an 80 percent vegetarian diet, I was working out a couple times a week—but I was drinking and smoking cigarettes. I truly believed I had the drinking part of my life under control. I had guidelines that I usually followed. In basketball we have a term for when a team plays on consecutive days, called "back-to-backs." Well, I felt that as a drinker, my back-to-back days were over. I was in my forties now, so I'd space out my drinking.

This strategy didn't always work; there were times when one of these spaced-out occasions turned into a couple-day spree. But the way I looked at it, it really wasn't a back-to-back, because I hadn't gone to sleep. That was my alcologic. I'd also think that if I said I was going out for a "light night" of drinking, I'd keep it under control. The way I would ask a drinking buddy to go out for one of these episodes would be, "Let's go out for a light night, you know, just a couple of beers." Usually it wasn't a couple of beers; usually things got out of hand. I wouldn't see my buddy for a long stretch of time. I wasn't a blackout drinker, I usually remembered everything that happened, but I'd wonder if I had said or done something to offend him. When I finally did see him, I'd ask if there was anything I needed to apologize for, and the response I usually got was something like "Oh no. I've been recovering from that 'light night' we had. Please don't call me if you really want to go out drinking!"

I had been drinking since the age of fifteen, and not once in my thirty-three-year drinking career did I ever feel I had a drinking problem. I thought I drank normally. In fact, I thought I was a hell of a good drinker. One of the guys I worked with used to joke, "I'll put our staff up against any staff in the league in a drinking contest and I have no doubt that we will win." This would always get a big laugh because I was the only one on the staff that drank. I have to admit I took pride in my drinking ability.

My drinking wasn't all fun and games. The late hours and not coming home at all really upset my wife, Sofia. She'd tell me that my drinking was not normal, that I needed to get some help. I didn't believe that was the case. I thought she was just saying things that wives say to husbands to keep them around the house more. It never registered that it might be true. I don't know how she tolerated me.

I also had some run-ins with the law. I was pulled over several times. On one occasion I was taken down to the police station where I blew into their Breathalyzer and passed. I had just had a few, so I was pretty confident that I'd be okay. The next time I was stopped, I had had a lot more than a few, but I decided that I didn't need to blow because I was stopped under false pretenses. It was 2 A.M. and I saw the police lights flashing ahead, where they'd stopped several motorists. I slowed down and cautiously drove through the area when all of a sudden I was pulled over too. I asked the officer why he'd pulled me over and he said, "You were speeding." I thought that was ridiculous, and I felt I hadn't broken the law, so there was no reason for me to blow. He said, "If you don't, you'll spend the night in jail." Part of me felt this was an injustice and the other part of me felt I probably wouldn't pass the Breathalyzer . . . so I spent a night in jail.

The media got wind of it and were waiting for me when I was released. The networks broke into the afternoon programming to show me coming out of jail. It was on the front page of the newspaper. I was very embarrassed and humiliated. When I got home, I gave Sofia and my two teenage daughters my side of story, again emphasizing how I was wronged. But when my son came home from elementary school and I saw the sad look in his eyes, I broke down. I could imagine what his classmates were saying about me and how that made him feel. I got down on my knees to hug him and I promised I'd never embarrass him like that again. I never was more sincere about something in my life.

Well, the videotape of my arrest was reviewed by the district attorney and he couldn't find anything in my behavior or speech that would prove that I was over the legal limit. The charges were dropped. For about a month, I was very careful not to drink and drive—but not long after, I was back to driving after I'd had several drinks. It didn't occur to me to think about the possibility of not drinking anymore.

Two years later, on a day when I had not had a drink for a couple days, I passed out while driving my car and I wound up on the median of a road. I was taken to a hospital where they ran tests, but they couldn't find anything that would explain what happened. A team of doctors conferred and suggested that I should change my lifestyle. My drinking reputation was well known. I said, "I haven't had a drink in a couple days!" I felt insulted that they'd even suggest that possibility.

My close friend Robert came to see me. He was like a brother to me and I knew he loved me. He told me that the gossip around town was that I was drunk when I had the accident. He also told me that one of the doctors that examined me, who he was close to, was extremely concerned about my health. Robert said, "Rudy, go ahead and do the rehab thing and get healthy. I care about you, and you know I'd never recommend anything that wouldn't be good for you."

I was really upset. I couldn't believe that people were spreading untrue rumors about me and that the doctors didn't believe me—but I reluctantly decided to go to rehab. I wasn't going to quit drinking forever. Why would I do that? I didn't have a drinking problem, so quitting was out of the question. The main reason I was going was to shut up these people who were nagging me about my lifestyle. I really didn't know what rehab was all about. My impression was it was sort of like a health spa. I wouldn't drink alcohol for a while and get healthy, and then I'd drink like those strange people who can leave a half a bottle on the table.

I went to a treatment center in Tucson, Arizona. For the first couple days I had no idea what was going on there. When they were talking about the "Big Book" I thought they were talking about the Bible. I didn't notice the steps to recovery that were printed on posters that hung in every room at the center. They were there, but I did not see them. I was very nervous and uncomfortable and constantly having to deal with the voice inside my head telling me how terrible I was for winding up here, so I had a hard time concentrating on anything.

They put me on some medications for the first couple of days that helped calm me and slow my mind down, and I was able to grasp some of the things they were explaining in the various lectures that the staff gave. I began to get a whole different picture about alcoholism. When they talked about the feeling of not being good enough and feeling not a part of and different from other people, I was shocked. I thought that those feelings only applied to me and that everyone else felt okay. One of the biggest reasons that I drank was to get rid of these feelings. As far back as I can remember, I have always had this menacing voice inside my head that was constantly criticizing me and comparing me to other people, with me always coming out on the short end. I believed this voice and had very low self-esteem. I lived in constant fear that people would find out that I wasn't the person I was portraying. When I wasn't drinking and I encountered people who I felt could see through my facade, which was just about everyone, I was a bundle of nerves and anxiety. When I drank alcohol, something amazing happened. Instead of the voice telling me negative and degrading things, it changed to a voice that said things like "Man, you are so suave" and "You sure are smart" and "You are a fantastic dancer." When alcohol was in my system, it changed me from Howdy Doody into James Dean. I believed I had found the magic elixir. Alcohol was my best friend. It could mask the way I was really feeling about myself.

It worked for me for a long time. As the years, then decades passed, the benefits diminished. The euphoria I felt in the first several years rarely reappeared; it became more like a boring numbness. It wasn't much fun, but it was still better than listening to the demeaning voice. After years of drinking alcohol, which is a depressant, I became a depressed person. Now, at this treatment center, I was hearing that if I applied myself to this program, I could find a solution to my problem. They said I could become happy, joyous, and free. I wanted it. I couldn't believe that I had changed my mind and now wanted to stop drinking.

They slowly decreased the dosage of medication they were giving me, and it had an effect on me. I could not fall asleep. As I lay in bed hoping to drift off, the voice in my head was having a field day. After not sleeping one second for two nights, I tried again a third night, and I almost fell asleep. My body was exhausted, but the voice was getting louder and meaner. When I did drift off, it jarred me awake, saying, "I'm not finished with you, you piece of crap. Look what you've done with your life!"

I went to the nurse on night duty and told her my problem. She gave me an audiotape player that played wind chimes. It was supposed to soothe and relax me, but I was so on edge the tinkling sounds of the chimes sounded like thunder. I turned it off and tried to sleep in silence, but I could actually hear my teeth. When they touched, it sounded like metal doors slamming. I was in agony.

I went back to the nurse and asked her if I could call my doctor back in Houston. It was 3 A.M. when he picked up the phone. I told him I truly wanted to get sober but I couldn't sleep, could he please ask them to give me some sleeping medication so I could get some rest so I could apply myself to this program? They gave me a Benadryl. I couldn't believe it. Benadryl never had any effect on me. It was like taking an M&M.

Another sleepless night. I was so fatigued I could barely walk. The other patients at the center would ask me if I slept and I would just shake my head no. My mind was so confused, if you asked me my name, I am not sure I could give you the correct answer. I had a hard time putting a sentence together. I was really embarrassed about my mental and physical state. I am six foot eight, a big man, and I was trying to isolate and stay away from the others at the center, which was impossible because it was such a small place.

After I didn't sleep for a fourth night, at six in the morning I was waiting for the director of the rehab. I told him what a great place he had, that I wanted to get sober, but that I hadn't slept in four nights. I asked him for some sleeping medication. To my utter disappointment, he told me that wasn't possible. He said that when he went through treatment, he did not sleep for seven nights. He told me that I was suffering from a spiritual malady, and what would really help me was getting a connection with God. I had no idea of what he was talking about. What did God have to do with me sleeping and getting sober? I had no knowledge of the steps of recovery yet. He told me he was giving a lecture on spirituality that morning and I needed to be there. I left his office completely defeated.

I dragged myself back to my room and lay in the bed staring at the Serenity Prayer on the wall. I repeated it twenty times, but it did nothing for me because I didn't understand it. My mind was racing. The voice told me, "Let's get out of here. There is a bar about a mile away. Get some alcohol and drink yourself to sleep." The treatment center was located in the desert and there were rattlesnakes, coyotes, tarantulas, and scorpions out there. I was a city boy, and that idea did not sound too good. Then the voice said, "See that window over there? If you jump through it and hurt yourself, they will come and medicate you." I couldn't believe the thoughts I was having. Was I losing my sanity? A wave of desperation went through my body, I collapsed into a heap on the floor of my room. I cried out, "Hell isn't someplace you go after you die. This is hell!"

Because I did not know what else to do, I took the director's advice and desperately pleaded with God. "I cannot do it any longer. I give up. Please help me." Suddenly something happened. The giant boulder I was carrying around rolled off my shoulders. The heavy burden was gone. I could physically feel it. My tired legs felt light. My mind stopped racing and I began to feel calm. All the worries and troubles that I had felt the past four days drifted away. They were no longer mine, I had turned them over to God. I did not realize it at the time, but I had done my first Third Step. My fatigue was gone. I went through all the activities of that day with a rejuvenated attitude, then willingly interacted with the other patients after our classes. That night as I retired to my bed, I reviewed the events of the day and was amazed at the drastic changes I felt, both physically and mentally, when I surrendered to God. I was so grateful, and I slept.

I felt I was very fortunate to have such a profound experience with my first surrender. When I got out of the rehab and integrated into the recovery community, I found that was not the case with most of the recovering alcoholics that I was getting to know. Their spiritual experience was more of the gradual, educational type. When I was asked to share in recovery support groups, I would often tell this story with great pride because it was so dramatic. There was a problem: I was only talking about the surrender I once made, but in reality I had gradually picked up the reins again and was trying to run the show. The program I was running, Rudy's program, was one recovery meeting a week, a session with a therapist, and church on Sunday. The meeting was not even a real meeting—it was set up by some caring alcoholics who knew I was worried about losing my anonymity in regular meetings.

After half a year the therapist told me he couldn't reach me so he turned me over to his assistant, who urged me to go to regular meetings. I wasn't drinking, and I didn't see why I had to rush into these things. After running my half-assed program for eleven months, I got the revelation that I had this alcohol problem figured out, there was no way in the world I would ever drink again. A week later, for no reason at all, after ordering fruit juice all day, at three in the morning, I ordered a beer. I was a month away from my one year chip and I drank. The next day I was filled with remorse. I couldn't believe what was happening. I went running to the therapist. She told me I had to get rid of my terminal uniqueness and do the program like everyone else. She introduced me to a young alcoholic who took me to my first real recovery meeting.

I've learned that I have to repeatedly surrender, sometimes several times a day. My concept of God has drastically changed from one that is critical and punishing to one that loves me to the limit even when I am doing wrong. How much I want to experience His love is up to me. His love is always there. I'm the one who puts up the obstacles, and by surrendering they are taken away.

RICHARD LEWIS

❧

Richard Lewis has been sober fourteen years and is one of the stars of the HBO series Curb Your Enthusiasm. *He's currently on the endless* Misery Loves Company *tour, and he's also the author of* The Other Great Depression: How I'm Overcoming, on a Daily Basis, At Least a Million Addictions and Dysfunctions and Finding a Spiritual (Sometimes) Life. *I met Richard on the set of* Drunks, *a movie I tried to put together as a producer. (The movie ended up being made without me, but the director was kind enough to offer me a role as a bartender.) Since then, Richard and I have remained friends and compadres, trudging this road of happy destiny. The subtitle of his book tells you a lot about Richard's intensity and energy, and reading this story, you get an even better sense of what he's like to be around. He's a great example of someone who relishes his creativity and his insanity, even in sobriety. For the interview, he asked me to meet him at one of his old Hollywood hangouts.*

I wanted to come to the Four Seasons because I used to drink here so much. I used to drink everywhere so much, but I used to go to all the hotels and drink, and all the guys who were there then are still there. So, what I did after I sobered up, I came back to all my old haunts and I ordered like seven or eight Diet Cokes and lined them up like shots. I wanted to prove to everybody that I was sober. I needed to do that because I was carried out of a lot of places. I'd come out of the bathroom looking like a mental case and they'd say, "Listen, drive carefully."

I've been sober fourteen years now, and it's been a pleasure to come back to the places where I was unconscious, thinking I was doing a lot of great work. Talk about the epiphany . . . you go onstage and you think, "Gee, I've been working for five days on this concept," and you remember one line. All of a sudden you work three hours sober and you just tear the roof off because you remember a hundred and fifty thousand things because you're clear-headed. I did so much more work in an hour sober than I did in five days when I was drunk preparing. I was killing myself. I thought I was relaxed.

I go to a lot of sober musicians' first concerts, and they're monsters. Of course they're nervous. Why would they not be? When I went onstage sober the first time, after all those years of drinking, I did not have a great set. I had a Letterman show six days after I got sober, and I was not going to cancel. I did not have a great show. He said to me, "Are you okay?" And for the first time I was okay because I was sober, but I was off that night because I was shaking like a leaf and I thought I'd never get it back again. I immediately asked my publicist to book me again. Immediately. They booked me six weeks later and I had one of the greatest shows in my life, because I needed it. But I'm still proud of that show, six days sober, clueless, frightened out of my mind.

I was addicted to everything: food, sugar, women, sex. Actually, my therapist called me an affection junkie. I needed people to love me. I didn't have that woman to have sex; I wanted her to love me, which is a big difference, a huge difference. I used to do dates from hell until I realized that *I* was the date from hell, which opened up a Pandora's box, a billion hours of material, when I finally took responsibility for my actions. I met a woman a few years ago, who's a friend of mine now. I went out with her for four months while I was drinking and I had no recollection of her being a girlfriend.

It reminded me of looking in the mirror many times. I'd be bloated and I've ruined the evening and it was humiliating, and I'd say "Look at you . . . you've got to stop this." But I had no intention of stopping. I had no tools for stopping. I just knew that my life was going to end eventually. I would lose my career, lose all my money, and lose the woman I was with. I didn't go as far as I'd be homeless, but I was heading that way. So I decided, I am not going to kill myself with a disease that I could stop. I asked people to help me, and I got help.

I knew I was a drunk, but I couldn't imagine not drinking. My therapist—I was a therapy junkie for almost three decades—told me later, she knew I was a drunk but she also knew I had to realize that myself. She asked me to keep a diary, and one good thing about this therapist was, she's the most ethical person I've known in the profession, and I trusted her. I'd been seeing this therapist for thirteen years and she said, "When you're drinking, just write down what you're thinking about and how much you're drinking. Just make a chart, and then when you come see me next week, we can look at the chart and see what happened." And I stopped seeing her. I had told her literally everything that made me feel uncomfortable, all of my secrets, and they weren't brutal, like "I dressed up like a pirate" or "I tried to rape someone." It wasn't that kind of stuff, but it was stuff that made me feel like crap. When she told me to keep a diary, I stopped calling her, after thirteen years.

That was the first real crack, the first real epiphany for me. It wasn't the headlines in the entertainment section—"Lewis Carried Out of a Restaurant" or "Lewis Breaks into Springsteen's Band Meeting" or whatever. It was when I stopped therapy completely after almost thirty years. See, I had always told her the truth. When I was afraid to go in there and say, "I had four bottles of Cristal before the *Today* show," when I would have been ashamed and humiliated to own up to that—that was when I knew I was a drunk. I knew it, but I kept drinking for another year and a half because I got angry when I realized that I had to stop. I could not imagine living my life without a drink.

I remember going to the doctor—I was scratching a lot—and he says, "You have a yeast infection." What does that mean? I don't have a vagina. He said, "No, it's in your penis. I'm going to give you a pill called Flagyl. It means you can't drink for five days." I was about to go to New York and I remember thinking, "My whole trip is ruined. Here I am, going to do the Letterman show and I can't drink on the plane." It took away the joy. There was no joy in being one of the most frequent guests of all time on Letterman. All I thought was "I'm going to be in Manhattan and I won't be able to go to the St. Regis, to one of the most beautiful bars, the King Cole Bar, because I can't drink. Why even go? Why even get on the plane? Why do I have a career when I can't drink?"

I didn't see it then, how insane that was. I drank more and I got more into drugs than ever before because I knew I had to get sober or I was going to lose everything, and I did not want to get sober. I decided I was going to go out on my own terms, even if it meant dying.

This is how much I didn't care about my life. I ate at a restaurant in Hollywood and I got hepatitis A food poisoning and I had to go to the hospital. This was when I was shooting *Robin Hood: Men in Tights,* and I had one scene left. I never felt sicker in my life. I go to my doctor and I am jaundiced and he puts me right into the hospital. Mel Brooks calls me and he wants me to finish this last scene. Mel kept calling me in my room at the hospital. He says, "Richard, we're going to pick you up on a stretcher, we're going to paint you so you're not yellow, and we're going to lean you up against the wall. You'll do your two lines and we'll take you right back on a stretcher." I hung up on him. He knows I have hepatitis and a fever of 106, and I think I'm dying. The phone kept ringing and ringing. "We're going to paint you! You're going to look so pretty!" So finally I told my doctor, "You got to call Mel and say I can't do it," so they did the scene without me. Mel Brooks is one of the funniest human beings of all time and I'd work on anything with him as long as I didn't have hepatitis.

Anyway, when I got out of the hospital my doctor, my internist of twenty-five years, he says I can't drink for a year. If I drink, it could kill me. Because of the damage to my liver, I could develop hepatitis C. I was scared, so I went cold turkey. I was not going to go to any alcohol programs or any kind of self-help group. I didn't need that. So after about six months into not drinking, I go to get my teeth cleaned. This is the longest I've gone without drinking for about twenty years. I told the guy who was cleaning my teeth, "I'm healthy now so don't worry, but six months ago I got hepatitis A." We're talking about it and I said, "Yeah, I can't even have a glass of wine for a year." He said, "Really? My doctor said six months." I said, "You're kidding." No, he'd had hepatitis A, and his doctor had said after six months you could do whatever you want.

He could have been wrong, he could have lied, it could have been whatever it was, but I risked my life on a dental hygienist over my physician of twenty-five years. I went to a bar and I drank. That's how important alcohol was. It was absolutely the center of my universe.

When I think about that now, it makes me sad. It makes me sad that I was willing to die for a drink.

One day I called a guy I knew who used to do a lot of drugs who had stopped. A famous guy, a real great musician. He lived about five minutes from my house and he zoomed over and—you have to understand, my house is like a museum. I have all these photographs of people I admire, including a lot of musicians, Jimi Hendrix, Miles Davis. So this guy came over and he said, "This is it for you, man. You got to get help, because it is over."

Later that day he faxed me a note, which I still have. He said, "You know, I'm looking around the walls of your house. You really have wonderful rock art, and most of these people inspired me." And the line that stuck out was this: "A lot of those guys left the set too soon. You don't have to." It was true. All the people that I have photographs of, 80 percent of them checked out in their twenties or thirties. I mean, Lenny Bruce was forty when he died. That was it, that was the night.

I called someone else I knew who had a lot of sobriety and I said, "You have to help me." He came over in ten minutes. He says, "I'm here to help you. Here's the deal. You're going to listen to everything I tell you. If you take a Benadryl after I tell you not to, I am putting you away. I don't care what gigs you have, I don't care if you're in a show. I do not care." And this guy was historically one of the most legendary junkies that ever lived. He had seven years sobriety at that point, and now he's got over twenty years. For almost a year, all I did was listen to this guy and do everything imaginable to learn about sobriety.

I'm not articulate enough to describe exactly what the psychic change was. All I can say is, for the first time there was something other than me that mattered. Because up until that point, practically everything I did, even on my nice days, everything always seemed to filter back to Richard. Richard did that, Richard helped him, Richard did this, Richard had intercourse with that famous woman. Whatever it was, even if I worked for charities or whatever, it had nothing to do with anything other than myself. A spiritual entity came to me that day. It almost felt like there was an aura around me, and that aura was not me anymore, and that aura was something that was going to keep me alive as long as I believed in it.

I am not a perfect person now. I am not a perfect husband, I am not a perfect friend, and no one is. But I didn't get sober to remain full of all the defects and all the fears and phobias that pushed me into covering up all this shit with booze and drugs. I do work on it, but some things are always there. There are certain things I am going to blurt out because I'm crazy. Not crazy in a way that I have to be sent away, but crazy as in, I'm an alcoholic and I think a lot of bad thoughts and I also want to screw up. I have to really fight hard not to shoot myself in the foot, and it's murder. It's murder, and the best way I've learned how to not do that is to help other people.

One of the things that has kept me sober when I'm on the road is when I get a phone call from some musician or some comedian who's in trouble. I drop everything. Nothing is more important than talking to this person. Then if you see them later and they say, "Boy, thanks for talking to me"—I mean, what's better than that? I could go to that refrigerator ten feet away and have a couple of vodkas, or I could have the luxury of helping that person.

It is such a gift to be able to help somebody other than just yourself. People did this for me. Who knows what was going on in their life, and they dropped everything. "Stop the presses, someone's going to die!" That's how I live my life now, and it's the greatest thing that has ever happened to me.

When things aren't going my way, I think really long and hard, "What is my part in the deal?" Never did that before. Never cared about it. I was the victim, so I'd just give in to that dark side of every addict that goes "You deserved it" or "You're going to screw it up so just go ahead and get it over with." A few years after I got married, I was unhappy and I remember walking around with this guy with a lot of time in recovery. He's been married a long time, and he just listened to me like a wise sober person. I'm saying, "I got married late in life and I don't know if I should have, I don't know if I'm staying or not." I'm talking about every possible aspect of everything that's bothering me, and he doesn't say a word until finally: "Do you realize what you're doing? You're discussing things that are bothering you, as opposed to going out and doing things that could really ruin your life. Do you know what kind of progress that is?"

That was a great epiphany for me. I used to do a joke when I first got sober—now that I had so much clarity, I despised myself even more. In a lot of ways it's true, but what it really means is, because I don't medicate these problems, I see them. When things happen to me, they're like spears that go right through me, and since I can't smoke a joint and have a couple of cocktails, I'm living with this stuff. Do I get irritable sometimes? Yes. Do I ruin my life? No.

It was murder the first three or four months. I hardly got out of bed. I was afraid to do almost anything. I talked to a lot of people on the phone, but I was afraid to leave my house. I was afraid to drive. I was petrified. I didn't know who I was. I was sober for four or five days, I felt like a baby. It took me a good seven or eight months to feel like Richard Lewis, but he turned out to be a totally different man than before. And I wasn't sure if I liked him, because obviously, I never really liked myself enough to help myself. That's when you really need to talk to people who have been at that exact place. I do not recommend isolating during that time. By nature, I am sort of a recluse, and being a recluse in early sobriety is just not healthy. Not a good idea.

But it's difficult for everybody. It takes time. It doesn't happen overnight, and there are still many things that I want to change. I was speaking to a good friend of mine. He's going to be eighty-two years old and the guy hasn't had a drink for forty-nine years. This guy is spectacular. He's the funniest man I ever met, without a question. I go to his house, we sit and talk, and it's just too good to be true. We talked about alcoholism, and he stopped drinking when he was thirty-two and so he has an interesting take, because at eighty-one he's very honest. He talks about his family, his parents, his life in sobriety, and has no tolerance now for people that don't treat him with respect. He will not be treated poorly by anybody. And that's a part of sobriety. I don't have patience with people who, out of the blue, are selfish and are rude to me. I try to get away from it. That's hard, because most of the population is pretty whacked. It's true.

I'm seeing things now and I'm hearing things now, and I can listen to people. I have never been a better friend. I have never been better at my craft, and I have never been a nicer person. If I can just live out my life doing my best work—that's important to me. I do foolishly expect applause sometimes for being a better person after fourteen years of sobriety. I'm no longer quite as self-centered or as selfish as I was, but that's not totally where it's at.

I was born a Jew, so I went to Hebrew school and I remember one line, "God is everywhere." I believe the philosopher Spinoza said that. I sense that God has touched everything in some way. When I go onstage, whether it's a concert or in a club, I tell the audience, "If it is only about the Shecky Greene tossed salads you're eating and my hour and ten minutes onstage, let's just drink the Kool-Aid and call it a lifetime." Why not just believe in something greater than ourselves? I mean, there's got to be more than just spinning around the universe. There's something bigger, bigger and better. That's God, bigger and better.

KATEY SAGAL

❧

Katey comes from a show-biz family. Her father directed episodes for lots of TV series, including The Twilight Zone, *and her mother was a film producer. Katey started out as a singer (including a tour as one of Bette Midler's backup singers), but she's best known for her starring roles in* Married . . . with Children *and* 8 Simple Rules. *I've always admired her work; she's got a great sense of comic timing, and I figured she'd be fun to talk to. I was right. We had a great conversation, about everything from parenting teenagers to how great she looks, but it wasn't until we were deep in the interview that I realized we had a good friend in common. This guy had been one of my friends in recovery, a role model and inspiration for hundreds of people, and he ended up dying of a drug overdose, alone in his house. That's one thing none of us can forget: anybody in this book, anybody in recovery could be gone tomorrow.*

I got sober twice, and the first time was very different than the second time. The first time I was in the middle of the love-of-my-life romance. I was pursuing my chosen profession: rock star. I played the piano and wrote songs, smoked my cigarettes and ate my amphetamines. I wore all black and I had this big hairdo, all ratted out, and black eye makeup. My boyfriend and I were complete drug and alcohol partners. I was just crazy about him. He would run off for days and I'd go screaming through Hollywood in my car, trying to find him. I had this red El Dorado 1969 convertible, and I'd drive around with the top down, half out of my mind.

For a couple of years, I knew I needed to get sober. I would use daily in a moderate way, and then I would go on these long binges, and after every one of those binges, I would tell myself, "Okay. You are not going to do this anymore. You just cannot do this anymore." Then time and time again, there I would be. Once I would start, I couldn't stop. It would be four or five days, and then I would stop because I'd just pass out. I was working. Rock stardom eluding me, I was on a television series, God knows how. The star of the series, I'll never forget her telling me on the set, "I'm sober." I looked at her and I said, "Me too." I was completely lying, totally lying. In hindsight, she was one of those little angels.

Anyway, my boyfriend's name was Spyder, and Spyder was in a band. All the people in the band were sober except for Spyder and me, and we were like these ghost people. Like night crawlers. Then he ran off with this speed freak dealer girl. I went to my first meeting looking for him because I thought his friends would be there so maybe he'd go there. I think that was my cry for help. I just knew that drugs and alcohol and him and everything . . . it was all just too much.

I go to this mutual support group, and there were all these people I knew there. I just cried and talked about Spider. But I stopped drinking and using that first time. Then I went off to New York, doing this workshop of a play, and I knew nobody there. I was in New York for three months and then I started using again. I remember at that time thinking, "Well, I need this. Nobody will know." The denial process. "This won't be a big deal. I can control this and it'll just be for tonight." As usual, it was never just for tonight. As usual, I was just lying through my teeth to everybody around me and somehow showing up for work. I mean I was like a little chemist. I could get myself to sleep and get myself awake and get myself to work.

When I got back from New York, the boyfriend was gone. I came back to my house—God knows how, but I had a house—I was standing in my living room, and I really understood the meaning of powerlessness. There were other people there, carrying on doing what we always had done, and it was so *boring*. The same conversations would happen. The same paraphernalia was going to get spread across the coffee table. The same alcohol was going to get spilled. The same music would get played. You put up with a lot of shit when you're loaded. *Boring!*

It was that moment when I just kind of lifted up out of the room. I was done there. Sad and done. And as much as I wanted to stop, I realized that I couldn't do it myself. I'd had the illusion of control because I'd had a couple of months clean, but six months later there I was, right back where I had been. I was scared. It was a moment of humility, realizing that I had no control. I don't even know how to describe that, except that it was terrifying to realize, "I can't control this. I can't listen to myself when I say, 'No. You are not going to do that anymore.'" I've always been a very strong-willed person, and I accomplished a lot through it. I'm really disciplined, very driven. I'm the oldest of five kids, my parents died very young, and I sort of raised myself, and I was always able to do whatever I set out to do. But there in my living room, I had the sense that this thing is so much bigger than me, and it's just going to swallow me up.

That was my moment, realizing how big addiction is, how overwhelmingly powerless I am over it, and how as smart a girl as I am, all the things I can do—I can't do this. I was thirty-one years old, and I'd been using, in some way, since I was fifteen. I wasn't totally out of control until those last six years. Then, having been clean for those two months, and seeing how quickly it returns the minute you open that door again . . . that really scared me. That got my attention. So I think my moment of clarity was just realizing that I'm not so fucking smart.

What I had to do was nothing short of changing everything. The deflation of the ego is really what is required, and that moment was the beginning of the smashing of my ego. This time, I had a different attitude when I walked into the meeting. I wasn't looking for my boyfriend anymore. I was still pretty heartbroken, I think, but that broken heart saved my life. With me, with the women I work with in recovery, so much of our thing is all intertwined: the guys and the drinks and the drugs, it's all one big mess. So I just got out of that drama. I went down there and I quietly sat in the back of the rooms. And I just listened. I didn't cry. The first time I cried every day, all the time. This time I was really happy to be there. I read the book right away. I did everything everybody told me to do.

My drug and alcohol use gave me a lot of bravado, so until I got sober I didn't even realize that I was afraid of *everything*. And every single thing I was afraid of has shown up, including success, including failure, including having a family, including a divorce. Including death. All of it. And I've walked through every single one of those things. Not always gracefully, but without a drink. And that's a miracle. I think that's the divine part of it. I still look at it in awe, with childlike eyes. I've had so many moments of clarity. I mean, they are constantly happening. When you're awake, you start to put the pieces together and you're like "Oh, that's why I did this. That's where that came from. And that's why . . ." You know, that's the fabulous part of being in recovery and being drug-free and drink-free. I mean it's scary too. It's brave. I don't think a lot of people really want to have much awareness. If you choose to live that way, you are going to get it. It's going to come on.

In recovery, I learned to take a look at my relationships, instead of always looking to see what you could do for me. Which was a little bit of my M.O. "Okay, I'll be nice to you, but what are you going to do for me?" That was hard to realize, that I didn't have a lot of friends in my life, that I was really manipulative. That's changed. Not totally. I mean, I am in show business. But I think my behavior has changed. I know how to be a friend, and I have friends. At the same time, I'm not as willing to tolerate some stuff as I used to be. I can't believe the bullshit I put up with just to get high, what I had to listen to. I don't have the time for it, for all that sad conversation. Not that I'm deep, all philosophical all the time. But if we can't talk about something real, I'm just not interested.

When you take a lot of amphetamines and drink a lot of alcohol, which I did, you spend a lot of time in your own head. My feeling self is much deeper now, much richer. I experience all that emotion I was so afraid of. I was this really emotional little kid, and I scared myself. It was too much, so I just shut it down. Now I feel more access to all that, to my heart, and my emotions, and who I am.

JIM RAMSTAD

⚘

Jim was first elected to Congress in 1990. Over the years, he's been named Legislator of the Year by the National Association of Alcoholism and Drug Addiction Counselors, by the National Mental Health Association, and (twice) by the National Association of Police Organizations. He's also been a mainstay of the DC recovery community since the first day he arrived. He stepped up and offered to work with my cousin Patrick on his recovery, and I know the relationship means a lot to Patrick. Jim really is one of the good-guy Republicans, and I was sorry to hear that he'd decided not to run for reelection in 2008. Whatever he ends up doing, I'm sure he'll follow the path of his own mentor, Harold Hughes, and continue giving back.

On July 31, 1981, when I awoke from my last alcoholic blackout, I was in a jail cell in Sioux Falls, South Dakota, under arrest for a variety of offenses stemming from that last alcoholic episode. I recall the fright—I feel it right now—being overwhelmed by fright. I was so frightened because I always anticipated that I would end my drinking days by killing someone else or myself in a car accident. That was my greatest fear, but that did not stop me from drinking.

I asked the jailer two questions. I said, "Was I driving a car last night?" and he said, "No." I asked him a second question: "Did I hurt anybody or kill anybody?" and he said, "No." After learning that I didn't kill anybody, I didn't hurt anybody, I wasn't driving a car, I went to the corner of the jail cell—and it was hot. It was a hot day in South Dakota, and it was even hotter in that jail cell. I remember just dripping in perspiration. I kneeled down in the corner of that jail cell and I repeated over and over again the twenty-third Psalm, and intermittently I would say the Lord's Prayer.

For the first time in my life I really heard the words from the Lord's Prayer, "Thy will be done." I heard myself say them for the very first time. The whole time I had been a practicing Christian and an active alcoholic, it was always "my will be done." It was always me. I was the center of the universe, not a higher power and certainly not Jesus Christ. I also remember saying over and over again, "Yea, though I walk through the valley of the shadow of death, I will fear no evil." I was in that valley, and I could see the shadow of death, and I wanted to be dead. But I prayed the Twenty-third Psalm and the Lord's Prayer for what seemed like hours that day, and the more I prayed, the calmer I felt. And then the anxiety I felt lifted—I felt a calmness that I'd never felt before. After twelve long painful years of abusing alcohol, the good Lord answered the question I had asked countless times: "Am I an alcoholic?" I was in such denial. I did not want to be an alcoholic, because I'd lost an uncle on my mother's side of the family and an uncle on my dad's side due to this disease. Two wonderful men, one a doctor and another a very successful contractor, both of whom died from this fatal disease, and I did not want to be like them. I did not want to be an alcoholic, and I did not want to die.

But the fact is I am an alcoholic. On July 31, 1981, the good Lord did a number of things. First of all, He answered the question. I remember saying to myself in that jail cell, "I really am an alcoholic." That is the first time I ever said that. I had denied it every time a girlfriend or my parents or my sister or a close friend suggested that I look at my drinking or that I might have a drinking problem. I just argued, "No way."

I also thought that spiritual awakenings were what made televangelists rich, stories they used to raise money from unsuspecting seniors watching on Sunday morning. Little did I realize that spiritual awakenings are real and that I would have one, though I didn't really understand it as a spiritual awakening that day. All I knew was this calmness, feeling more at ease than I could remember, there on my knees in that jail cell.

Harold Hughes* writes about his spiritual awakening after he had lost everything. He was a truck driver abusing drugs and alcohol, and eventually he lost his job, he lost the love of his wife and his family, and his house was being foreclosed on. He decided that the only honorable thing left to do was to commit suicide. We used to have a Wednesday meeting together. He became my first DC sponsor, and he told me, "Jim, I couldn't do anything right, so I decided the only thing I could do was kill myself."

He loaded his shotgun and he got into the bathtub at his house and he put the barrel in his mouth, cocked the gun, and pulled the trigger—and it jammed. And when he wrote about it later, he said that in that quiet bathroom, "a warm peace settled deep within me and my emptiness and self-hatred seemed to evaporate like moisture spots under a hot bright sun." These were his words. "God was reaching out and touching me. A God who cared, a God who loved me, a God who was concerned for me despite my drunkenness. Like a stricken child lost in a storm, I have suddenly come into the warm arms of God."

And that is exactly what I felt. That God was reaching down and touching me, a God who cared about me, a God who loved me despite my drunkenness. That I could be totally honest with Him and with everybody else—including myself—about my alcoholism. It was a great relief and a great release. It was a great feeling of freedom and of love.

I went back to Minneapolis the next day, and I went into treatment at Saint Mary's. There was a counselor there who was just wonderful. He walked into my group room the first day and he said, "You think you're a big shot, don't you?" There was a chalkboard there, and he drew concentric circles on the board, with a little circle in the middle with an X for me.

---

* Hughes served as the governor of Iowa from 1962 to 1968. During his second term, he became friends with Robert Kennedy, who persuaded him to run for the U.S. Senate in the 1968 election. He made substance abuse issues a centerpiece of his legislative program, organizing and chairing the first subcommittee on alcoholism and drug abuse and pushing for legislation to recognize and treat these as illnesses. He retired after one term and continued helping people through private foundations and religious organizations. He died in 1996 at the age of seventy-four. His 1979 autobiography, *The Man from Ida Grove: A Senator's Personal Story*, is an honest and inspiring book.

He said, "This is you, at the center of the universe. But you're not that important. Nobody is. You know, the most important political person in this country died in 1963, and everybody missed him and we all grieved for the loss, but life goes on. Even the greatest political leader of the free world at the time, he was assassinated, and we recovered from that. So you're just not that important."

This put it all in perspective. I was always thinking constantly, thinking about how to control things, how to get what I wanted. But what he was saying was, turn it over to a higher power, and I've been doing that—not perfectly, not every day and every minute—but I've been trying to do it ever since.

I've set my goals on public service ever since meeting President Kennedy in the Rose Garden. Bill Clinton was there that day too. We've both got those pictures of us with the president, and after that day I geared everything I did toward that goal. My major, my extracurricular activities, being captain of the team and president of student council—it was all about building a record and a résumé. I never wanted to admit weakness, and I saw alcoholism not so much as a disease but as a real weakness. And it took a long time to overcome that, even in my own recovery.

Of course, while I was in that jail cell, I still did not want this to be made public. I still was hoping that as I went back to Minnesota, that it would not be made public. Well, we hit the ground and the press was awaiting me at the airport because some reporters had heard that the young state senator from Minnesota had been arrested for disorderly conduct and resisting arrest and who knows what else.

Seeing it in print, seeing it as a lead story on television news, I knew there was no place to run or place to hide. And again, that became part of my relief, that I didn't have to hide it. I could just say, "Yes, I am an alcoholic," and deal with it. Treatment really helped me to do that, to deal with my alcoholism, but it was all about honesty. It all started with honesty.

I was sick and tired of lying, living a life of lies. I was sick and tired of that lifestyle. And I was afraid of dying like my uncles had, because I knew what happens if you don't arrest this disease. If you don't recover, you die.

I didn't need any more fearful data than seeing two uncles die of this horrible disease. When I was a young boy, I watched my uncle dying in the state mental institution. He had the tremors and the DTs and it was a horrible death. I will never forget that.

So I think it was a combination of being sick and tired and afraid. I wanted to live a more fulfilling, real life. Not too long ago, Patrick Kennedy shared this about his own life and I could certainly relate. He said his public persona and his private persona felt one and the same in a way that they never had before. I felt the same. I remember during my drinking, I would stand in front of the mirror and say, "Why can't I be Jim Ramstad? I do not want to be the drunk I see in the mirror." I never wanted to be that person. I wanted to go out and have a few drinks with friends and be normal, but I never was.

But that first month in treatment, I started to feel like Jim Ramstad. My head was a little clearer each and every day. I felt more real and more comfortable each and every day. I just soaked up everything—every lecture, every group, every evening with my friends who were in treatment. I loved treatment. I really enjoyed it. It was a very comforting, therapeutic experience, and I particularly liked the spiritual component. We had a really good chaplain. Some people look at treatment as a tedious regimen, something to just get through. I looked at it as an enjoyable, soothing, therapeutic experience.

In that jail cell and for a time in treatment, I assumed my political career was over. I had embarrassed myself and humiliated myself, and who is going to vote for a drunkard in a jail cell? But I remember thinking, "I need to get well or I'm not going to be around and in public office anyway. I can go back to practicing law or find something else to do, but that's not my concern right now. My concern is recovering from this disease and staying sober, because otherwise I'm going to die like my uncles." So I really took treatment very, very seriously.

There was a state senator from the other side of the aisle who hated my guts. I beat his best friend to get to the Senate and he had no time for me. He wouldn't even speak to me, let alone give me a hearing on any of my bills, and he was the first call I got at Saint Mary's. The counselor gave me the message with his name on it, and I crumpled it up and I threw it in the wastebasket and went to the next lecture. I don't remember what it was exactly, but I heard something that made me think, "At least return the guy's phone call." I assumed he was going to take me to the ethics committee, but something told me to just do the right thing and call him back. So I called and he said, "You and I have had our differences politically, but I just want you to know something you probably don't know about me. I'm a recovering alcoholic, and I'll come down there tonight, tomorrow, whatever time you want, if you want to talk." This guy was not at all warm or fuzzy—but he was there for me.

There was one guy in my district who was a big American Legion member, and he always used to try to stop me from serving a pancake breakfast or being active in Legion even though I was a member of the American Legion. I am still. I will never forget, there was a luncheon at his Legion Post after I got out of treatment, and of course he was there. I saw him get up all the way at the other end of this long, big hall, and he walked down to me and stood there with his arms crossed. I figured he's going to slug me. He said, "You know, Ramstad, I never liked you. You got three strikes against you. First of all, you're a goddamn politician and I hate politicians. Secondly, and even worse, you're a goddamn Republican politician and I hate Republicans. And thirdly and worst, you're a lawyer and I really hate lawyers."

He uncrossed his arms, which were about the size of two-hundred-year-old tree trunks, and I figured he's about to slug me. He brought his arms up and reached around and hugged me. And he said, "But now that you're one of us, welcome to the club, brother." He had this big smile on his face, and I had tears coming down my face. I've almost got them right now, remembering it.

I could tell stories like that all night. Little did I know that's what would happen after I got real. Rather than being rejected, I was more accepted than ever before by people from all walks of life.

KALE BROWNE

⚬

Kale has been a friend of mine since we did a scene together on the soap opera
All My Children *in 1992. I was a private detective and he was a murderer
coming back from the grave—what do you want, it was a soap! From that day
to this we have traveled the road of recovery together, and I would say there is
nobody on the planet who has helped me more. His honesty, compassion, and
patience have sustained and inspired me. As an actor, Kale played the roles of*
Michael Hudson on Another World *and Sam Rappaport on* One Life to Live.

Describing the specific ways my behavior has changed would take
a whole book in itself, but if I was going to boil it down, I'd say
two things are different. One, I know now that by helping others
I get the help I need. Two, since I'm not the center of the universe anymore,
I treat people with respect most of the time, and I'm not afraid to own my
own problems. The result of that is that most people are happy to see me
coming and sorry to see me go, and I know it, and it's real. That is the polar
opposite of my life when I drank.

I'd gone to the doctor in the East Village with the steel door, the kind with
a little window, like a bookie joint. Everyone in the waiting room had the
shakes when they came in and a prescription in their hand when they left,
myself included. I don't remember what they were—some kind of uppers,
I'm sure—but I took a few pills and went to my acting class with Uta Ha-
gen. What a great lady. She threw me out of class that day, saying, as I recall, "You can fool the critics but you can't fool me." I didn't have a clue
what she meant.

At the time, I was living with Kathy, a high-priced call girl/wayward actress from Nashville. I'd made it my duty to rescue her from this Mafia guy who'd been paying for her apartment. I guess she was a lost soul like me. She was perfect: a beautiful southern damsel in distress, and best of all, she didn't mind my drinking. At least, I thought she didn't. I didn't realize she simply had no idea how much I drank. I was shocked when she came back from a trip and asked about this half-gallon of vodka we kept in the freezer. It had been full when she left, and now it was almost empty. "Did you drink that whole bottle in two weeks?" I was embarrassed and cornered, so I lied and told her that friends had come over while she was gone. They drank it. She seemed happy with that, but now I was on alert; if she was ticked off about me possibly drinking a half-gallon in two weeks, for sure I wasn't going to tell her I drank a half-gallon every two *days*. And that was at-home drinking, before going out to do the serious drinking. If I couldn't be honest with myself about how much I drank, I sure as hell couldn't be honest with her.

Anyway, that week I was home more than usual. For some reason I'd quit my job waiting on tables. Every morning Kathy would give me some shit about messing up the kitchen in the middle of the night. I'd deny it, and rightly so. I didn't eat in the middle of the night, and I'd never leave a mess. It was only the two of us in a one-room studio apartment, so I don't know who I thought did it. Elves, maybe. I didn't care. "Just get the fuck off my back, or you'll go on the list."

I had this list in my head of the people who'd embarrassed me, who didn't understand me. The fuckers who'd hassle me about stupid shit, like maybe stealing their booze or money or drugs. My response was always "I didn't do it. Shit happens. Get over it." Then I was out the door to find some new place where people weren't so paranoid and suspicious. Sure, things kind of disappeared when I was around, but *I* certainly didn't do it. Of course, I had done all those things and more, but if I believed I hadn't, then I hadn't, period.

If my denial about stealing was rock solid, my denial about my drinking was ironclad. I had a real capacity to disassociate myself from whatever I did, so that I could believe I hadn't done it enough to deny it convincingly. I must have begun to suspect that booze was a problem, because around this time I'd started to lie about going to meetings during a couple of those late-night drunken phone calls to whoever lived far away and still took my calls. I don't know how I even knew about meetings. I'd only met one guy who went to meetings, and he was a total loser.

People just don't understand. As far as alcoholics are concerned, they aren't afraid of the truth. Everyone else is.

I think Carl Jung is right about the need for an alcoholic to experience some kind of psychic change if they're ever going to recover. For me, a psychic change means a new way of looking at things, a paradigmatic shift in awareness or consciousness or perception that's totally unpredictable and completely unfathomable up to the moment it happens.

Even though it happened over thirty years ago, I remember the moment it happened to me like it was yesterday.

One night I go to bed and pass out as usual, and next thing I know I'm standing in my kitchen, looking into Kathy's eyes. I knew a couple of things simultaneously: we were in the middle of a conversation, and whatever it was about, I'd just said something completely insane, because she had that look on her face like a puppy gets when you make a high-pitched whistle and they cock their head to one side and look at you like "What the fuck was *that*?" In that nanosecond, I saw myself through her eyes. I saw not the guy I'd convinced myself I was, but—accurately—who and what I'd become. A stranger. A monster. Out of control.

I didn't know it then, but that was the beginning of the end. I couldn't lie to myself anymore. I mean after that night, I really couldn't. I knew what I'd become. It no longer mattered if I convinced you I didn't have a problem. I *knew*.

I remember turning away from her, toward the only light in the kitchen, a sickly candle-flicker behind me. I saw what our conversation was about. I'd been cooking a grilled cheese sandwich on the stove, without benefit of a pan. Directly on the burner. There was this silence, just the hiss of a grilled cheese becoming charcoal.

I know now that blackouts are considered a sure sign of the disease of alcoholism. Normal drinkers don't seem to have them. It's when your body walks and talks, and maybe drives or gets arrested or worse, without your knowledge. Whatever makes you aware of you isn't in there. As a friend once put it, "Blackouts are like leaving the house with all the doors and windows open. Anyone can walk in and do whatever they want."

This happened right around June 16, 1977, my twenty-eighth birthday. I was doing a play on forty-second Street. The theater had a bathroom with one of those old overhead ceramic tanks, up high, right at the ceiling. Every day I'd hide a pint of vodka in the tank, and drink when I took a bathroom break. I'd be loaded by lunch. Somehow I confessed that I couldn't stop drinking to this wonderful woman, Claire Heller—God bless her—who was producing the play. I have no idea why I told her. I'd never told anyone. I think she must have asked me about my drinking.

Turns out she had a friend who was in recovery, and get this, he was one of the three other people in the play. She told me I could ask him for help if I needed it. I called him, and he took me to one of those recovery meetings. I stayed sober a week, and I was so happy I wasn't an alcoholic anymore, I got a pint of vodka and went to see a noon show of *Star Wars*. I'm sitting in the back row of this theater, drinking this bottle, and as I finished, I started crying. It hit me that I was an alcohol addict, just like a drug addict. I *had* to drink. Me thinking I was choosing to drink was just bullshit.

I went back to meetings, but even then I didn't stop drinking until July thirteenth. I know I had my last drink, one lousy beer, on July 13, 1977, because it was the night of the big blackout in New York. I was doing a production of *Butterflies Are Free* and in the middle of the play the lights went out. My character was blind, and I ad-libbed what I think was my all-time best: "Mom, somebody turned off the radio." We finished the play, as I recall, but what I remember clearly is that earlier that night I'd bought two 16-ounce Coors to drink before the show, and I never got to the second. The first one had gotten me so drunk I could barely walk. I was in that stage where I could drink a quart of vodka and not get stoned or, as on this night, get plotzed on one beer. I knew my drinking had chewed me up and spit me out.

In order to stay sober, I've had to become a totally different human. Nobody knows how somebody like me gets sober. I couldn't stop and couldn't conceive of stopping. I was without hope. There was no way, through my own power, that I could change. Then it happened, zapped out of the blue. I'm in the kitchen, having this experience, which is the beginning of the end. You can't make that happen. It just does. I now believe that things happen in this world that defy easy explanation. It's certainly not a matter of virtue, because my dad was a great guy, and he was dead at fifty-four from complications of alcoholism. All I did that he didn't do was I got to a place where I really wanted to stop but I couldn't.

Before that moment in the kitchen, there is nothing that anyone could have said to get through my denial. My denial was impenetrable. That's why that moment, when it happens, is so profound. Some people get put off by the whole spiritual thing in the program, but I think it's as simple as, they didn't know what else to call it. Stopping is not a mental experience—at least it isn't for an alcoholic of my type, because I decided to get sober a hundred times and it never lasted. Getting sober is not a physical experience either. There's no predictable cure for chronic drinkers except total abstinence, and if that was easy, more people would do it. If you're doing it on will alone and you don't change inside . . . well, the only person who's as miserable to be around as an active drunk is a sober drunk who needs a drink.

When I was drinking, I wasn't afraid of anything. That was the point. After I was sober a while, that's when I discovered I was full of fear. It never occurred to me that I'd never had sober sex until I did, and I had a lot of feelings about it. I hadn't worked without a drink in a long time, because I was afraid to. Turns out I was afraid of pretty much everything, in some way. That's why the idea of living sober was so terrifying. I think that's why the long-term success rate for most people who try to stop by themselves—at least, alcoholics of my type—is so bad. Stopping isn't really the problem. Living sober and surviving sobriety . . . that's the problem.

I have no idea if God ultimately exists or not; I choose to believe because it's like the wind—you can't see it, but you can see its effects. I've seen too many miracles, too many incredible coincidences, too many lives restored, to not believe in an intelligent universe that responds to intention. There's an axiom that says, "I see the world as I am, not as it is." When I'm toxic, the world looks toxic to me, and my effect on people feels poisonous. When I'm in a good place, the world ain't so bad. Believing in a loving God with a great sense of humor is how I stay in a good place.

MARTIN SHEEN

In a career that's spanned over four decades, Martin has played hundreds of roles, but he's best known for three: Kit, the seductive killer in Badlands; *Captain Willard, the tormented would-be assassin in* Apocalypse Now; *and President Bartlet in* The West Wing. *I first met Martin at the Kennedy compound in Hyannisport, when he was coming back from sailing with my Aunt Ethel. This was not long after he'd had his heart attack during the filming of* Apocalypse Now, *and he looked like he was about to have another one. He said, "Coppola couldn't kill me, but your aunt almost did."*

Martin's activism on behalf of peace and social justice goes back as long as his career, and his passion and commitment have only gotten stronger over the years. I know he's been a great friend and supporter of Patrick Kennedy's work on mental health and insurance parity issues. When Martin and I sat down at his house in Malibu for the interview, he told me the only reason he'd agreed to talk about his—and his family's—history with addiction was because he'd read Symptoms of Withdrawal. *He said, "If you could be that honest, so can I."*

I was drinking quite often, and when I drank, it gave me permission to do things that I normally would not do. I had a moral frame of reference. I never played around or anything except when I drank. I was one person here in this house and I was quite another person out there, ass-kissing and trying to get the job, and if I didn't get the job or I got a bad review, they all suffered. If I was sleeping late, it was "Don't wake him up, don't get him upset," because I was a rageaholic, and you know that is the word. But no one out there ever saw my rage, unless I got a part where I could ratchet it up. Then you'd see some anger or some rage behavior through a character. The real rage, that was here in this house.

If I could change anything in my life, it would be the violence that I did to my children—the extremely rare physical violence, the more frequent emotional violence, and of course the spiritual violence. If I was at the last breath of my life and I was offered one wish, that's the thing I would ask for. Please let me take back the violence. Let me heal the wounds that I inflicted with my behavior, my alcoholism, my ego, my dishonesty. The people I love the most paid the price for all that.

The moment I'm going to share with you, there are two witnesses to it, Janet and Charlie. Charlie was a very dear, very shy kid. Because he was so sensitive, because my anger affected him so much, I would overcompensate. I would either be too nice to him or too mean to him.

Charlie was a very good baseball player, just a wonderful athlete generally. When he was about fifteen, a sophomore in high school, we were playing basketball at the house. He had never beaten me one-on-one. I used to be pretty good. But that day, he had me. He was whipping me, and I kept coming back and coming back. He had to win by two, right? He was one up, and I missed a shot and he got the rebound, drove around the back, zinged that thing, and got it. He was dancing around, and I said, "No, no . . . we play by the rules, right?"

"Yes, but I won!"

"No, you stepped on the line right here. You went out of bounds."

I could not let him have it. He beat me fair and square, and I could not let him have it, and he was so furious. That's the ego. That's what he had to deal with in me, what the whole family had to deal with.

One morning about a year later, he came in to our bedroom. Maybe we were out the night before, maybe I was hungover, I don't remember the specifics—just that we were sleeping late and he came barging in. *Boom!* The door flies open and he says, "I need some money for lunch." I wake up, "What the hell is this?" and he said, "Come on, I'm late. I need some money!" and he was not pleased. No "May I?" No "Please." Nothing.

Janet said, "Well, darling, get something out of my purse over there." He grabbed the purse and looked in and said, "There's nothing in here!"

and he threw the purse down and he said some vulgarity, used the F-word. That set me off. I am stark naked and I bolted out of bed and I said something awful. I said, "You little son of a bitch!" I was going to knock him cold with everything I had. He turned to look at me and he threw his head back, and as my hand was flying toward him, just flying right at his face, I opened it and I hit him in the chest hard enough that I knocked him down on the floor. He looked up at me, and for the first time in my life I saw myself. I saw the mirror, I saw me. I saw what I looked like in his eyes. I was a monster. I was this raging lunatic who would physically assault his son, this little boy.

He started scooting on his elbows and his ass, trying to get away from me, and I just lost it. I kept pursuing him, saying, "Oh, Jesus, I am sorry. I am so sorry. Forgive me," and he was not having it. He was cursing me and trying to get away, just desperate to get away from me, and I kept following him. When he got to the kitchen, he got up and he headed for the door and I said, "Please, no, wait, Charlie, I am so sorry. Forgive me." "You asshole," he said, and he opened the door and I followed him out. I said, "I'm not going to let you get away. Please don't leave. I'm going to follow you." I just reach for him, and I'm naked, and the guys and kids, his friends, are all watching the scene. He's dodging around the car, trying to get away, and we're both weeping, and finally he just stayed still long enough, I walked in, and I just hugged him and held him and I kissed him and I said, "Forgive me . . . just forgive me," and that was it.

It made all the difference in both of our lives and it changed me forever. I began to realize that I had done this kind of thing to all of them, all my children, for all their lives. I had emotionally traumatized them with my violence, with my temper, with my ego. It was all about me, and if they were anything, they were decorations. I began to become aware of how I had hurt my kids with my ego and with my desperate desire to be liked. Well, loved, really. Being an actor is about being loved. If you're not loved, unless you get big box office or something, you can't work here. We know that. We all know that. So you try desperately not to offend anybody, and then you treat your family like shit, and that's what I was doing. I hurt my children most obviously by raging at them and I hurt my children subtly by not looking at them. By not looking across the table and seeing them. That happened most with Charlie. He would be in terrible, terrible shape, and I would rage and I would weep, "Look what you're doing to me!" What have I done to him? I taught him how to do it. I taught him everything he knew. I never got into the drugs in that way, but I used to drink with the lads on a few occasions, not falling-down drunk but certainly not presentable either.

But because of that incident when he was sixteen, he knew I had a good heart. He knew I was a desperate man. He knew I was addicted.

I became very aware of my drinking, but I thought I deserved to drink. I deserved to get drunk every now and then. After all, wasn't I carrying this burden? I'm entitled. If anyone's entitled, certainly it's me, and I don't do it that often, and I rarely do it at home.

It took me a long time to stop because I always felt, in a lot of ways, that someday I'm going to have a life. This is not it right now. I've got to raise these children, I've got to have this career, I've to do all this stuff, but this isn't really my life. Someday I'll be myself, but what's happening here isn't me.

That's changed. I know this is me, this is my life, and I'm grateful for it. Janet and I have been together, through all the ups and downs, and she has become my hero. I adore her. I adore my children, I adore my grandchildren. Gosh, I just couldn't have it any better.

We did three interventions with Charlie, and the final one, I said, "Well, I need some help here." He had broken his parole and I knew it. He left the hospital, and they gave me what he'd left behind. I saw what he took for the overdose. I got to see it, I owned it. I had the evidence that he'd broken his parole. I said, "Janet, I've got to go out and see the judge. I've got to see the sheriff." Oh, Jesus. That was the most difficult thing I've ever done, but I knew that I had to do it. I was thinking, "Who am I going to invite to the funeral? What am I going to say?" This was the last thing I could try.

The sheriff called Charlie, because he was barricaded in his apartment, a penthouse where the elevator opened inside the apartment, one of those places, so he knew who was coming and going. I gave them the number. I did the only thing that I could do.

The sheriff got him on the phone and said, "We'd prefer to have you come in, but if not, we are going to have to come and get you. There's a warrant for you, okay? And your dad is here. He wants to talk to you."

They put me on the phone, and he started on me. Oh, Jesus, it was bad—"You Judas, how could you do this to me?" I listened and I said, "Well, what are you going to do?" He says, "I'm coming in tomorrow. I got a lawyer and I've already got it set up." I said, "Hang on, wait a minute. Would it be okay if I came?" There was a pause and he said, "Sure, why not." And he hung up.

The next morning, I was there at the courthouse. He looked like a zombie, and when he came into court, he walked right up to me and kissed me on the lips. He knew what had happened, and why it happened. He knew that after that morning when he was sixteen, I would never hurt him again, and that was the difference. That was the most important moment in my life because it took someone that I adored to show me myself. What have I done to these kids all these years?

The difference between despair and hope, I think, is a flash. It could be a stranger's smile, or somebody stopping to let you by, or just some measure of human kindness. Oscar Wilde wrote about being brought down to court and the huge crowd that gathered, a mob. He was a celebrated figure, and now he's being publicly humiliated for being gay and so forth. He saw his lover, Bosie, in the crowd, and they made eye contact, and then Bosie turned away. Wilde wrote about it and he said the most extraordinary thing: "There had been men who did less that were allowed into heaven as an act of mercy, and you refused it to me."

I think it's that kind of natural—and I do think it's natural—human expression of kindness and generosity that can make all the difference. One of the best lessons of recovery is the lesson that you need to do something for someone. Do something nice for someone, and don't tell anybody. That's the hardest thing, because our ego wants credit, we want people to talk about us in a good way, and I think that's what drives away the spirit.

Einstein's lesson, the reason he did all his work, was he wanted to know if it's a friendly universe. That's the bottom line of all his study—is it friendly out there? He did his work and he said yes, it is friendly, and I do believe it is. There is a future. There's a future, but we foreclose it with our fear. I think fear is some measure of despair, fear of being human and being vulnerable. But it's only when you allow that, when you allow yourself to be vulnerable, to get broken, even—that's the only time the spirit can get in. It's that thing Hemingway talks about. "The world breaks everyone and afterward many are strong at the broken places."

That morning when I hit my son, I was broken. I was totally broken. I don't know if I spoke for a week. I got very reflective. I saw myself really clearly and didn't like what I had seen, and that was a blow to the ego. But more than that, I realized that my life was at stake and maybe the lives of my children. My spiritual life was at stake. It took a long time, but I started to make the changes I needed to make. I realized that it's a process, and my world started to change.

Whether we're conscious or unconscious of it, the world is exactly the way it is because we made it that way, and we are equally capable of changing it. But we have to see it first. You have to realize you're looking at the problem, you're a part of this horrible problem. You can't do anything until you change yourself, and you're the only one you can change. I've never changed anyone. Everything I do, I do it for myself.

MAX CLELAND

❧

Georgia native Max Cleland was an only child, and his childhood hero was the Lone Ranger, yet he's lived a life of service to others. He enlisted in the U.S. Army during the Vietnam War and reached the rank of captain. Four days after actions that earned him the Silver Star and the Bronze Star, a battlefield accident changed his life. After he returned home, no one would hire him. He won a seat in the Georgia State Senate and became such a strong advocate for veterans' issues that Jimmy Carter named him head of the Veterans Administration. After Reagan took office, Max returned home and served as Georgia's secretary of state until 1996, when he successfully ran for the U.S. Senate. In 2002 Max lost to his Republican challenger after a nasty campaign that included television ads pairing Cleland with Osama bin Laden and Saddam Hussein. Since then, he's advised other politicians, but he says he'll never run for office again. Max's story shows the profound power of fellowship to heal wounds of all kinds. Max is the only person in this book who doesn't identify as an alcoholic or addict. He quit drinking in 1975 when he realized he could too easily hide behind the bottle. His story may illuminate different circumstances from the others in this book, but his struggle resonates powerfully.

T homas Jefferson described the presidency as "a splendid misery." That's what politics has been for me—a splendid misery. In over forty years of public service, I've had powerful splendor, powerful achievements, powerful ups and downs; and along with that, I've had powerful physical, mental, and emotional misery. Hemingway wrote about his war, World War I, in *A Farewell to Arms*, and Arthur Schlesinger Jr. used a quote from the book to introduce *A Thousand Days*, about

Kennedy's presidency: "If people bring so much courage to this world the world has to kill them to break them, so of course it kills them. The world breaks everyone and afterward many are strong at the broken places. But those that will not break it kills. It kills the very good, and the very gentle, and the very brave impartially."

Hemingway was right. The world breaks us all. If you haven't been broken by life, just wait a while. All of us get broken one way or another, at some time or another. And many people do grow strong at the broken places, but many do not, and that's the mystery.

How do you recover from being blown the hell up? How do you recover from losing both legs and your right arm? I was always the tallest guy in my class, and I was right-handed. I shot basketball right-handed, and I was honorable mention All-County Basketball. I batted right-handed, I threw a baseball right-handed, and I lettered four years in baseball. I was second in the state in my class in tennis singles. So running with a ball was my life. Then I joined the U.S. Army and jumped out of airplanes in airborne training. I really was feeling my oats when I was a young man. At the age of twenty-five, all that ended.*

I'm not sure how I missed becoming one of the fifty-eight thousand dead listed on the wall. There are some physical answers. I was so close to the grenade that the flesh was burned so much that I didn't bleed to death right there. There was an immediate helicopter medevac to the division aid station and then a field hospital where they did surgery. Five hours and five doctors and forty-two pints of blood later, I woke up.

Then came a powerful struggle, an uphill battle, clawing my way back to some sense of dignity. Struggling through days and months of not knowing what in the world I was going to do in life. Was I going to be able

---

* Max was injured during the Battle of Khe Sanh. He'd just disembarked from a helicopter on a mission to set up a radio relay station. He bent down to pick up a grenade he assumed had dropped off his flak jacket. The grenade exploded, destroying his lower legs and right arm. Thirty years later, one of the men who'd been on the scene revealed that the grenade had belonged to another of the soldiers on the helicopter, a young private who'd loosened the grenade pins on his own flak jacket.

to walk on artificial legs? Drive a car? Was I going to be able to date or dance or anything? Nobody could tell me.

All my life I've had fixed goals, stars to steer by. I've had worthy things to do—serve my country, join in the military, become an officer, go to jump school, volunteer for Vietnam, whatever. When I came back, I focused all that into a different kind of service by running for office and serving in government. I wanted to be proud of myself, and I wanted other people to be proud of me too. I tried to live a good life. I tried to do well, and do good.

When I lost that election in 2002, I went into a massive depression, a deep misery. I had never struggled with my own emotional health, my own mental capacity, my ability to think and make decisions. But that was gone. I couldn't focus. I couldn't work. I couldn't function mentally anymore, and I had always depended on my mind to bail me out. I wound up before a psychiatrist and counselors, and they started talking to me about brain chemicals. Recovering from this meant I had to do stuff I had never done before in my entire life. I was on all kinds of medication, which I had never experienced before in my life. I was struggling to recover my sense of self, my sense of identity and all that. It's one thing to recover physically. It's another thing to recover from absolute total hopelessness and despair.

I felt like my life had been worthless. Going to Vietnam had ended in a terrible tragedy—for me and for the country. Then, thirty years of politics ended for me with a massive, sudden-death experience on election night. I was thrown out of office and on the street and back again where I was before—no money, no future, no hope.

That loss triggered the initial experience of life blowing up in my face, instantly. I felt again the sense of being totally helpless and totally vulnerable. That fear is lodged in the base of my brain. My body knows it. I know it. That's my greatest source of panic and anxiety. Fighting that kind of deep fear has its own consequences. It sucks up all the brain chemicals that make you feel good and comfortable and let you have fun. I dropped like a rock because of massive anxiety and fear.

I'm coming out of it by the grace of God and the help of friends. I'm working through it. I have been broken every way you can be broken. But

I'm still here. I'm still alive. That's the mystery and the miracle. Somehow, life can heal us—if we allow it to, and if we live that long. God can heal us. A power greater than myself helped restore me to health and some sense of sanity. The Good Lord pulled me out of my pit rather than me pushing my way out. Now my job is to try to show up and be still and try to be led.

I realized in 1975 that alcohol and I were never going to mix. I was dating an alcoholic, and it caused me so much pain to see somebody I cared for in this out-of-control situation. I had never known anybody who just couldn't control their drinking. God knows, I've been in the military, and I knew what getting drunk was. I knew what raising hell was. I had done it. I knew that I myself could become an alcoholic. But in 1975 I realized I didn't want any part of alcohol, ever again. I quit drinking. I've had to fight so hard for a life of dignity and respect; fight so hard to function as a "normal" human being—have a job, drive a car, live independently, communicate with people, function and be relevant in society. All that has taken powerful amounts of energy and struggle. I think I knew I wouldn't have enough energy to fight alcohol and my normal battles too. I had to let that go.

Viktor Frankl was an eminent psychiatrist in Vienna who was sent to concentration camps in World War II. Talk about odds—he was the one in twenty-eight that survived. He came out of that experience and he wrote about what he saw, saying, "To live is to suffer. To survive is to find meaning in suffering." The book is called *Man's Search for Meaning,* and that's what life itself is—man's search for meaning, for purpose and direction and guidance. My toughest times in life are when I don't have a sense of purpose, when I don't have clarity, when the lights go out.

Now I've come to a point that I've never been at before. I believe that whatever happens in the future is okay. I've literally turned it over, as they say, to the Good Lord, to the universe. That's surrender, which always has been tough for me because I've tried to control things in order to have a sense of what my trauma counselor calls SOS—safety, organization, and stability. I need safety, organization, and stability in my work environment, in the people around me, in my circumstances in life. If I don't have that, I'm right back in Vietnam. I'm right back blown the hell up, fighting for my life and fighting for every breath.

But now . . . whatever happens, happens. I'm not trying to control everything anymore. My goals are more fundamental. I'm trying to get some serenity and sense of peace in the mornings so that I can handle the day and function and function well. I just try to turn the rest over to my higher power, the Good Lord or whatever.

When you go through trauma, one of the brain chemicals that's affected is dopamine, which is one of the feel-good chemicals in the brain. When you've been on alert too long, on adrenaline overload, you're low on dopamine. A swig of whisky, a shot of a drug, and you feel better until you need the next swig or the next shot. When you're facing the aftermath of trauma, it's easy to start down the slippery slope of self-medication. If you have PTSD, the trauma has happened and now it's over, but your body doesn't know it's over. Your brain chemicals are messed up from the high adrenaline levels, from being always on the alert, fighting for your life.

I created the Vet Center program in 1980 to deal with the emotional aftermath of war for the veterans returned from Vietnam. Today, Iraq and Afghanistan veterans are swamping the VA's two hundred vet centers. The divorce rate among U.S. Army officers has more than doubled. Physical abuse among military families is dramatically on the increase. So are suicides. Being at war for so long is taking a tremendous toll on families. Even if the soldier comes back from war uninjured, they come back a different person. They've still got the same body, still got the same name, but they are different. They don't know how they're different, but they know they've changed, and their spouse knows they've changed. Many times it's the spouse that gets this soldier into treatment. One of the guys who saved me on the battlefield forty years ago and who now is a counselor in a vet center has told me that if you can get the soldier struggling with PTSD off the drugs and off the alcohol, they can survive. Otherwise, the situation is not good. This is deadly serious stuff, not to be toyed with.

I look at the slippery slopes I've been down, on the battlefield and on the political battlefield. I've been blown up on both. I truly am lucky to be here, and I know I didn't get here on my own. I needed the powerful help of others then, and I need the help of others now just to survive day to day. And where that takes me, I don't know. That's the surrender part of it, letting go of the outcomes. I've always worked my rear end off to either achieve the goal I set for myself or die trying. Now I don't have any goals other than to try to get more sane and more stable and to look after myself better and look after my daddy, my only living blood relative left.

A friend of mine, a doctor, is fond of saying, "Circumstances create depression. Chemicals perpetuate it." You've got to get your brain chemicals and your life balanced right. That's my day-to-day struggle now: not to achieve some goal in the future but to survive well today. I've done a turnaround in what's important to me. I've had to find new coping skills. It's been a long road back. A fellow Vietnam veteran who's also a counselor says, "People put their lives back together brick by brick by brick." That's what I've been doing. It's clarity, not so much in one bright shining moment, but clarity that comes slowly the way the dawn comes or the fog lifts.

You can't give others assurance unless you've had a little of it yourself. I have a wonderful group in Washington, a fellowship of people whose lives have crashed and burned. Some are there for alcohol problems. Some are there for drug problems. Some are there for depression problems. Some are there for life problems—loss of a family member, where their grief is just taking them over. But all of us in that room have been powerfully successful. Admirals, generals, senators, congressmen, highly achievement-oriented, highly accomplished individuals. However, back to Hemingway's line, "the world breaks everyone." These people, my brothers, we've all been shipwrecked. We all want to get back home; in order to recover, we all work to get better together, get stronger together. We do it by reaching out to others. We hold hands firmly and pray that we're going to make it to the shore. That's the power of the group.

Tom Daschle had a good line about when he came to the U.S. Congress, as a freshman from South Dakota. He went to talk to Claude Pepper, a House leader from Florida and an eminent fighter for health care. Claude sat Tom down, as older members of Congress will do when you're a young whippersnapper, and Claude said, "Son, there are two types of people on Capitol Hill, and they're not *R*s and *D*s, Republicans and Democrats. They're *C*s and *D*s, Constructive and Destructive."

I think that's the demarcation, not just in Congress and the Senate but in life. That's the plumb line. If you try to live a constructive life, for you and for others, you'll be on the right side, the correct side of the aisle. And if you get on the destructive side . . . well, make amends for it as best you can, and fight your way back to the constructive side.

My grandfather used to say, "If somebody gets up in church and prays extra long, go home and lock the smokehouse door." Good thought. When my grandmother got criticized for not doing enough in the church, she pointed out that the Bible says, "Let your light shine," not *make* it shine. So now I have to work a little bit harder to let my light shine, which is a paradox. I just do the best I can to tend my light. When and where it shines is going to be up to the Good Lord, not up to me. And that's a relief.

There's great power in peer-group counseling, or what they generally call support groups. Somebody who's walked in your moccasins can talk to you in a way that's credible. I remember lying there at Walter Reed, and people would walk in with two legs and two arms and pat me on the head and say, "You're going to be fine," and then they'd walk out. I'd say, "What the hell do you know?"

When I saw a double-leg above-the-knee amputee walking on artificial limbs with a beautiful woman on his arm, I thought, "Son of a bitch. If *he* can do it, *I* can do it." He became kind of a mentor long before I knew all of these terms—support group, therapy, mentoring. Long before I knew any of that, I was thinking, "I'm pretty screwed up here. Is there anybody else in my situation who's done well with their life, who's making it? If so, I'll make it. If they can do it, I'll do it. I *will* do it." When I saw that guy, that World War II veteran with this beautiful woman, that gave me hope. That gave me strength.

The guys on the ward, we were all young officer amputees, young tigers. Airborne, Rangers—hard-core, dedicated soldiers, and we had all been seriously wounded. We were all there together, keeping each other afloat. When one was down, the others would come over and pick him up. We all stuck together. I'm still in touch with some of those guys forty years later.

That's the way my group is now. I know if I really get in trouble, if my head gets too far up my rear end, I can call one of those guys and talk to them and they will understand. It won't be a foreign language to them. We've all been in basically the same place, and we're all working hard to try to get to a better place. My clarity has come inch by inch, brick by brick, struggle by struggle, clawing my way back up the hill to a life of decency and dignity and meaning, where I can just enjoy the day. Man, if I can enjoy the day, that's the biggest victory of all.

I talked to my daddy the other day. He's ninety-four, and he's drowning in grief after losing my mother after sixty-six years. Can you imagine trying to come back and recover at ninety-four? I know how tough it is at sixty-six. It's a lot tougher than it was at twenty-five. But little by little, he's doing better. There's a healing even with him. That's a miracle. He went to the most broken place in his whole life at ninety-four, and yet he's recovering. That's a miracle and a mystery; it's an answer to prayer. I pray for that every day. I pray that I can help facilitate the process. But ultimately it comes from another source. It comes from the belief that life's worth fighting for, worth showing up for, worth living after all.

ELAINE STRITCH

⤺

The phrase "living legend" gets thrown around a lot in show business, but if it applies to anyone, it applies to Elaine Stritch. For more than sixty years, she's been a star on Broadway and a scene-stealer in Hollywood, known for her quick wit, her bold singing style, and her great legs. But her brash public persona hid a stage fright so crippling that she literally couldn't go onstage without a drink. Elaine talks about that—and a lot more—in her one-woman show, Elaine Stritch: At Liberty. *In 2002 the show won just about every theater award there is, and when we talked, she was on her way to London for another round of performances there. For many years, she was an amazing friend to my mom. In fact, she reminds me of my mother at her best, and I wanted her in the book for that reason alone. But because of her age and her talent and her years in recovery, Elaine doesn't take shit from anybody. She's not a people-pleaser. Plus, she's busy, and scheduling the interview wasn't easy; for a long time I wasn't sure I'd get it. In the end, I did—and it was great.*

I f somebody, anybody, ever happens to say to you, "Hello hello hello, oh my God, you haven't changed a bit!"—if that ever happens to you, you are in big trouble. Change, folks, is good news, especially the kind of change that hits you when you put down the sauce, when a Tanqueray martini, straight up, very dry, with two olives, is finally, at best, in your life a memory. Man, oh man, oh Manischewitz (sorry)—that is *change.*

In 1979, along with my alcoholism, I became an insulin-dependent diabetic, and I'm telling you if I never worked another day in my life at my chosen profession, I would be fully occupied from morning till night looking after myself, coping with diabetes. It is, believe me, the pits! Even with my various addictions, I happen to be a giant disciplinarian. How did that happen? So I got very good at controlling my blood sugar. A few months rolled by and I said to myself, "If I can control the diabetes, how 'bout I control the booze? Enough of this total abstinence nonsense— *control*. That is the operative word."

So two drinks a day, on- or offstage, two drinks a day. Two, two, two, two drinks a day. It doesn't work. Not when you want eleven. Not when you start shopping for wineglasses in the vase department at Bloomingdale's. However—if you'll pardon the pun—I gave it a shot—and it worked!

Until one night at a dinner party given on the St. Regis roof in memory of Jackie Gleason, out of the blue, Lucille Ball asked me to say a few words about Mr. Gleason. I said, "Sure, why not?" and then it hit me. "Oh my God, I've already had my two drinks for today. What the hell am I going to do?" I was so goddamned dependent on alcohol to enable me to do "my thing"—to enable me to do *any* thing.

So I had three drinks that day, and here is my Jackie Gleason story: During the rehearsals of a TV show I did with Jackie Gleason, he invited me to have dinner with him at Toots Shor's. I was so excited! My God, I must have changed my clothes maybe eight, maybe nine or ten times. I finally made a decision. Black. All black. Black dress (Dior), black tights, black shoes, black hat, black bag, and, oh, a single strand of pearls. Very New York. I'll be fine.

I hit the street, grabbed a cab, and I was off to Toots Shor's. I made my entrance, and Jackie Gleason, holding court at the bar, took one look at me and proclaimed, with what seemed to be body-mike projection: "Who died, pal?"

Well, my Jackie Gleason story was a huge success so I had to celebrate, didn't I? So I had four drinks that day, and then I had five drinks that day, and on and on and on, and so it always goes.

I got home that night and climbed into my four-poster bed. The next morning I found myself on the floor, my nightdress in disarray, the phone off the hook. I was in an advanced stage of a major diabetic hypoglycemic attack, and I needed sugar, in any way, shape, or form. I needed *sugar*.

All of a sudden, I'll be damned if there wasn't yet again God, so quickly. My doorman, trying to deliver a package to me marked URGENT and getting no answer, used his passkey. He found me, grabbed a quart of orange juice out of the fridge in my bedroom, and I was back in business.

A moment of clarity—I think so! The party was over; it was time to call it a day.

After twenty-one years of sobriety come September 2008, I am beginning to get a pretty good sober look at myself. I like a lot of what I see and I don't like a lot of what I see. But I am dealing, and rumor hath it, I am definitely changing for the good—one day at a time.

Oops, I blew it! I blew it! Okay, I *am* a recovering alcoholic and my name is Elaine Stritch.

Even though it's not really related to recovery, I'm leaving in a story Elaine told me, about a couple of dates she had with my uncle. It's just too good not to share.

Oh, by the way, Chris—I had two dates with your uncle Jack, did you know that? I was nineteen years old. The first date was my idea. I saw him at a cocktail party, as they say, across a crowded room. Some enchanted evening? You had better believe me. I noticed he was about to leave the party and, Chris, he was so adorable, you want to know what I did? (After two martinis, it wasn't difficult.) I just up and asked him where he was going. "Just for a bite at the Carlyle up the street, a little Bobby Short and then home, I guess."

"Is it okay if I come with you?"

And Jack Kennedy said, "Why in the world not? Fine with me."

The second date was a glorious evening at the Stork Club. We got back to my apartment on Fifty-second Street and I invited your uncle Jack up to have a nightcap. "Elaine," he said, "if going up to your apartment and having a nightcap means having scrambled eggs and listening to Glenn Miller records, then I have to say no."

I was very young and very inexperienced, if *you* know what I mean, but *I* knew exactly what he was talking about. "Well," I said, "I guess that is what I had in mind." He kissed me good night, turned me over to the doorman, and, back in his limo, made a U-turn on East Fifty-second Street and drove off into the night. I got into my elevator and I remember saying to myself going up, "What a straight shooter. I'll bet the house he is, *definitely* and *without a doubt,* going places!"

DeJuan Verrett

DJ has been sober three years after spending eighteen years in federal prison. In the two years he's been free, he has released the CD Outta Myself *and is working on a book about his life entitled* An Inside Job. *DJ's moment of clarity happened while he was in solitary confinement and powerfully demonstrates that a psychic change can happen to anyone, anywhere.*

My understanding was that God had put me in prison, God had let me grow up in the projects, God had made sure I never knew my father, God let me get shot and get stabbed. Why would He let that happen to me? And why would I want Him in my life?

But while I was in prison, I had a moment when I realized my understanding was wrong. God isn't the cause of my problems; that's my head and my will. God isn't the one telling me that I'm worthless; that's my head and my will. God is in my heart, and my heart has never led me to sell drugs. My heart has never led me to shoot people. As long as I let my heart lead me, I'm okay.

I grew up in Harbor City, California, and I went to prison when I was nineteen years old. What happened was, I gave three of my childhood friends a kilo of cocaine apiece and they got caught. They set me up with the feds. I came home and the feds right away kicked in my door and found a bunch of money. There was so much cash coming in, I'd just stack it up, stack it up, stack it up, stack it up. There was the money, but there were no drugs in my house. I'm thinking, "Hey, I'll beat it. They'll confiscate the money, but I'm a first-time, nonviolent offender. I'll beat this." It didn't happen like that.

The prosecutor wanted me to give up all my connections and I said, "I don't do that." My friends are all going to testify against me. My blood brother is going to testify against me. We'd grown up together, and neither one of us had a real brother. One day we were watching an old John Wayne movie, and John Wayne and this Indian guy cut their fingers and mixed their blood together and said now they were blood brothers. That's what we did, and he was testifying against me.

I'm still thinking I'll beat this, or maybe get five years or something like that. I was so arrogant. This was a federal charge, *United States v. Dejuan Verrett.*

To make a long story short, I was sentenced to eighteen years in the Bureau of Prisons, and as of June 2008, I've been out two years.

Being in prison was like being out of prison. I had my young homies. I ran weed, I ran coke. I made wine out of oranges and potatoes and rice and shit like that. I'd make ten gallons and keep three for myself. I'd drink until I passed out, and my crew would take me back to my cell and watch me. After a couple of years, I got transferred to Oakdale, in Louisiana. I know I'm going to need my coke and my weed and my alcohol. I need to establish myself so I can do what I've been doing. I got some beef rib bones in the kitchen and I took them to the washer, put it on spin cycle, and sharpened the beef ribs. That's what you do in prison, because bones won't set off the metal detectors. So I gave these knives to one of my new young homies. He used one on somebody, poked him a few times, and he got caught. He told them I'd given him the knife.

Now me, I had priors of using the knife in prison, and I was a California gang member, so they give me 270 days in the hole, in a special housing unit, SHU—you say it like "shoe." I'd been in Oakdale twelve days.

So I'm detoxing in the SHU. No alcohol, no drugs. Well, I'm asthmatic, so I could get Sudafed from the physician's assistants. I took them all at once, just to try and keep my buzz going, and I overdosed and nearly died.

Now the SHU is an eight-by-ten room. There's a bed with a plastic mattress maybe three inches thick. There's a metal toilet-sink-mirror, all one piece, all stainless steel. The only thing you can wear is a T-shirt, boxers, and socks. They give you a roll of toilet paper and you can use that as a makeshift pillow.

After I overdosed, the corrections officer told me, "Verrett, you keep fucking up and they'll four-point you—put you spread-eagle on a concrete slab and tie you down like that." I was there for three weeks and I had nine months to do and I didn't see how I could do it.

I woke up in the middle of the night. I have no drugs at all anymore and no alcohol, and I have to take a piss. I stood up, and it was like one step from my bunk to the toilet. I leaned forward to pee and my hand touched the cold mirror. I looked up, and all I could see was my eyes. Just my eyes. I stared into those eyes, and something happened right here, in my heart. It was like every cell in my body was waking up. When I looked in the mirror, I saw freedom.

I got some toilet paper and I blotted out the mirror so I could stand there and see just my eyes. Then I positioned myself in front of the sink with my cigarettes and I just talked to myself. I needed someone to talk to, I needed somebody to understand, and there was nobody else. I spilled my guts to that person in the mirror, and he just listened and listened and listened.

I tell this guy in the mirror everything I have ever done, all the things I'm sorry for doing. I tell him, "I don't want to be like this. Why can't I stop drinking? When I start drinking, shit goes wrong—why can't I just stop? Why can't I drink like regular people?" I just kept talking. I said, "What do I need to do? I cannot continue being like this." And that's what brought the liberation, and let me go on. I talked about my childhood, how much I hated growing up in the projects, growing up without a father, and I let everybody off the hook for that. I let my codefendants off the hook. I just let go of all this anger. It was weird, it was crazy. I finally told somebody all my secrets and my fears, and it felt so good. I felt at peace.

I lay down and went to sleep, and in my sleep, I started reading in my dreams. I am reading all this new information from this book called *Encyclopedia Britannica*. Now I didn't know what *Encyclopedia Britannica* is, but I'm reading that stuff in my sleep. And then in my dream, I felt God say, "I am going to help you do this nine months. You will sail by yourself, but I am going to help you do this."

The next morning they brought around the book cart and I said, "I want something to read. I don't want any Jackie Collins, none of that garbage." Then I looked down at the bottom of the cart and I said, "What are those books right there?" He said, "Those are the *Encyclopedia Britannica*, *A* to *Z*." I said, "Can I have the first one?" and I started reading. I didn't know what the hell an abacus was. It's a counting machine. I am reading everything, about days of the week, how Thursday is named after Thor, this god with a hammer—Thor's day. I read about the Gregorian calendar, the Aztec conquest, the continental crust, surface temperatures of the stars, manifest destiny. I read *A* to *Z*. The letter *Z* comes from the Greek letter *zeta*.

My nine months went by so fast.

When I got out of the SHU, I tried to hang on to that moment of clarity, but the thing is, you need a program to keep it going. I didn't have a program. Things started going wrong, and one day my cellmate was brewing some wine and I said, "Let me have a cup." He said, "You don't drink anymore." I said, "Man, fuck that." I took a drink and I couldn't stop. I drank for twelve more years until July second, 2005. I went to sleep the way I did most of the time. I was drunk, and my buddies put me in the bunk, and the room is spinning until I pass out. In the middle of the night I woke up, the same way I had twelve years before, needing relief. I got up to pee and I saw myself in the mirror again and I said, "Fuck, man, you ain't accomplished anything." On July third I woke up and my first thought was, "God, what do I need to do? Just tell me what to do." It was coming from the heart.

I went outside and I saw these people with the pink box and I thought, "Doughnuts . . . I haven't had a doughnut in fifteen years. I wonder if they have those twisted things, crullers." So I follow the people with the pink box. I thought they were church people or something and I'd go sing a couple of Hallelujahs and they'd give me a doughnut.

They said, "This is a recovery meeting for alcoholics. Come on in. You want a doughnut?" I'm like, "Yeah, I'll take a doughnut." So I sat back and I listened to these stories of how hopeless and how unmanageable their lives were, how they had lost everything—kids, homes, jobs, money. This one man talked about living in a big beautiful house, a million-dollar house, and going from that to sleeping in a field next to cows to stay warm, because a cow's body temperature is 105 degrees. Listening to him, I realized it wasn't about being imprisoned or not; it's about losing a life because of the disease of addiction.

So I kept going to meetings, but it took me two months to stand up in that group in prison and say, "My name is Dejuan and I am an alcoholic." They did not laugh at me. Now back in compound, when my homie boys called me an alcoholic, everybody would laugh, but in the rooms of recovery, they didn't laugh, they embraced me, you see what I am saying.

I call getting out of prison "coming back to America" because it was like leaving one country and going to another one. The day I went home, I walked straight over to the phone booth outside the prison gate, and people from the program were right there waiting for me.

I was scared to death. I don't know how to live. I sold drugs and I drank, that's all I knew how to do. I used to run to go to meetings because I didn't know what else to do. I'd wake up at six o'clock in the morning, catch the bus, run a half a mile, and get there early so I can help set the chairs up. And I learned, and I changed. I'm a totally different person than I was before July 3, 2005.

It was hard to find a job, and it was hard to escape my past. My friend in recovery told me two things. He said, "You used to be willing to go to any lengths to get the drugs and the alcohol, so you've got to be willing to go to any lengths to keep your recovery." And he told me, "Your past is going to be your greatest asset, if you choose to make it that way. Go out there, get in the action, and do what you need to pay your bills. Every day it'll get a little better." And it has.

See, if he'd told me, "You're going to write a book, you're going to be on TV," I wouldn't have believed that. But that's what's happened. And I'm always at service. I had a friend call me the other day, a friend who was there when I got out. She called me the other day and she's smoking crack. I went down to her and I asked, "How can I help?" She says, "Just listen to me." I sit down and listen. I know how powerful it is to have someone listen.

And I know what it's like to be a gangbanger and what that leads to.

One day I was in Inglewood passing by a building and I saw some weights outside in the yard. Something made me pull over, and I saw this guy and asked, "Is this a gym or something?" It's a continuation school for kids who have trouble in regular high schools. I talk to this guy for a while and he says, "Do you want to talk with the kids?" and I said yeah. So I walk inside there, and I saw all the little young gangbangers and I'm like, "What's up, youngster? Where you from?" "I'm from nowhere."

I've been working with the kids in Inglewood for damn near a year now. All they wanted was somebody who would listen to them, somebody they can relate to, and I can do that. I took thirty-five of them to a university campus and let them see—"This is what's ahead of you if you want it. It might not be this school but it could be something like this. But you got to want it, and you got to work at it." So they're like, "Oh! You in school now?" I say no but then—I'm telling all the kids "go to school go to school" but I'm the one who's not going to school. So that's why I enrolled.

Every single time I brush my teeth, in the daytime and in the night-time, I think about the man in the mirror. I hold tight to that moment, and I hold tight to my sobriety. I'm very grateful and I'm very humble. My thing is to be of service, to help those who suffer, because somebody helped me.

EPILOGUE

The day I finished this book and sent it off to the publisher my manager called to ask if I had seen a show called *Intervention*. The producer was interested in talking to me about hosting another show they wanted to do on recovery. I told him I hadn't seen the show but would meet the producer because he was from Boston and his cousin used to work with my sister at Jordan Marsh. I have a deep and unwavering trust in things that come out of nowhere. My girlfriend, whose beauty is surpassed only by her taste, told me *Intervention* was one of her favorite shows on television, and after watching a few episodes I had to agree. I met the producer for lunch at the Polo Lounge at the Beverly Hills Hotel. That was the only thing "Hollywood" about the lunch; the guy got two phone calls while we were eating, but one was from his wife and the other was from his mother. He explained he wanted me to host a one-hour interview show, focusing on what the lives were like now for some of the addicts and alcoholics who had found recovery as a result of being on *Intervention*. The fact that I had never done anything like host a talk show didn't seem to bother him at all.

Two weeks later I found myself standing on a darkened Hollywood soundstage in front of a live audience, three interventionists, and six brave souls who had hit bottom on national television, waiting for the lights to come up and the show to go on. Everyone was relying on me to do a good job.

Whose idea was this anyway? Clearly somebody had made a big mistake. I don't know how to do *THIS*! As I was about to raise my hand and ask to be excused, one of the interventionists, Candy Finnegan, ambled over and whispered, "How's your book coming?"

"I turned it in to my publisher two weeks ago," I said, trying to stay focused on the terror at hand.

"I had a moment of clarity," Candy continued, not realizing how attached I was to being fully focused on my fear.

"Really," I said not very enthusiastically.

"Yeah. I was forty-nine days sober and I was on a plane with my kids going from Wichita to Denver heading right into a tornado. I could see it just off the right wing. We were bouncing all over the place, everyone was panicked. I rang the bell for a flight attendant who showed up at my seat with a handful of throw-up bags. I told her that barfing was not my problem—drinking was, and implored her to make an announcement over the intercom asking if there was anyone on the plane who knew Bill W., which all of us in recovery know is code for another person in recovery. I told her I had to talk to another recovering alcoholic because if I didn't I might drink—or worse. She leaned down, grabbing both armrests on my seat, getting right in my face, and said, 'Honey, stand up and look for him yourself.'

"I looked into her eyes and said with the urgency of desperation, 'I need you to do this or I'm going to drink.'

"My kids were looking at me like dogs on a freeway as the flight attendant walked to the front of the plane, reluctantly picked up the microphone, and asked if there was somebody who knew Bill W. to please ring their call button.

"The silence was deafening."

She went on to say, "Now understand, Chris, I had been sober for forty-nine days. I had heard all about God and the turning-it-over stuff, but until that moment on the plane, squeezing my kid's hand like it was the last thing I might do in this life, I never really got it. I closed my eyes and went to a place I had never gone before. It was my surrender. For the first time in my life I asked for help, leaving the results up to something greater than me. Just as I did, the plane turned out of Kansas and the turbulence stopped. Just like that—it was over. I looked up from my prayer and as I did the cockpit door opened and the captain stepped out. He walked over to me and said, 'Did you ask for me?'

" 'No sir, I asked for someone who knew Bill W.,' I said.

" 'That's me. I'm a friend of Bill W.,' he said. 'Don't worry, everything is going to be okay; you and your kids are in my hands.'

"I thanked him and told him that he needed to get back up front to fly the plane. As he left, my five-year-old son looked at me and asked, 'That wasn't God was it?'

" 'No, baby, but close enough,' I said."

I thanked Candy for the story.

"I figured you needed it," she said. "Just remember, you're not alone."

ACKNOWLEDGMENTS

My thanks to Laurie Liss for the inspiration to do such a book and Maureen O'Brien for having the vision to see its potential and the courage to buy it. To my collaborator, Jan Werner, for working much harder than she was obliged to, and for the skill and empathy with which she cared for these stories. To our editor Marjorie Braman, who inherited this project but treated it as if it was one of her own, giving us her invaluable experience and insight. To the friends who encouraged, inspired, and helped us along the way, especially Ken Cross, Kale Browne, David Black, Bill Teuteberg, Sara McNitt, Matt Eakin, and Tim Tankosic. To the good folks at Caron Treatment Centers, who have dedicated their lives to helping addicts and alcoholics realize their moments of clarity. I want also to acknowledge the people who made this process really, really, really difficult—you know who you are. And lastly, I want to express my profound gratitude to all of those who shared their moments of clarity with me, for your honesty and the trust you placed in me. Your courage to publicly claim your recovery in the hope that others might be inspired to find a better life is breathtaking.

WORKS FROM
CHRISTOPHER KENNEDY LAWFORD

SYMPTOMS OF WITHDRAWAL
A Memoir of Snapshots and Redemption

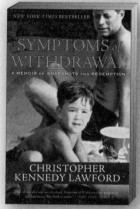

ISBN 978-0-06-113123-3 (paperback)

"Sometimes in this narrative you might think you've taken an elevator to hell and you wonder how this young man survived at all. He did—and we are fortunate to have his story in prose that is jazzy, rocking, sometimes dark but, in the end, bright with hope." —Frank McCourt

HEALING HEPATITIS C

Christopher Kennedy Lawford and Diana Sylvestre, MD

ISBN 978-0-06-178368-5 (paperback)

A personal and comprehensive sourcebook for confronting the stigma, misinformation, and fears about Hepatitis C.

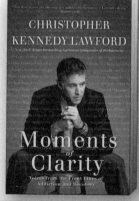

MOMENTS OF CLARITY
Voices from the Front Lines of Addiction and Recovery

ISBN 978-0-06-145622-0 (paperback)

"Revelatory epiphanies are as mysterious as they are sublime. . . . Each story holds the individual fascination of its particular circumstances; all of them get their oomph from punchy compression and plainspoken honesty." —*Kirkus Reviews*